STRUCTURE & SURPRISE:
Engaging Poetic Turns

STRUCTURE & SURPRISE:
Engaging Poetic Turns

Edited by
MICHAEL THEUNE

Teachers & Writers Collaborative
New York, New York

Library of Congress Cataloging-in-Publication Data
Theune, Michael, 1970–
Structure and surprise: engaging poetic turns / Michael Theune
ISBN-13: 978-0-915924-27-1 (ppk.–alk. paper)
ISBN-10: 0-915924-27-7 (ppk.–alk. paper)

2007900082

Teachers & Writers Collaborative
520 Eighth Avenue, Suite 2020
New York, NY 10018-6507

Cover and page design: Sylvia Ruud
Cover photo: Zinnia, 1998 Copyright Tom Baril
Printed by Victor Graphics, Inc.
First printing

ACKNOWLEDGEMENTS

As the number of its contributors indicates, the publication of *Structure & Surprise* largely was a communal endeavor, and I thank all of these writers for their insightful and inspiring work. However, many others, whose names do not appear elsewhere in these pages, also were involved in the making of this book. The ideas for this book were sparked by the many fine teachers with whom I have had the great fortune to work, including Jack Ridl, Jorie Graham, Ellen Bryant Voigt, and Ed Hirsch. The book project was given shape and direction by a team of excellent editors at Teachers & Writers Collaborative, including Christina Davis, Chris Edgar, Amy Swauger, and Catherine Barnett, and the project was made possible in part by a grant from Illinois Wesleyan University, which provided me a Junior Faculty Leave in fall 2005. All along, this project and I myself were sustained, assisted, and enlivened by conversations with family, friends, and colleagues at Illinois Wesleyan University and elsewhere. My deep gratitude to *all* of these contributors.
—Michael Theune

Structure & Surprise: Engaging Poetic Turns was funded by a grant from the National Endowment for the Arts.

Teachers & Writers Collaborative programs are made possible in part by grants from the New York State Council on the Arts, the New York City Department of Cultural Affairs, the Manhattan Borough President's Office, and the Manhattan City Council Delegation.

Teachers & Writers Collaborative is also grateful for support from Booth Ferris Foundation, Bydale Foundation, Carnegie Corporation of New York, Cerimon Fund, Consolidated Edison, E.H.A. Foundation, Agnes Gund & Daniel Shapiro, Jeannette and H. Peter Kriendler Charitable Trust, JP Morgan Chase Foundation, New York Times Company Foundation, David Rockefeller Fund, The Scheide Fund, Smith Barney (Citigroup Foundation), Starbucks Foundation, Steele Reese Foundation, Washington Mutual Foundation, and members and friends of Teachers & Writers Collaborative.

CONTENTS

The Poetic Turns

Introduction

MICHAEL THEUNE

Poetic structure is, simply, the pattern of a poem's turning. As such, poetic structure identifies a vital feature of poems: the best poems very often include convincing, surprising turns. T.S. Eliot calls the poem's turn "one of the most important means of poetic effect since Homer," and in a lecture called "Levels and Opposites: Structure in Poetry," Randall Jarrell claims that "a successful poem starts from one position and ends at a very different one, often a contradictory or opposite one; yet there has been no break in the unity of the poem." More than almost any other aspect of poetry, it is structure that reveals how poems remain whole and unified even as they move, leap, turn.

And yet, for all its importance, structure has received very little attention in recent poetry-writing pedagogy. In part, this is because structure often is considered, at best, synonymous with form. The occasional chapter called "Poetic Structure" in a poetry handbook usually contains information on poetic form, the musical and rhythmic aspects of poems. And, generally, to whatever extent structure and form have been thought to name separate aspects of poems, structure is considered ancillary to form. For example, when taught at all, the turn most often is taught as a part of the sonnet, and so the sonnet's turn—or *volta*, as it is sometimes called—is treated as just one more feature, along with rhyme scheme and line count, of the sonnet's many formal demands.

However, the turn does not belong solely to the sonnet tradition. In fact, as suggested by poet-critic Ellen Bryant Voigt in her essay "The Flexible Lyric," all kinds of poems turn and these poems can be classified according to the ways they turn, regardless of form. Whereas form provides one set of categories for classifying poems—one that includes categories such as sonnet, villanelle, pantoum, and ghazal—structure introduces new categories, including, but not limited to, the kinds explored in this collection of essays: ironic, emblem, concessional, retrospective-prospective, elegiac, dialectical, and descriptive-meditative.

Structure's taxonomy categorizes poems in a way that is at once radically new and strikingly familiar. Structure's taxonomy is new in that it makes connections between many seemingly disparate poems. For example, poems with radically various forms can be linked by a common structure. One of the following chapters links, among other forms, a sonnet and a haiku; another joins an epigrammatic two-line poem with a long poem of incantatory repetitions.

For all its ability to make unfamiliar connections, structure itself is not unfamiliar, and this is what makes structure so vital. Whereas form can so often seem a strange, merely "poetic" activity, structural turning is, if not obvious, then to some extent familiar. Almost no one regularly thinks or speaks in sestinas or pantoums, but almost everyone regularly engages in structured thinking and speech, and many everyday speech acts enact particular structures, contain effective turns. For example, even if one has not consciously considered the retrospective-prospective structure, anyone who has ever confessed anything about their past—privately or to another person—in order to then make new resolutions about the future has employed just this structure in their thought or speech. So this structure can be efficiently and effectively pointed out, shown to be relevant, and put to use in poems. Similarly, even if one has never heard of the ironic structure, its turn from set-up to punch line is not a foreign concept to anyone who has heard or told a joke. Structure offers a whole new way to conceive of poems that is at once paradigm-shifting, highly sophisticated, *and* readily apparent and available.

As suggested by the reference to the structure of jokes, structure does not necessarily mean simply order and rationality. Rather, structure's primary concern is the art of the turn and often this means making *surprising* turns. Some structures, even logical structures or structures with very pragmatic ends, can be wonderfully counterintuitive. For example, it seems detrimental to employ concessions that admit certain weaknesses in an argument before trying to make that argument. However, poems that make use of such a concessional structure strengthen arguments by establishing the goodwill of the speaker and limiting the scope of debate. Structure reminds and encourages us to see and to make poems that maneuver in such surprisingly new ways.

But structure in a poem is not necessarily built out of conventional logic. As Randall Jarrell notes, "Poetry constantly uses logic for the details of structures . . . constantly haunts about the shape of logic. . . . But for poetry logic is merely one method of organization, one among many others. . . ." Poetic turns also can be narrative or dramatic. Just as a turn might signal a move from premise to conclusion, a turn might also consist of a transition from one emotional state to another. In fact, poetic turns can even consist of mistakes. Jarrell states that "We can learn more about poetic structure from logical fallacies than from logic," advising poets to "go to the political orator, the advertising agencies . . . but let the logician molder in his icebox."

Numerous significant thinkers recognize that structure's primary goal is to lead to surprise. According to poet-critic A.D. Hope, "the art of modulation" is "key" to composing longer poems, and his list of "all the architectonic skills" that depend on this art includes proportion, harmony, connection, *and* surprise. Poet-critic Mary Kinzie says, "The very keystone of logic" is "the art of making transition—the art of inference and connection, the art of modulation and (hence) surprise."

The notion of poetry as a combination of structure and surprise significantly challenges some longstanding, deeply-ingrained ideas about poetry. It also offers an alternative to—a counterpoint for—some current poetry-writing pedagogies. Still very much embedded in a late-Romantic phase, poetry often is conceived of as "the spontaneous overflow of powerful feelings," as William Wordsworth so famously wrote more than 200 years ago. As such, poetry is thought of as a kind of magical process in which a poem springs forth from the poet's inner self. More than a century after Wordsworth's claim, the surrealist practices of psychic automatism and automatic writing—writing processes through which a poet supposedly can make direct contact with the subconscious—developed from theories such as Wordsworth's. The writing that issued forth flowed, moving quickly, enacting skittering movements of mind. By the 1960s, Allen Ginsberg's poetic dictum "First thought, best thought" praised the immediacy and impulsiveness of poetry.

But just as Wordsworth's formulation is incomplete insofar as it does not indicate the fact that most poems flow *from* somewhere and *to* somewhere, Ginsberg's formulation is incomplete insofar as it does not indicate, as do each of the many poems included in *Structure & Surprise*, that poems often contain *second* and *third* thoughts. And whether or not *those* thoughts are "best" usually has a great deal to do with structural issues, with how they relate to—how they leap away from yet connect to—initial thoughts.

Such structural concerns have not been taken up by much current poetry-writing pedagogy, which more often focuses on poetic flow and form. Many books and Web sites give writing exercises designed to generate text via largely surrealist procedures and offer a host of forms for shaping the raw material generated. While such methods very usefully encourage production and invention, incorporating an understanding of poetic structure into these exercises pushes "exercise" to a deeper art. Knowledge of structure gives both writer and reader a vital perspective and means from and with which to read, understand, assess, and reconceive one's own—and anyone else's—work. Knowing poetic structure makes new demands on poets and poems, but it also offers a useful new tool. Acquainted with turns, one can better see and even *imagine* a draft's structural possibilities, and further draft, critique, and revise accordingly.

To the extent that it is true, as Stephen Dobyns writes, that "We write, finally, to be free of things, not to express ourselves; to become articulate, not to mumble to ourselves; to drive our feelings and vague ideas into consciousness and clarity," it also is true that "Structure is our primary means of achieving articulateness and consequently of communicating our discoveries."

Structure & Surprise has three interconnected and increasingly sophisticated goals:

- To increase awareness of the significant presence of structure in poetry, thus further revealing the many dimensions of poetry.

- To allow for better, more complete readings of poems, thus creating new expectations in poetry readers.

- To inspire and guide the creation of new poems.

To achieve these goals, each of the first seven chapters in *Structure & Surprise* presents a poetic structure. The first five chapters present two-part structures: ironic, emblem, concessional, retrospective-prospective, and elegiac. The sixth and seventh chapters present three-part structures: dialectical and descriptive-meditative. Each chapter provides a succinct definition of the structure; a brief historical examination, if available; close textual analyses; discussion of any structural variants; and a section of supplemental poems. The eighth and ninth chapters do not provide information on specific kinds of turns but rather, developing from very recent investigations into structure, highlight peculiar characteristics of the turn. "The Mid-course Turn" emphasizes how radical poetic turns can be, and "Substructure" is a reminder to pay attention for subtle structures in seemingly "difficult" poetry.

Structure & Surprise, however, is in no way intended to be the final word on poetic structure; rather, it is meant to be a revealing and generative introduction. In fact, it is virtually impossible to imagine a final word on poetic structure. Structures intersect and overlap to such an extent that there are too many connections for any one effort at organizing the various structures to be the only organization possible. Additionally, there are, of course, countless other structures than those presented here. The structures presented in this book are simply some of the most common. As a recognition of the existence of other structures, this book includes a section called "Endless Structures," composed of fourteen short texts written by some of today's most exciting poets. In this lively section, poets whose work is wildly diverse each discuss one of their own poems and its structural concerns. Some of this section's essays refer back to structures already examined in earlier chapters. Others are new and demonstrate how idiosyncratic and yet universal poetic structures can be. As this section suggests, there are endless possibilities for poetic structures.

In order to show as clearly as possible how the ideas in this book can be used to encourage new writing, the last chapter, "Inspiration, Guides, Exercises," gathers together ways for the practicing poet to play with structure in both early and later drafting stages. Ideally, a larger notion of structure, combined with these specific exercises, will invite writers to try new ways of both generating and working with their raw material.

Finally, it is a pleasure to direct readers of *Structure & Surprise* to other writers who already have revealed, explored, established, deepened, and complicated the vast world of structural possibilities: T.S. Eliot, Randall Jarrell, A.D. Hope, Mary Kinzie, Ellen Bryant Voigt, and Stephen Dobyns. *Structure & Surprise* is the pragmatic outgrowth of their work and hopes to further the conversations begun so eloquently by these articulate thinkers. Please read the works listed in "Further Reading" for deeper exploration, to understand where many of the ideas examined in this book came from, and to continue the dialogue begun here.

The Poetic Turns

CHAPTER ONE

The Ironic Structure

CHRISTOPHER BAKKEN

W.B. Yeats famously claimed that "We make out of the quarrel with others, rhetoric, but of the quarrel with ourselves, poetry." A poem with an ironic structure is, in essence, a poem that has an argument with itself. It offers two points of view, or two conflicting attitudes toward a single subject, and allows the playful tension of those contradictory impulses to stand.

Poems employing an ironic structure begin with positive assertions and assumptions of truth but end by undercutting such assertions and certainties, sometimes rather abruptly and surprisingly. This decidedly simple poetic mechanism—which might be thought of as the process of rising and falling, or inflating and deflating, or dreaming and waking—is capable of producing great intellectual and dramatic energy. Though examples of poems employing an ironic structure date back to the beginnings of poetry, the ironic structure has proven especially popular in the poetry of the last two centuries, embodying as it does a particular attitude toward the world that we associate with modernity.

The manipulation of tone is at the heart of any poetic activity, which makes irony a crucial weapon in any poet's arsenal. Yet there is an important distinction between the most common type of irony we encounter—*verbal irony*—and the kind of *structural irony* under consideration here. *Verbal irony* is produced by saying one thing while meaning or implying the opposite. Perceptive readers or listeners will "hear" irony because they understand that the truth of what's being said is intentionally undercut by the context in which it is said. For example, if you step outside your house on a February morning into a diagonal sleet, with a ten-below-zero wind chill churning in your face, and you say to your wife, "Nice day!," she'll know, because she is just as disgusted as you are, that you are not proposing a picnic. In *An Introduction to Poetry*, X.J. Kennedy explains that this kind of irony is "a manner of speaking that implies a discrepancy. If the mask says one thing and we sense that the writer is in fact saying something else, the writer is using an ironic point of view." Often this disparity results in good-natured humor, since what is actually said differs from the straightforward truth in such an exaggerated way. But of course this kind of irony can be exaggerated even more, so it moves away from sarcasm into ridicule and scorn.

Structural irony, in contrast, is a way of organizing a series of utterances so that what is first proclaimed is suddenly or systematically undermined by what follows. Charles Bernstein's tiny poem "Shaker Show" enacts this in two lines:

> Now *that* is a chair
> I wouldn't want to sit in.

The irony emerges when we perceive the contrast between these two utterances, when we perceive the imbalance between them. In this way, structural irony suspends and stalls a conclusion. If verbal irony is to be immediately perceived, structural irony will typically surprise us more gradually. This is not to say it cannot happen quickly, as in the Bernstein example or in the m loncar poem included in the Supplemental Poems at the end of this chapter. In these examples, we recognize the same kind of reversal that works to fuel the punch lines of jokes or gives limericks their signature finish. Such comic forms help remind us that we often have debates with ourselves over things that are decidedly silly and mundane, as in: "I will floss today. No, I will not floss today." But for such mundane facts to rise to the level of thought-provoking irony, a kind of wit and comic timing must be at work and the structure must be built upon enough of a reversal to surprise the reader at the outcome.

Of course, structural irony is not in any way limited to the comic or absurd, as is demonstrated by Margaret Atwood's arresting little poem "you fit into me." Atwood's entire four-line poem is built upon a basic ironic structure and a single simile. In fact, this simile is offered to us twice, with startling modifications:

> you fit into me
> like a hook into an eye
>
> a fish hook
> an open eye

The first line of this short poem effectively introduces us to the poem's context: the fitness of a "you" and a "me." With the title in mind, it's hard not to read the poem, at least initially, as a love poem, one with a decidedly erotic edge. The opening two lines build the title's statement into a figure of speech: the fitness of "you" and "me" is likened to that of a "hook" and an "eye." Such a declaration can be taken quite positively. What kind of connection could be more symbiotic and comfortable than a hook and eye fastener? The hook and eye require one another to serve their combined purpose of drawing together two pieces of fabric or the two lapels of a jacket. Read sexually, as an image of penetration, the first two lines suggest erotic fitness of the very best kind: compatibility, natural rightness, pleasure.

But the final two lines deflate such possibilities violently and entirely. We may not, these lines announce, read "hook" and "eye" with any ambiguity at all. If the opening lines might be thought to define the terms of a relationship, the last two lines radically redefine those terms, since they redefine the simile itself. What could be more awful than a fish hook with its barbed tip encountering a vulnerable "open eye," which must watch itself being destroyed? There is no humor to this reassessment. The reader is left grasping at an image of utter incompatibility, of sexual violence. The ironic comparison of these two viewpoints—one affirmative, one profoundly negative—might even be thought to mimic two perspectives on the same relationship, bringing new meaning to the old cliché that "love is blind." The power of such a poem resides in part in the simplicity of its ironic structure, the surprise of that harsh undercutting, which resonates beyond the brief space of the poem.

Dorothy Parker's short poem "Comment" is another example of a poem employing a basic ironic structure. This poem drives toward its final undercutting with a limerick-like quickness:

> Oh, life is a glorious cycle of song,
> A medley of extemporanea;
> And love is a thing that can never go wrong;
> And I am Marie of Roumania.

The first three lines constitute rather broad assertions about decidedly broad and abstract concepts—"life" and "love"—and Parker understands that we might *want* to believe such positive truisms. After all, don't we turn to poetry for wisdom and truth? But clearly Parker herself cannot believe in them at all, since she is certainly *not* Marie of Roumania. With the outright lie of the poem's fourth line, the false truths of the first three lines suddenly light up like neon platitudes. This is not merely a statement of two points of view, of thesis/antithesis, because antithesis clearly has the last word here. The actual sentiments of a poem organized with an ironic structure, then, almost always rest upon the poem's conclusion. Here the poem's final "Comment" is to disclaim any absolute, positive certainties about life or love. According to the logic of the poem, any attempts to comment so broadly about existence will be facile, if not foolish, about as close to the truth as her last line.

This kind of philosophical skepticism represents a decidedly modern attitude. According to literary critic Anne Mellor, in her book *Romantic Irony*, this kind of skepticism became central to artistic production beginning with the Romantic poets—those artists who had to recreate the terms of art after the cataclysmic French Revolution and American War of Independence. These poets no longer took for granted the idea that the world was divinely ordered, that God was ever-present in the natural world, that religion shaped the backbone of society. We still see great spiritual longing and questing in Romantic poetry, but in the context of an increasingly secular world.

This paradox informs the very structures of Romantic poetry, resulting in what Mellor calls "Romantic irony." Mellor claims that the Romantic ironist "must acknowledge the inevitable limitations of his own finite consciousness. . . . Even as he denies the absolute validity of his own perceptions and structuring concepts of the universe . . . he must affirm and celebrate the process of life by creating new images and ideas."

Such poetry reflects the ongoing tension between disbelief and belief, between rejection and celebration, and often the very structure of a poem helps the poet exhibit this tension creatively. "The artistic process," Mellor continues, "must be one of simultaneous creation and de-creation." The ironic structure—with its building up and knocking down, its dreaming and waking—becomes the perfect instrument for a great Romantic ironist like Lord Byron, whose long poem *Don Juan* exemplifies this complicated problem.

Byron's poem is composed in a seemingly unstoppable series of *ottava rima*, an elegant eight-line stanza rhymed in an ABABABCC pattern. The energy of the first six lines—which are propelled forward by the alternating ABABAB rhymes—comes crashing up against the final rhyming couplet, which is designed to bring the stanza to a conclusion, to close with certainty. Bryon adapts *ottava rima* to his own purposes, however, often turning the stanza into an ironic structure by forcing the first six lines to build toward a concluding statement, then dismantling the possibility of settled conclusions in the final couplet, often to great comic effect. As critic Hoxie Neale Fairchild once said, Byron had a mind "too idealistic to refrain from blowing bubbles, and too realistic to refrain from pricking them."

Byron's protagonist, Don Juan, is at the outset too earnest, naïve, and ordinary to be taken very seriously by the poem's wildly rhyming narrator, or by the reader, no matter how profound some of the poem's themes might appear to be. The ironic structure of the stanzas alone makes this abundantly clear, as in this stanza from Canto I describing Don Juan's meditations upon love:

> He pored upon the leaves and on the flowers
> And heard a voice in all the winds; and then
> He thought of wood-nymphs and immortal bowers,
> And how the goddesses came down to men.
> He missed the pathway, he forgot the hours,
> And when he looked upon his watch again,
> He found how much old Time had been a winner.
> He also found that he had lost his dinner.

The first six lines of the stanza place Juan in the realm of an idealized pastoral landscape—an Arcadia this young lover wanders while contemplating his beloved, Julia. What he projects upon that landscape is the dreamy stuff of pagan Greece and Rome, the kind of things any reader of Homer or Virgil might imagine. But Juan's longings are hopelessly overwrought and silly, purely conventional. The bubble of that kitschy pastoral daydream is burst by the entirely mundane final two lines—bringing our hero, now hungry, having "lost his dinner," back to earth.

Structural irony actually helps Byron produce the stanzas that make up his lengthy poem; every burst bubble is followed by another breath of affirming inflation. Byron addresses this idea in this stanza from Canto IV of *Don Juan*:

> Nothing so difficult as a beginning
> In poesy, unless perhaps the end;
> For oftentimes when Pegasus seems winning
> The race, he sprains a wing, and down we tend,

Like Lucifer when hurl'd from heaven for sinning.
  Our sin the same, and hard as his to mend,
Being pride, which leads the mind to soar too far,
Till our own weakness shows us what we are.

For Byron, the problem of beginning—and ending—in "poesy" has ulti-mately to do with knowing how far the poet should reach. The first six lines of this stanza contrast the two case studies of Pegasus and Lucifer. Pegasus, our mythic symbol of rising, represents artistic aspiration, the ambition that makes poets want to reach for the stars. Lucifer, our mythic symbol of falling, represents the consequences of reaching. Though these feel at the outset like contrasting examples, in the end both attempt to rise and both fall, landing upon Byron's final couplet. The problem is "pride," the cou-plet claims, since it "leads the mind to soar too far." Our "weakness" is overreaching, a flaw that eventually "shows us what we are," namely crea-tures of the earth, of the low. This stanza sums up Byron's philosophy and his aesthetic. Although he maintains an ironic understanding of the uni-verse, Byron knows we are not ever satisfied with earth. For him poetry will be made out of endless attempts to rise but it will also reflect the ever-leveling force of gravity, which pulls even the greatest poets back to earth.

Here's a famous stanza from Canto VII of *Don Juan* where the author ponders the purpose and aim of his poetry another way:

And such as they are, such my present tale is,
  A non-descript and ever varying rhyme,
A versified aurora borealis
  Which flashes o'er a waste and icy clime.
When we know what all are, we must bewail us,
  But, ne'ertheless, I hope it is no crime
To laugh at all things, for I wish to show
What after all, are all things—but a show?

The idea of the world we are being offered here is not very optimistic. If we live in the equivalent of a "waste and icy clime," and we understand this fact, "When we know what all are," what is left to do but "bewail" our situa-tion and even ourselves?

Byron's declarations here are both shocking and disheartening. He sees the poet—like the rest of us—living in a fallen world, and he understands it would make sense for poets to expend their creative energies lamenting our fallen condition. But in truth, much of *Don Juan* is dedicated to ridiculing poets who make this kind of whining, this "cant," their central project. (His contemporaries William Wordsworth and Samuel Taylor Coleridge get skewered several times.) The thrust of this stanza may first move us toward a sobering sense of existence, but the final couplet begins dismantling that notion, rejecting it. Why must we "bewail" when we could be laughing? If our existence is nothing but "a show," an illusion perpetuated to keep us miserable, then all we must do is realize that fact and laugh at it! Clearly Byron believes, at least in part, that the world is at best disorderly, and at worst "a waste," but he hopes to produce a poetry that "flashes" over that wasteland like the famous Northern Lights, the *Aurora Borealis*.

At every step in the long progress of *Don Juan*, closure is avoided. This applies to individual stanzas, but also to the narrative itself. Our hero cannot rest for long before circumstance, fate, or just the author's own restlessness puts Don Juan back on the path of another adventure. Byron is like a shark: if either he or his poem stops moving he'll suffocate. As Byron himself once put it, "I can't stagnate." As the example of Byron proves, this process of creation and de-creation can be very productive for the poet. Rather than being a dead end, the rise and fall of the ironic structure can lead to a kind of improvisational poetic momentum.

For a poet like Byron, the quarrels with himself tend to work their way out humorously. The narrator of *Don Juan* has the courage to admit his own limitations, and to laugh at his own foolishness and that of others. A high proportion of the stanzas that make up *Don Juan* remind us of the importance of humor in a world where most hard conclusions come at the expense of living without the blindfolds of overwrought idealism and existential clichés. This kind of ironic reversal operates so insistently in Byron that we cannot help but understand it as the author's unique and hilarious perspective.

As we have seen, the ironic structure imitates or enacts a sense of uncertainty about the world. The following poem, Constantine Cavafy's "Waiting for the Barbarians," records a series of questions and answers between two speakers who are poised on the very edge of such uncertainty:

What are we waiting for, assembled in the forum?

The barbarians are due here today.

Why isn't anything happening in the senate?
Why do the senators sit there without legislating?

Because the barbarians are coming today.

What laws can the senators make now?
Once the barbarians are here, they'll do the legislating.

Why did our emperor get up so early,
and why is he sitting at the city's main gate
on his throne, in state, wearing the crown?

> Because the barbarians are coming today
> and the emperor is waiting to receive their leader.
> He has even prepared a scroll to give him,
> replete with titles, with imposing names.

Why have our two consuls and praetors come out today
wearing their embroidered, their scarlet togas?
Why have they put on bracelets with so many amethysts,
and rings sparkling with magnificent emeralds?
Why are they carrying elegant canes
beautifully worked in silver and gold?

> Because the barbarians are coming today
> and things like that dazzle the barbarians.

Why don't our distinguished orators come forward as usual
to make their speeches, say what they have to say?

> Because the barbarians are coming today
> and they're bored by rhetoric and public speaking.

Why this sudden restlessness, this confusion?
(How serious people's faces have become.)
Why are the streets and squares emptying so rapidly,
everyone going home so lost in thought?

> Because night has fallen and the barbarians have not come.
> And some who have just returned from the border say
> there are no barbarians any longer.

And now, what's going to happen to us without barbarians?
They were, those people, a kind of solution.

The stage setting here—forum, praetors, emperor, barbarians—helps us place this poem in the ancient world, or at least in a society simplistically divided between a distinguished "us" and a barbaric "them." In this poem, the ironic structure serves to build suspense and then deflate all that suspense in the final lines. The simple question-and-answer format illustrates the fact that civilization as the speakers know it is about to be destroyed. Each of the questions points to the strangeness of the situation, since every common activity of life in this place is being disrupted. The senators aren't legislating; the orators aren't orating; and everyone, even the most bureaucratic among them, is dressed to the nines. All of this is happening, the answers tell us each time, because "the barbarians" are coming closer and closer with each passing minute. The poem is structured to build toward the arrival of these barbarians, to make us yearn to see what their arrival will bring. After all, they are barbarians!

But all the energy of that suspense dissipates suddenly in the poem's final lines when Cavafy reveals his surprise: "night has fallen and the barbarians have not come." This is the first of three deflations really, since we fall even farther upon reading the next lines, which reveal that perhaps "there are no barbarians any longer." And the first speaker—always full of questions—finds he must answer his own question in the poem's final gesture: indeed, what will happen to these people without barbarians? "They were," he concludes, "a kind of solution."

After so much building up, this feels like a rather flat, enigmatic conclusion. Clearly, the meaning of the final line emerges from the ironic structure itself. Almost every gesture of the poem illustrates the way this culture defines its idea of itself, in this case by relying upon a group of other beings, "the barbarians," to serve as examples of what they are not. Each question, with its underlying assumptions about the lowly barbarians (those easily bored beings simple enough to be "dazzled" by jewels), betrays the speaker's desperate need to reaffirm his culture's superiority, its assumed difference from the barbaric barbarians. But all that comes crashing down in the poem's ironic final gesture: the barbarians don't come at all, and what's left in their absence? What "solution" did the barbarians serve? The meaning of that final line arises out of this irony—the speakers, so dependent on the fact that they are *not* barbarians, haven't taken the time to define themselves in any other meaningful way. When the barbarians don't arrive, these citizens prove hollow, and their idea of what defines them collapses inward. The ironic structure allows Cavafy to illustrate poignantly this shallow, racist mentality and at the same to satirize it and to reveal its emptiness in these citizens' own words.

Uncertainty—or more specifically a desperate longing for certainty—is also the central theme of the next example of the ironic structure. If Cavafy's poem was primarily social, Robert Frost's poem, "The Most of

It," is primarily philosophical and spiritual. Like many of us, the character depicted in this poem begs to know what's "out there," wants desperately to see into invisible places, wants an answer from the universe:

> He thought he kept the universe alone;
> For all the voice in answer he could wake
> Was but the mocking echo of his own
> From some tree-hidden cliff across the lake.
> Some morning from the boulder-broken beach
> He would cry out on life, that what it wants
> Is not its own love back in copy speech
> But counter-love, original response.
> And nothing ever came of what he cried
> Unless it was the embodiment that crashed
> In the cliff's talus on the other side,
> And then in the far-distant water splashed,
> But after a time allowed for it to swim,
> Instead of proving human when it neared
> And someone else additional to him,
> As a great buck it powerfully appeared,
> Pushing the crumpled water up ahead,
> And landed pouring like a waterfall,
> And stumbled through the rocks with horny tread,
> And forced the underbrush—and that was all.

The irony in this poem is suspended until the very last moment. In order to understand how this poem comes to its conclusion, it is helpful to think of the poem as having an introduction and conclusion (or lack of conclusion), even if they are not divided by a stanza break.

The first nine lines act as a kind of preface, providing us with the background information we need to register the importance of what happens in the rest of the poem. Already with the opening line, we know we are dealing with a character who stands at a rather odd angle to the universe. "He thought he kept the universe alone," we are told. Shall we take this as a statement of ultimate solitude? Or shall we emphasize that word "thought," and realize that such a "thought" is rather preposterous—after all, none of us keeps the universe to himself. In either case, the next lines offer us a reason for why he might think this. When he stands at the edge of a lake, upon a "boulder-broken beach," the only voice he hears when he cries "out on life" is his own echo, come back to him from the "tree-hidden cliff across the lake." He is never satisfied with that "mocking echo." Clearly he wants more than that. He is tired of "copy speech," of echo, and wants instead "counter-love, original response." "And nothing ever came of what he cried," we are told, "Unless . . . ."

This depressing pattern of behavior—his forlorn shouting and echo-ing—is finally broken in the remaining lines of the poem, which consist of one long, suspended sentence. With this prefatory information behind us, we are now prepared for the surprise arrival, but of what? We cannot be sure that what follows actually "came of what he cried," since that word "Unless" keeps us from being very certain, but what comes is at least an "embodiment that crashed / in the cliff's talus on the other side." We are meant to imagine the man's astonishment here. After all, he's been repeat-edly asking the emptiness for an answer for his cries "out on life" and at last he might be receiving one. Frost maintains suspense by postponing the ar-rival of this "embodiment," letting it swim slowly toward us, employing comma after comma to slow this revelation.

The buck that emerges from the water, though beautifully "pouring like a waterfall," is not immediately satisfying. There is a note or two of dis-appointment: what arrives is not even human, is not "someone else addi-tional to him." And how is "a great buck" an answer to the man's appeal? Here, the power of the ironic structure comes into play. We are invited to ponder the meaning of such a strange crescendo. Perhaps we wish to see the buck, a creature of enormous grace and strength, as confirmation that a be-ing—a god?—with such attributes controls the universe? Perhaps we are tempted to see the buck as an image of wildness, or nature's unflinching power over man, but still a response of some kind. Frost carefully orches-trates the poem's final lines to allow us such inflated interpretations, but he will not be content to let them stand. The buck does not stop and utter any satisfying moral—even Keats' Grecian Urn at least gets to speak! The buck has already moved on, having "stumbled through the rocks with horny tread." Frost's frank four-syllable conclusion, "and that was all," brings us crashing back to reality. All we get in answer from the universe—if we get anything—is this: either it was just a buck, or it meant something more, or it was nothing at all. There is simply no way to tell. Like Byron, Frost has an ironic understanding of the universe, one that allows for the possibility of mystery and wonder but at the same time checks such possibilities with recurring notes of skepticism. His poem enacts this philosophical attitude right before our eyes, playfully baiting us into believing more, or perhaps less, than we should.

If skepticism were a religion, and believing *less* was one of its central creeds, the English poet Philip Larkin would have been at least an arch-bishop. One final example, Larkin's astounding poem "High Windows," is worth brief consideration here, since this poem illustrates a variation on the ironic structure. Each of the poems we have considered so far has fol-lowed a by now familiar pattern: inflation followed by ironic deflation. But the ironic structure can also proceed in the opposite direction, whereby a series of deflations and mundane reckonings are undercut by a sudden and illuminating inflation.

Larkin's poem begins low—even the poem's diction is low, marked by words we're more used to hearing in locker rooms—and it continues to de-scend from there. Published in 1967, in the midst of a sexual revolution, "High Windows" explores the complicated relationship between sex and religious morality. The poem depicts the progressive loosening of sexual mores by giving us the perspective of three generations—the speaker finds himself right in the middle, caught between the "kids" and "everyone old":

> When I see a couple of kids
> And guess he's fucking her and she's
> Taking pills or wearing a diaphragm,
> I know this is paradise
>
> Everyone old has dreamed of all their lives—
> Bonds and gestures pushed to one side
> Like an outdated combine harvester,
> And everyone young going down the long slide
>
> To happiness, endlessly.

For the old, it might seem like paradise to be freed from the "bonds and ges-tures" of religion, to put such moral strictures out to pasture like some use-less farm machinery. The "long slide" that once led (where else?) to hell, now appears to lead, through a clever enjambment, to "happiness."

But the speaker remembers that his own generation once pursued its own freedom, pushing against the moral constraints passed on to them by another generation, and he steps back to gaze from that even older perspective:

> I wonder if
> Anyone looked at me, forty years back,

And thought, *That'll be the life;*
No God any more, or sweating in the dark

About hell and that, or having to hide
What you think of the priest. He
And his lot will all go down the long slide
Like free bloody birds.

The poem has offered us two "slides," two descents into what could have been depravity and damnation, if seen from a fundamentalist point of view, but that are instead descents into happiness and freedom. These double descents have also revealed something earth-shattering to the speaker: all sexual restriction is predicated on a fear of God, but even the previous generation recognized the possibility that there is "No God any more." Just as the poem is about to come to rest upon that gigantic deflation, leaving us to expect a declaration of sensual anarchy, or nihilism, the poem swings upon the hinge of an ironic reversal:

And immediately

Rather than words comes the thought of high windows:
The sun-comprehending glass,
And beyond it, the deep blue air, that shows
Nothing, and is nowhere, and is endless.

The terms of this sudden rising are deeply ambiguous. We should not mistake the radical shift in tone for absolute certainty or a symbolic religious conversion. Nor can we entirely dismiss the sublimity of this attempt to peer through "the sun-comprehending glass" into what's beyond. Just as the speaker recognizes his freedom from the idea of divinity, religious guilt, and fear, the poem is blasted with awe. In "High Windows," the speaker is tempted to believe more than he should—or is it less? What we are offered is nothing more and nothing less than an image: the air beyond the glass "shows / Nothing, and is nowhere, and is endless." Whether we read this as a statement of affirmation or negation, of an instinctual impulse toward belief or the final banishment of it, we recognize that the poem has lifted off from where it started with the kind of power that can only come from the deepest kind of surprise.

This wide array of examples demonstrates the flexibility and power of the ironic structure, which helps produce the comic levity of the transparently clear short poems, but also the gravitas of the more filigreed longer poems. While the ironic structure's pattern of rising and falling is easy to recognize, and while it might seem rather easy to employ, these poems also demonstrate how different poets use an array of complicated poetic and rhetorical devices to build upon that simple foundation. It is important to recognize that in each case, what is undermined at the poem's finish has been first built up to (or slid down into, as in the case of Larkin's "High Windows") very concretely and convincingly, in such a way that allows the reader to become engaged in the poem's affirmations, and therefore deflated by the conclusions. Cavafy uses his highly rhetorical series of questions and answers and his extravagant Hellenistic setting, for example, while Frost chooses to concoct an elaborately philosophical preface, with its almost convoluted syntax and diction, to draw us into the quarrel at hand. Byron titillates and teases us with the wild rhymes of his *ottava rima*, over which he has achieved a mastery that is hard not to find irresistible. As many of the poems in Supplementary Poems will demonstrate further, with subjects ranging from fast-food coffee and Caribbean schooners to hedgehogs and the Holocaust, what the ironic structure offers poets is an occasion for complicated simplicity. This simplicity will more often than not produce poems nimble enough to juggle weighty ideas—conclusions and decisions that can be suspended in air, or playfully bobbled, or decisively dropped, or laughed right off the stage.

SUPPLEMENTAL POEMS

For Once, Then, Something
Robert Frost

Others taunt me with having knelt at well-curbs
Always wrong to the light, so never seeing
Deeper down in the well than where the water
Gives me back in a shining surface picture
Me myself in the summer heaven godlike
Looking out of a wreath of fern and cloud puffs.
Once, when trying with chin against a well-curb,
I discerned, as I thought, beyond the picture,
Through the picture, a something white, uncertain,
Something more of the depths—and then I lost it.
Water came to rebuke the too clear water.
One drop fell from a fern, and lo, a ripple

Shook whatever it was lay there at bottom,
Blurred it, blotted it out. What was that whiteness?
Truth? A pebble of quartz? For once, then, something.

The Mower
Philip Larkin

The mower stalled, twice; kneeling, I found
A hedgehog jammed up against the blades,
Killed. It had been in the long grass.

I had seen it before, and even fed it, once.
Now I had mauled its unobtrusive world
Unmendably. Burial was no help:

Next morning I got up and it did not.
The first day after a death, the new absence
Is always the same; we should be careful

Of each other, we should be kind
While there is still time.

ohio
m loncar

besides spilling the better half, as well as the steamier half,
      of mcdonald's best try at a cup of coffee on my crotch,
            the ride out of ohio passed without incident.

Incantation
Czeslaw Milosz

Human reason is beautiful and invincible.
No bars, no barbed wire, no pulping of books,
No sentence of banishment can prevail against it.
It establishes the universal ideas in language,
And guides our hand so we write Truth and Justice
With capital letters, lie and oppression with small.
It puts what should be above things as they are,
Is an enemy of despair and a friend of hope.

It does not know Jew from Greek or slave from master,
Giving us the estate of the world to manage.
It saves austere and transparent phrases
From the filthy discord of tortured words.
It says that everything is new under the sun,
Opens the congealed fist of the past.
Beautiful and very young are Philo-Sophia
And poetry, her ally in the service of the good.
As late as yesterday Nature celebrated their birth,
The news was brought to the mountains by a unicorn and an echo.
Their friendship will be glorious, their time has no limit.
Their enemies have delivered themselves to destruction.

Berkeley, 1968

History
Tomaz Šalamun

Tomaz Šalamun is a monster.
Tomaz Šalamun is a sphere rushing through the air.
He lies down in twilight, he swims in twilight.
People and I, we both look at him amazed,
we wish him well, maybe he is a comet.
Maybe he is punishment from the gods,
the boundary stone of the world.
Maybe he is such a speck in the universe
that he will give energy to the planet
when oil, steel, and food run short.
He might only be a hump, his head
should be taken off like a spider's.
But something would then suck up
Tomaz Šalamun, possibly the head.
Possibly he should be put in formaldehyde, so children
would look at him as they do at fetuses,
protei, and mermaids.
Next year, he'll probably be in Hawaii
or in Ljubljana. Doorkeepers will scalp
tickets. People walk barefoot
to the university there. The waves can be
a hundred feet high. The city is fantastic,

shot through with people on the make,
the wind is mild.
But in Ljubljana people say: look!
This is Tomaz Šalamun, he went to the store
with his wife Marushka to buy some milk.
He will drink it and this is history.

The Dancing
Gerald Stern

In all these rotten shops, in all this broken furniture
and wrinkled ties and baseball trophies and coffee pots
I have never seen a postwar Philco
with the automatic eye
nor heard Ravel's "Bolero" the way I did
in 1945 in that tiny living room
on Beechwood Boulevard, nor danced as I did
then, my knives all flashing, my hair all streaming,
my mother red with laughter, my father cupping
his left hand under his armpit, doing the dance
of old Ukraine, the sound of his skin half drum,
half fart, the world at last a meadow,
the three of us whirling and singing, the three of us
screaming and falling, as if we were dying,
as if we could never stop—in 1945—
in Pittsburgh, beautiful filthy Pittsburgh, home
of the evil Mellons, 5,000 miles away
from the other dancing—in Poland and Germany—
oh God of mercy, oh wild God.

What I Did on a Rainy Day
May Swenson

Breathed the fog from the valley
Inhaled its ether fumes
With whittling eyes peeled the hills
to their own blue and bone
Swallowed piercing pellets of rain
Caught cloudsful in one colorless cup

Exhaling stung the earth with sunlight
Struck leaf and bristle to green fire
Turned tree trunks to gleaming pillars
and twigs to golden nails
With one breath taken into the coils
of my blood and given again when vibrant
I showed who's god around here

Sea Grapes
Derek Walcott

That sail which leans on light,
tired of islands,
a schooner beating up the Caribbean

for home, could be Odysseus,
home-bound on the Aegean;
that father and husband's

longing, under gnarled sour grapes, is
like the adulterer hearing Nausicaa's name
in every gull's outcry.

This brings nobody peace. The ancient war
between obsession and responsibility
will never finish and has been the same

for the sea-wanderer or the one on shore
now wriggling on his sandals to walk home,
since Troy sighed its last flame,

and the blind giant's boulder heaved the trough
from whose groundswell the great hexameters come
to the conclusions of exhausted surf.

The classics can console. But not enough.

CHAPTER TWO

The Emblem Structure

MICHAEL THEUNE

The emblem structure has a rich history with roots in significant traditions of Western art, theology, science, and philosophy. A two-part structure, it begins with an organized description of an object and culminates with a meditation on that same object. In this way, the emblem structure moves from sight to insight, from perception to reflection.

The structure's curious name refers to a genre of Renaissance art that combines a brief, often cryptic motto, a visual image—typically a print derived from an embossed surface, or an *emblema* in the original Latin—and a poem explaining the meaning of the image. Collected in *emblemata*, or emblem books, the emblem poem, the shorthand name for poems employing the emblem structure, was incredibly popular. These poems were used for all manner of entertainment and instruction: to assist priests in prayer and meditation, to give political advice, and to teach children proper manners.

At the center of the emblem tradition is the philosophical and theological concept of an ordered universe, a universe that can be both observed and "read," its meanings deciphered. Many Western doctrines and concepts embody, reflect, and convey this idea. One such doctrine is that of the "two books." According to many Christian thinkers, God wrote two books for humankind's edification: the book of scripture, that is, the Bible, and the book of nature. Just as one might turn to scripture for understanding, guidance, or healing, one might also turn to nature. In *Religio Medici*, a seventeenth-century memoir and spiritual testament, Sir Thomas Browne states, "There are two bookes from whence I collect my Divinity; besides that written one of God, another of his servant Nature, that universall and publik Manuscript, that lies expans'd unto the eyes of all."

In the following nineteenth-century emblem poem, Oliver Wendell Holmes clearly believes that the things of this world are signs of the divine:

The Chambered Nautilus

This is the ship of pearl, which, poets feign,
   Sails the unshadowed main,
   The venturous bark that flings
On the sweet summer wind its purpled wings
In gulfs enchanted, where the Siren sings,
   And coral reefs lie bare,
Where the cold sea-maids rise to sun their streaming hair.

Its webs of living gauze no more unfurl;
   Wrecked is the ship of pearl!
   And every chambered cell,
Where its dim dreaming life was wont to dwell,
As the frail tenant shaped his growing shell,
   Before thee lies revealed,
Its irised ceiling rent, its sunless crypt unsealed!

Year after year beheld the silent toil
   That spread his lustrous coil;
   Still, as the spiral grew,
He left the past year's dwelling for the new,
Stole with soft step its shining archway through,
   Built up its idle door,
Stretched in his last-found home, and knew the old no more.

Thanks for the heavenly message brought by thee,
   Child of the wandering sea,
   Cast from her lap, forlorn!
From thy dead lips a clearer note is born
Than ever Triton blew from wreathèd horn!
   While on mine ear it rings,
Through the deep caves of thought I hear a voice that sings:

Build thee more stately mansions, O my soul,
   As the swift seasons roll!
   Leave thy low-vaulted past!
Let each new temple, nobler than the last,
Shut thee from heaven with a dome more vast,
   Till thou at length art free,
Leaving thine outgrown shell by life's unresting sea!

"The Chambered Nautilus" moves clearly and distinctly from the first three stanzas' observation and description of the empty, spiral shell of a dead chambered nautilus to the final two stanzas' meditation on and revelation of the meaning of the shell, its "heavenly message."

All emblem poems are arguments. The descriptive section lays the groundwork for the ensuing meditation. In "The Chambered Nautilus," for example, Holmes' description, especially in the second and third stanzas, focuses on the fact that the chambered nautilus is a mollusk that builds larger and larger segments of its spiral shell. This takes on the symbolic, metaphysical resonance proclaimed in the poem's final stanza. Observing the ever "more stately" product of a creature's patient, lifelong toil, Holmes encourages himself, his "soul," to do and be likewise, to live in ever better, ever "nobler" ways, to move properly, confidently, bravely toward death and the promise of a glorious afterlife.

A key feature of Holmes' argument is the nautilus' anthropomorphosis. The nautilus is a "tenant" who has mental processes similar to a human's: "he" is capable, at least, of "dreaming." What he builds seems less a shell and more a human construct, a "ship," or a "crypt," or a "temple," or a "home" complete with "ceiling," "archway," and "door." Holmes further anthropomorphizes the nautilus by not indicating how he died. We don't know if he was beached or perhaps eaten by another creature. Such details would make the nautilus seem less human. By avoiding such details Holmes can make the fate of this sea creature seem relevant to the fates of humans while also portraying death not as a terrifying rupture, but as an apotheosis, a glorious consummation, a freedom that makes *life*, not death or dying, seem filled with unrest.

"The Chambered Nautilus" is a very Christian poem. It likely only persuades and comforts a reader who already believes that our difficult world is one small part of a much larger cosmic scheme that includes a more significant, glorious, and permanent spiritual world beyond this one. But the emblem poem's structure is extremely flexible and lends itself to secular revelations as well. Robert Frost's "Design," for instance, employs an emblem structure to construct an argument against what is called in philosophy and theology "the argument from design":

I found a dimpled spider, fat and white,
On a white heal-all, holding up a moth
Like a white piece of rigid satin cloth—
Assorted characters of death and blight

Mixed ready to begin the morning right,
Like the ingredients of a witches' broth—
A snow-drop spider, a flower like a froth,
And dead wings carried like a paper kite.

What had that flower to do with being white,
The wayside blue and innocent heal-all?
What brought the kindred spider to that height,
Then steered the white moth thither in the night?
What but design of darkness to appall?—
If design govern in a thing so small.

Most famously advanced by William Paley in the eighteenth century, the argument from design tries to prove God's existence by arguing that the world, with all its intricate relations and arrangements, obviously seems designed, which would suggest that it must have been created by an intelligent, powerful, and likely good—or at least orderly—designer, that is, God. However, by focusing on a moment of death, and considering death as a serious flaw in any supposed universal design, Frost arrives at conclusions very different from Paley's. Either, Frost states, there is a design to the world—a frightening, morally reprehensible, diabolical "design of darkness"—or else, as is suggested by the "If" in the last line, there is no design at all.

Though the outlook and conclusions of Frost's "Design" are radically opposed to the outlook and conclusions of Holmes' "The Chambered Nautilus," the poems have identical structures. Frost's poem, too, begins in perception and ends in revelation. Its initial octave depicts death, and its closing sestet meditates on the significance of that depiction. Much of the death scene is ironically innocent: the death occurs in the morning, the flower that is the stage for this scene is called a "heal-all," the color white is pervasive. The deadly spider is described very much like a baby, "dimpled" and "fat," or a child carrying "a paper kite." Thus, the world the poem evokes seems at best a cruel joke. It becomes easier to believe the poem's elements are not the product of some good God but a diabolical prankster, or, alternatively, to think that we should not take stock in such universal readings at all.

Though with "Design" Frost offers a monumental critique of some of the philosophy behind the emblem tradition, the tradition continues. Even in the twenty-first century, poets continue to find new subjects, new features of the world, that speak significantly to them, and their poems con-

vey the messages of these oracular objects and occurrences. Poet Jorie
Graham opens her book *Never*, published in 2002, with the following em-
blem poem:

Prayer

Over a dock railing, I watch the minnows, thousands, swirl
themselves, each a minuscule muscle, but also, without the
way to *create* current, making of their unison (turning, re-
                                        infolding,
entering and exiting their own unison in unison) making of themselves a
visual current, one that cannot freight or sway by
minutest fractions the water's downdrafts and upswirls, the
dockside cycles of finally-arriving boat-wakes, there where
they hit deeper resistance, water that seems to burst into
itself (it has those layers), a real current though mostly
invisible sending into the visible (minnows) arrowing
                        motion that forces change—
this is freedom. This is the force of faith. Nobody gets
what they want. Never again are you the same. The longing
is to be pure. What you get is to be changed. More and more by
each glistening minute, through which infinity threads itself,
also oblivion, of course, the aftershocks of something
at sea. Here, hands full of sand, letting it sift through
in the wind, I look in and say take this, this is
what I have saved, take this, hurry. And if I listen
now? Listen, I was not saying anything. It was only
something I did. I could not choose words. I am free to go.
I cannot of course come back. Not to this. Never.
It is a ghost posed on my lips. Here: never.

Describing a school of minnows largely subject to the whims of the water
they're in, Graham interprets this vision as having something significant to
say about and to the human. We, too, are subject to forces beyond us, and
so we might adjust our incessant demands for unlikely ideals such as "pu-
rity" and embrace the scintillating presence of flux and transformation in
our world and in our lives. Like Holmes and Frost, Graham describes her
subject in such a way that it leads seamlessly into the meditation. For exam-
ple, calling the minnows "muscles" streamlines the poem so that it shows
quite plainly that will and strength, the work of the muscle, does little, if

anything, to change one's place in the world. Graham's fragmentary, en-jambed yet mellifluous lines even seem to duplicate the odd movements of the isolated yet multitudinous and flowing minnows.

Though each is a clear example of an emblem poem, Holmes' "The Chambered Nautilus," Frost's "Design," and Graham's "Prayer" are very different poems. Not only do they meditate on different things and develop very different conclusions, but they also differ both formally, ranging from a complex stanza form to a sonnet to free verse; and tonally, from trium-phant to stoic to a whispered incredulity. Other important variants in the emblem tradition indicate further possibilities for innovation. For exam-ple, not all emblem poems move from perception to reflection. The follow-ing emblem poem by W.H. Auden reverses this structure:

Musée des Beaux Arts

About suffering they were never wrong,
The Old Masters; how well they understood
Its human position; how it takes place
While someone else is eating or opening a window or just walking dully
  along;
How, when the aged are reverently, passionately waiting
For the miraculous birth, there always must be
Children who did not specially want it to happen, skating
On a pond at the edge of the wood:
They never forgot
That even the dreadful martyrdom must run its course
Anyhow in a corner, some untidy spot
Where the dogs go on with their doggy life and the torturer's horse
Scratches its innocent behind on a tree.

In Brueghel's *Icarus*, for instance: how everything turns away
Quite leisurely from the disaster; the ploughman may
Have heard the splash, the forsaken cry,
But for him it was not an important failure; the sun shone
As it had to on the white legs disappearing into the green
Water; and the expensive delicate ship that must have seen
Something amazing, a boy falling out of the sky,
Had somewhere to get to and sailed calmly on.

Here, meditation—though highly imagistic, employing details from some of Pieter Brueghel's other paintings—precedes description. The structural reversal powerfully reminds us of the significance of the meditation in the emblem tradition and of the interrelation of meditation and description.

Another significant variation in the emblem tradition is a poem by Emily Dickinson:

> There's a certain Slant of light,
> Winter Afternoons—
> That oppresses, like the Heft
> Of Cathedral Tunes—
>
> Heavenly Hurt, it gives us—
> We can find no scar,
> But internal difference—
> Where the Meanings, are—
>
> None may teach it—Any—
> 'Tis the Seal Despair—
> An imperial affliction
> Sent us of the Air—
>
> When it comes, the Landscape listens—
> Shadows—hold their breath—
> When it goes, 'tis like the Distance
> On the look of Death—

Observing a quickly fading ray of winter sun, Dickinson makes clear that this sighting is significant. Emotionally powerful, it oppresses like the music from a massive church organ. Associated with "Despair" and "affliction," it inflicts a "Heavenly Hurt." However, Dickinson's poem differs from so many emblem poems in that no specific lesson is imparted. The sighting offers nothing to "teach." In fact, this momentary light seems to disrupt mental categories, making some sort of "difference" deep in the mind, "Where the Meanings, are . . . ." Though Dickinson's poem has in it much unknowing and mystery, it is not confused or confusing. Dickinson writes a brief, haunting, mysterious poem about a brief, haunting, mysterious subject. Hers is not, as some poets might see, a grand, enlightening vision of heavenly hosts, or a glorious epiphany or radiant visitation by angelic orders proclaiming the unambiguous Word of God, but rather a momentary anti-epiphany, a glimpse at fleetingness itself, at death.

Almost the opposite of Dickinson's concise, cryptic poem, and also very unlike many of the other emblem poems examined thus far, is Elizabeth Bishop's "The Fish":

> I caught a tremendous fish
> and held him beside the boat
> half out of water, with my hook
> fast in a corner of its mouth.
> He didn't fight.
> He hadn't fought at all.
> He hung a grunting weight,
> battered and venerable
> and homely. Here and there
> his brown skin hung in strips
> like ancient wallpaper,
> and its pattern of darker brown
> was like wallpaper:
> shapes like full-blown roses
> stained and lost through age.
> He was speckled with barnacles,
> fine rosettes of lime,
> and infested
> with tiny white sea-lice,
> and underneath two or three
> rags of green weed hung down.
> While his gills were breathing in
> the terrible oxygen
> —the frightening gills,
> fresh and crisp with blood,
> that can cut so badly—
> I thought of the coarse white flesh
> packed in like feathers,
> the big bones and the little bones,
> the dramatic reds and blacks
> of his shiny entrails,
> and the pink swim-bladder
> like a big peony.
> I looked into his eyes
> which were far larger than mine
> but shallower, and yellowed,
> the irises backed and packed

with tarnished tinfoil
seen through the lenses
of old scratched isinglass.
They shifted a little, but not
to return my stare.
—It was more like the tipping
of an object toward the light.
I admired his sullen face,
the mechanism of his jaw,
and then I saw
that from his lower lip
—if you could call it a lip—
grim, wet, and weaponlike,
hung five old pieces of fish-line,
or four and a wire leader
with the swivel still attached,
with all their five big hooks
grown firmly in his mouth.
A green line, frayed at the end
where he broke it, two heavier lines,
and a fine black thread
still crimped from the strain and snap
when it broke and he got away.
Like medals with their ribbons
frayed and wavering,
a five-haired beard of wisdom
trailing from his aching jaw.
I stared and stared
and victory filled up
the little rented boat,
from the pool of bilge
where oil had spread a rainbow
around the rusted engine
to the bailer rusted orange,
the sun-cracked thwarts,
the oarlocks on their strings,
the gunnels—until everything
was rainbow, rainbow, rainbow!
And I let the fish go.

Far from being a remote observer, the speaker in Bishop's poem actively participates in the investigation of her subject. She catches the fish, holds it, inspects it, imagines its innards. And she ultimately discovers the specific significance of this very particular fish: those fishing lines, symbols of past struggles overcome. Once this discovery is made, the poem moves, at the line "I stared and stared," to account for the power of what has been discovered, offering not a clear statement of meaning but a testimony to the power of the discovery. The poem's speaker gains no new information but receives instead a new way of seeing things, a triumphant and hopeful outlook.

Ralph Waldo Emerson states, "Every moment instructs, and every object: for wisdom is infused into every form." As all of the poems in this chapter, including those in Supplemental Poems, make clear, there is virtually no end to the possibilities for the emblem poem; subjects for the emblem poem are as limitless as the things of the universe. Nature may provide material for further emblem poems, as it does in William Cullen Bryant's "To a Waterfowl." But so do, as in Mark Doty's "A Display of Mackerel," a grocer's produce; and, as in Miranda Field's "Miraculous Image," a religious icon. And so can theoretical physics, politics, or hardware; there are emblem poems waiting to be written on quasars and super strings, depleted uranium missiles and abandoned landmines, rivets and crowbars. And the description need not be primarily visual. Any of the senses might animate an emblem poem. Taste could initiate an emblem poem on taking a sip of cold, sweet-sour lemonade.

There is no limit to what emblem poems can communicate. They can, for example, argue with each other, deliver timeless truths, suggest ideas of historical contingency. Their meditations, which can take the shape of prophecy, lament, question, or proclamation, are as vibrant and diverse as their descriptions. W.H. Auden folds acts of description into his meditation. Elizabeth Bishop shows a transformed worldview. At the very end of *Walden*, in a paragraph that reads like a prose poem, Henry David Thoreau crafts a meditation that slowly emerges from the poem's last rhetorical question so that it actually enacts the same process—a gradual emergence—described in the poem's first half! As all of the poems here attest, the emblem poem's meditation is a vital part of a structure that animates terrifically various poems.

To a Waterfowl
William Cullen Bryant

Whither, 'midst falling dew,
While glow the heavens with the last steps of day
Far, through their rosy depths, dost thou pursue
   Thy solitary way?

Vainly the fowler's eye
Might mark thy distant flight to do thee wrong
As, darkly seen against the crimson sky,
   Thy figure floats along.

Seek'st thou the plashy brink
Of weedy lake, or marge of river wide,
Or where the rocking billows rise and sing
   On the chafed ocean side?

There is a Power whose care
Teaches thy way along that pathless coast—
The desert and illimitable air—
   Lone wandering, but not lost.

All day thy wings have fanned,
At that far height, the cold, thin atmosphere,
Yet stoop not, weary, to the welcome land,
   Though the dark night is near.

And soon that toil shall end;
Soon shalt thou find a summer home, and rest,
And scream among thy fellows; reeds shall bend,
   Soon, o'er thy sheltered nest.

Thou'rt gone, the abyss of heaven
Hath swallowed up thy form; yet, on my heart
Deeply has sunk the lesson thou hast given,
   And shall not soon depart.

He who, from zone to zone,
Guides through the boundless sky thy certain flight,
In the long way that I must tread alone,
   Will lead my steps aright.

A Display of Mackerel
Mark Doty

They lie in paralleled rows,
on ice, head to tail,
each a foot of luminosity

barred with black bands,
which divide the scales'
radiant sections

like seams of lead
in a Tiffany window.
Iridescent, watery

prismatics: think abalone,
the wildly rainbowed
mirror of a soapbubble sphere,

think sun on gasoline.
Splendor, and splendor,
and not a one in any way

distinguished from the other
—nothing about them
of individuality. Instead

they're *all* exact expressions
of the one soul,
each a perfect fulfillment

of heaven's template,
mackerel essence. As if,
after a lifetime arriving

at this enameling, the jeweler's
made uncountable examples,
each as intricate

in its oily fabulation
as the one before.
Suppose we could iridesce,

like these, and lose ourselves
entirely in the universe
of shimmer—would you want

to be yourself only,
unduplicatable, doomed
to be lost? They'd prefer,

plainly, to be flashing participants,
multitudinous. Even now
they seem to be bolting

forward, heedless of stasis.
They don't care they're dead
and nearly frozen,

just as, presumably,
they didn't care that they were living:
all, all for all,

the rainbowed school
and its acres of brilliant classrooms,
in which no verb is singular,

or every one is. How happy they seem,
even on ice, to be together, selfless,
which is the price of gleaming.

Miraculous Image
Miranda Field

When an effigy cries,
    the wood she's carved from rots.
Tears, tight-reined, migrainous
    implosions. Two trenches
of decay down the cheeks,
    the dress wearing itself
away, the heart's embroidered
    harness. And inside
never intended to be seen,
    naked, breathing,
wormholes, striations of the grain.
    What holds the parts in place:
glue of knackered hooves.
    Such havoc the pierced hands
wrestle—the soft blue mantle of Heaven

melts about the body,
the body shriven, its gilt
   stars of scabbed paint
flaking off. Leaven.
   How our undressings lift us ...
A sacred thing undone grows brave,
   a convict with nothing
in the world to lose—
   the baby sheds his baby fat,
his gold hair calms, mouse-brown.
   Epiphanies glance off him then,
a human thing, and hungry.

From *Walden; Or, Life in the Woods*
Henry David Thoreau

Every one has heard the story which has gone the rounds of New England, of a strong and beautiful bug which came out of the dry leaf of an old table of apple-tree wood, which had stood in a farmer's kitchen for sixty years, first in Connecticut, and afterward in Massachusetts—from an egg deposited in the living tree many years earlier still, as appeared by counting the annual layers beyond it; which was heard gnawing out for several weeks, hatched perchance by the heat of an urn. Who does not feel his faith in a resurrection and immortality strengthened by hearing of this? Who knows what beautiful and winged life, whose egg has been buried for ages under many concentric layers of woodenness in the dead dry life of society, deposited at first in the alburnum of the green and living tree, which has been gradually converted into the semblance of its well-seasoned tomb,—heard perchance gnawing out now for years by the astonished family of man, as they sat round the festive board,—may unexpectedly come forth from amidst society's most trivial and handselled furniture, to enjoy its perfect summer at last!

CHAPTER THREE

The Concessional Structure

MARY SZYBIST

A poem that employs the concessional structure has two parts: beginning with a concession, it admits something that is (or seems) counter to the position it ultimately unfolds. Concessional poems seek to persuade, and poets, like chess players, know something about strategy. Accomplished chess players often begin their games with gambits: they know how to sacrifice a pawn or other piece in an opening move in order to gain an advantageous position. In poems, concessions are common gambits. The act of conceding can be risky, but done well the gesture gains far more than it sacrifices. Concessions can gain an audience's attention and trust. Most importantly, they can strengthen the force of an argument and its overall persuasiveness.

Consider, for example, the following assertion:

> By heav'n, I think my love as rare
> As any she belied with false compare.

By itself, this is not an especially persuasive declaration of love. The speaker claims that his beloved is as exceptional as any woman, any other "she," whose beauty has been falsely exaggerated. Place these lines at the end of a well-crafted concession, however, and the effect is rather different:

> My mistress' eyes are nothing like the sun;
> Coral is far more red than her lips' red;
> If snow be white, why then her breasts are dun;
> If hairs be wires, black wires grow on her head.
> I have seen roses damask'd, red and white,
> But no such roses see I in her cheeks,
> And in some perfumes there is more delight
> Than in the breath that from my mistress reeks.

I love to hear her speak, yet well I know
That music hath a far more pleasing sound.
I grant I never saw a goddess go;
My mistress when she walks treads on the ground.
    And yet, by heav'n, I think my love as rare
    As any she belied with false compare.

William Shakespeare's Sonnet 130 typifies the concession gambit: the speaker first admits that his mistress does not live up to the ideals of beauty that other poets claim for their mistresses; he concludes by declaring his love for her. Shakespeare is, of course, mocking the Petrarchan tradition of love poetry in which male speakers hopelessly idealize the female objects of their affection. These love poets often used the technique of the blazon (or blason) to praise the body of the female beloved by describing it in detail, part by part, sometimes starting with the hair and moving spatially downward to the eyes, nose, mouth, neck, and so forth. The formula rendered the beloved as astonishingly ideal and therefore extraordinarily desirable. Here Shakespeare uses the same blazon mode in order to break that formula. As Helen Vendler explains in *The Art of Shakespeare's Sonnets*, "This mock-blazon pretends to be a denigration, but is in fact a defense of the woman as she is, as *rare* as any."

The fact that the concession pretends to be a denigration is certainly a risk. The majority of my students have insisted, on first reading the poem, that it is insulting to the mistress, and the final couplet initially does little to assuage them. There are, however, no insults here. The speaker never says that his mistress' eyes are not bright; he only acknowledges that they are "nothing like the sun." Through his concessions the speaker simply refuses hyperbole and thereby earns credibility. ("Reek" did not carry the same negative connotation in the seventeenth century that it does today. It meant something closer to the more neutral "breathe." Likewise, the word "mistress" meant something closer to "girlfriend" or "beloved"; it didn't suggest a woman on the side.) The speaker sees plainly that his mistress isn't really very much like a delicate flower or an ethereal angel, and he knows her voice is nothing like music—yet he loves to hear her speak. *His* mistress doesn't need the embellishment of false comparisons. The concession is at once a defense of his own mistress and an attack on the sincerity of other poets. If they do not represent their beloveds accurately, how can we believe their claims of love? The fact that this speaker takes care to speak only the truth about his mistress suggests that he is not exaggerating when he swears "by heav'n" that he loves her. The speaker knows intimately the smell of his mistress' breath and the color of her breasts. The concession shows us that he loves her not *despite* but *for* her human reality.

Concession has been an essential tool in argument at least as far back as the ancient Greeks, who considered it an integral part of the classical argument. They knew that they could undermine the opposition's best points by simply conceding them, and they knew that they could, likewise, persuasively minimize their own weaknesses by straightforwardly admitting them. A straightforward admission will hurt an argument far less than an attack from the other side. Most of us intuitively understand this. "Granted," we say, "That is sometimes true," or "You're right about this, *but* . . . ." We hear concessions around us in everyday speech and in popular songs.

> Don't know much about history
> Don't know much biology
> Don't know much about a science book
> Don't know much about the French I took
>
> But I do know that I love you
> And I know that if you love me too
> What a wonderful world this would be

As a declaration of love, these lines from Sam Cooke's "Wonderful World" may be less weighty than those from Shakespeare's sonnet, but the concessional move is similar. The speaker's final claims about love appear, or at least attempt to appear, more trustworthy in light of his concessions. The speaker *knows* he doesn't know much about most subjects, and therefore asks the "you" to believe his single claim of knowledge. The concessions ask us to believe that the speaker is telling a straight story, not selling a false bill of goods.

As in Shakespeare's sonnet, the speaker of Harryette Mullen's "Dim Lady" can be accused of neither cover-up nor false promotion. Her updated version of Shakespeare's famous sonnet to his reputed "Dark Lady" likewise defiantly concedes that her beloved does not conform to popular ideals:

> My honeybunch's peepers are nothing like neon. Today's special at
> Red Lobster is redder than her kisser. If Liquid Paper is white, her
> racks are institutional beige. If her mop were Slinkys, dishwater
> Slinkys would grow on her noggin. I have seen table-cloths in

Shakey's Pizza Parlors, red and white, but no such picnic colors do
I see in her mug. And in some minty-fresh mouthwashes there is
more sweetness than in the garlic breeze my main squeeze wheezes.
I love to hear her rap, yet I'm aware that Muzak has a hipper beat. I
don't know any Marilyn Monroes. My ball and chain is plain from
head to toe. And yet, by gosh, my scrumptious Twinkie has as
much sex appeal for me as any lanky model or platinum movie
idol who's hyped beyond belief.

The ideals that this "honeybunch" falls short of have to do with stereotypes
of beauty, with the spectacular, the larger-than-life, ivory-skinned,
bleached-blonde idols that the marketing world hypes "beyond belief."
The speaker admits, "My honeybunch's peepers are nothing like neon."
Neon is the stuff of commercial displays; the beloved in Mullen's poem
doesn't belong to that sensational realm. The beloved "wheezes" garlic and
is "plain from head to toe," and yet she is sexy and "scrumptious." The fact
that she isn't eye-popping—with skin as bright as Liquid Paper and lips as
red as a Red Lobster special—is beside the point. It has nothing to do with
what makes her desirable. In a world of Las Vegas showgirls and platinum
movie idols, this speaker will take his (or is it her?) "dim lady," thank you
very much. His "main squeeze," his "ball and chain" doesn't belong to the
overblown language of commodity, but to the slang, colloquial, playful lan-
guage that we reserve for our nearest and dearest. Presumably the speaker
wouldn't call his lady's mouth a "kisser" unless the speaker was in the habit
of being kissed by it. And it is not presumptuous, I think, to assume that
this speaker is in the habit of kissing his honeybunch's "noggin" and unre-
markable "mug." Here, as in Shakespeare, the concessional portrait the
speaker paints of his beloved is not based on delusional idealization but on
clear-eyed and intimate knowledge.

Another particular power of the concession is its ability to create
goodwill. Conceding a point to the opposition provides assurance that a
speaker has considered and appreciated opposing arguments. A concession
is the opposite of an attack. Attacks place the listener, the "other," on the
defensive; concessions reach out to the listener. Well-crafted concessions
have the power to captivate skeptical listeners by admitting the negative
and simultaneously to clear space for the speaker's own affirmative vision.

One approach that possesses the power of concession without all the
attendant risks is the speculative or provisional concession. On these occa-
sions, the speaker concedes a point to the opposition hypothetically: "*Let's*

say it's true that she's no good for me," a speaker might begin, or "*Suppose* our happiest years really are behind us." Andrew Marvell's "To His Coy Mistress" (in Supplemental Poems) is a famous example of this. *If* there were "world enough, and time," his mistress's coyness would be entirely appropriate. Of course, after conceding this to her, he goes on to insist that time is fleeting and therefore they have no time for such coyness. Linda Gregg also employs this strategy in her poem "Gnostics on Trial":

> Let us make the test. Say God wants you
> to be unhappy. That there is no good.
> That there are horrors in store for us
> if we do manage to move toward Him.
> Say you keep Art in its place, not too high.
> And everything, even eternity, is measurable.
> Look at the photographs of the dead,
> both natural (one by one) and unnatural
> in the masses. All tangled. You know about that.
> And can put Beauty in its place. Not too high,
> and passing. Make love our search for unhappiness,
> which is His plan to help us.
> Disregard the afternoon breeze from the Aegean
> on a body almost asleep in the shuttered room.
> Ignore melons, and talking with friends.
> Try to keep from rejoicing. Try
> to keep from happiness. Just try.

The two parts of the concessional structure are clearly present. The poem begins by conceding, for the sake of argument, that the world is a terrible place and ends by praising the world.

"Gnostics on Trial" reverses the order of Gerald Manley Hopkins' "God's Grandeur," which begins with a straightforward proclamation: "The world is charged with the grandeur of God." Nevertheless, Gregg crafts a similar argument. As the title announces, the poem sets out to consider and test the Gnostic idea that the physical world is an irrevocably fallen world, to put the Gnostics "on trial," but rather than begin by challenging them the speaker hypothetically grants that the Almighty wills our unhappiness in a world where "there is no good." Instead of directly attacking Gnostic dualism, the speaker makes room for it, invites it in, considers it. However, once she has reached out to her Gnostic listeners by carrying out the thought experiment of this bleakness, it becomes but a small task to admit some small delight, some good—that "afternoon breeze from the Aegean," say—back into the world. The desolate vision with which the poem begins acts as a foil, making such gems as the afternoon breeze and "talking with friends" stand out. It's as if the opening concession answers a dare: okay, the speaker says, let's say that what you believe is true. Then she turns the dare back on her audience. Even if it is true, "Try to keep from rejoicing" in melons, in that breeze on your almost sleeping body, in the authentic pleasures that are still left to us. The speaker discovers, and the poem argues, that the beauty of the living world is even more apparent against the backdrop of that bleak Gnostic vision.

Not all concessions initially reveal themselves as concessions. In such poems, the opening statement may seem to be the straightforward and central position of the speaker. Consider Marianne Moore's famous and rather sly use of concession in her poem "Poetry":

> I, too, dislike it.
>> Reading it, however, with a perfect contempt for it, one discovers in
>> it, after all, a place for the genuine.

It's easy to identify Moore's two-part concessional structure. The first sentence, which certainly seems a counterintuitive way to begin a defense of poetry, is critical of poetry; the second sentence renders it praiseworthy. Moore's opening concession seems especially daring in a poem of this length. (This is her final revision of the poem, which is significantly shorter than earlier published versions.) She doesn't give herself much room to recover from, much less transform, the dislike she straightforwardly admits. Nevertheless, the opening concession serves the poem and its argument in multiple ways. Partly, the power comes from the surprise. We expect poets to defend, not condemn, their art. Moore refuses to feign what she is "supposed" to feel, and by doing so she gives us permission to free ourselves of similar pretensions. Yet the gesture is more significant than just an opening gambit to gain our attention or even our trust. It's not simply a concession that is then cast aside in favor of more powerful points.

Concessions like this can draw listeners in before they realize just what kind of argument is being made. These concessions subvert the expectations of argument; they don't establish an oppositional relationship between the speaker and her audience. Moore's speaker seems to be commiserating with us, not arguing, and certainly not preaching about the virtues of poetry. In *The Imaginative Argument*, Frank L. Cioffi stresses how important it is to "empathize with your opposition, attempting per-haps to inhabit its consciousness." In asserting her dislike, Moore not only acknowledges poetry's detractors, but counts herself as one of them. She becomes her opposition. This would be a much different poem if the open-ing stated "They dislike it" or, simply, "I dislike it." By aligning herself with readers who find poetry objectionable, she *conjures* our objections. She in-sists upon them.

Only after Moore admits and conjures this dislike for poetry does she move on to defend it, for it isn't by tiptoeing around such dislike that she arrives at her affirmative but precisely by moving through it. One must read poetry "with a perfect contempt for it" *in order to* discover the genuine within it. She begins by assuring poetry's detractors that she is on their side, and she ends by telling them they are really very close to being on her side, on poetry's side. Compared, presumably, to the syrupy poetry cheerleaders who profess their love for the genre, those who read with "contempt" are in a much better position from which to discover the true genuineness that poetry holds. It is essential that the opening concession in this poem isn't a verbal trick. The speaker never tries to minimize or qualify her dislike. A genuine appreciation of poetry only emerges from a genuine dislike.

As both Gregg and Moore demonstrate, the concessional structure is a particularly able vehicle for unfolding paradox. However, not all poems that employ this structure center on paradox. Sometimes the structure em-bodies a real change in vision. Thus, another variation of the concessional structure begins with speakers conceding that they once disliked or opposed the position that they then go on to praise or support. The rhetorical strength of this "conversion concession" is well known. It's the basis of the conversion testimonial, which has long been a staple of everything from the most profound spiritual memoirs to advertisements for cleaning products. Political conventions love to parade out both politicians and citizens who once belonged to the opposing side. One of the risks of this strategy is that the speaker can appear unreliable. If the speaker seems easily swayed, he undermines his authority. The speaker must convince his audience that his conversion was provoked by the strength of the new position, not by the weakness of his previous convictions. If the speaker can persuade the audi-ence, particularly an audience under the sway of his *former* belief, that his transformation was the result of a deeper and more mature understanding, he has the ability to speak to them from the inside. He can assure his oppo-

nents not only that he understands them but that he was recently one of
them. David Lehman's "The World Trade Center" is a good example:

> I never liked the World Trade Center.
> When it went up I talked it down
> As did many other New Yorkers.
> The twin towers were ugly monoliths
> That lacked the details the ornament the character
> Of the Empire State Building and especially
> The Chrysler Building, everyone's favorite,
> With its scalloped top, so noble.
> The World Trade Center was an example of what was wrong
> With American architecture,
> And it stayed that way for twenty-five years
> Until that Friday afternoon in February
> When the bomb went off and the buildings became
> A great symbol of America, like the Statue
> Of Liberty at the end of Hitchcock's *Saboteur*.
> My whole attitude toward the World Trade Center
> Changed overnight. I began to like the way
> It comes into view as you reach Sixth Avenue
> From any side street, the way the tops
> Of the towers dissolve into white skies
> In the east when you cross the Hudson
> Into the city across the George Washington Bridge.

Since the destruction of the towers, no one needs to be coaxed to see them
as national symbols. Lehman, however, wrote this poem after the first at-
tack on the World Trade Center and well before September 11, 2001—
though I, for one, have found the poem more moving since that day. In
light of the World Trade Center's destruction, the opening concession
sounds almost sacrilege, almost like a confession, and the power of the con-
cessional gesture often overlaps with the power of confession. Both con-
cessions and confessions often involve saying the things that are the
hardest to admit. Like confessions, concessions can shock and alarm their
listeners. Both gestures have the capacity to captivate readers and com-
mand their attention.

What makes something a concession rather than a simple confession is
strategy. There is an *argument* at stake. The concession demonstrates an
understanding of the opposition's perspective and, therefore, reaches out

to listeners, particularly unsympathetic listeners, in order to gain their trust and prepare them for the emerging argument. Here, Lehman reaches out to discriminating New Yorkers. He offers solid reasons that he, too, disliked the "ugly monoliths." Given their architectural flaws, such objections are virtually a badge of good taste. Furthermore, Lehman heightens his credibility by establishing himself as a man of long-held convictions. He held the same opinion for twenty-five years, and he never suggests that his *tastes* have changed; it is the world that has changed. Once the towers came under attack, the poem argues, they began to symbolize not just America's artlessness and lack of style, but America itself. The architecture didn't change, but its symbolic weight did. Imagine how much less compelling this poem would be as straightforward patriotic praise for the towers. Praise is all the more powerful when it comes from reluctant sources.

Another significant variation of the concessional structure is the double concession. Ann Townsend provides a particularly gutsy example of this in "A Trick of the Eye," a poem in which she twice concedes personal weaknesses that sound strikingly confessional. It's worth noting that she opens her first book *Dime Store Erotics* with this poem, and therefore she opens her book with this concession: "I have no imagination but what I steal." It's a huge risk. Do we really want to read a poet who admits to being so imaginatively unoriginal? Isn't the project of a first book of poetry to try to prove to readers that a poet has something imaginatively fresh to offer?

A Trick of the Eye

I have no imagination but what I steal.
    I think of it when I walk past
the strangely fashioned chair
    in the furniture store window,

whose back is shaped and painted
    like a shocking red poppy,
green stem upright
    where the spine might press back,

black heart where the shoulders would yield—
    how the painted chair looks best
behind shop glass, how I want to make
    that shapeliness myself,

with small brushes and held breath,
   how my shaky hand fails the design,
my inventions and patterns
   only incomplete hieroglyphs,

how surprised I am, just the same.
   Someone else can always do it better.
Against the sharp spring air,
   a line of chairs waits by the auction house,

blond wood and broken rush seats.
   If I watched for long
they would be gone, taken home
   to be made new by a man with paint

and a make-up brush to capture the small detail.
   And then what would I do?
I would not recognize them again.
   But somewhere in a crowded room

an implausible bunch of grapes
   painted on the seat
surprises the guest when she sits.
   She thinks she'd had too much wine already

or that someone has spilled her food.
   And the one who painted the chair
would do it all over again,
   just to see her skin flush

from the nervous touch of the new,
   the way it does when we're caught
in the wrong place,
   with something crude.

The speaker concedes not only that she has no imaginative originality, but that, despite her desire to create, "someone else can always do it better." On one level, laying herself bare in these concessions is a gambit for our trust. Not many poets would admit such things. On another level, these are defensive moves. Imagine, for example, that your friends implore you to play a song on an instrument that you haven't touched in years. You'd probably be quick to acknowledge that you are out of practice. They're more likely, after all, to be impressed by your abilities when their expectations have been lowered. So Townsend both minimizes and defuses her weaknesses by admitting them from the start and then by going on to compose a scene that offers ample evidence of a fresh and agile imagination.

Beginning in the sixth stanza, everything in the poem takes place in the speaker's imagination. "*If* I watched for long," she begins [my italics], "they would be gone, taken home / to be made new . . . ." Of course, the scenes she imagines are largely a re-assembly of materials. They're not images cut whole cloth from her own mind, and thus, this becomes an argument about just what imagination is. Human originality has to do with how we re-make; artists *must* steal their materials. We can't create, for example, a whole new language for our art any more than we can create a whole new genus of flowers. Still, the way botanists can mix and match to create endless varieties of roses, artists can mix and rearrange and re-make to create new and vital visions. The person who "fashioned" the chair was imitating a poppy, and therefore "stealing" a vision, an image, and crafting it in a new—and cruder—way. It's not the pure, the untainted that, in Townsend's vision, has power to captivate. It isn't real grapes that have the power to shock the woman who sits on the painted chair. It is the painted grapes that hold the power of surprise. This poem seems to begin as self-denigration but it becomes, in its own quiet way, a defense and a celebration of imaginative stealing in all its imitative crudeness.

A final variation is the reversal of the concessional structure. Notice how Charles Wright uses concession not as an opening but as a conclusion in his poem "The Monastery at Vršac":

We've walked the grounds,
                    inspected the vaults and the old church,
Looked at the icons and carved stalls,

And followed the path to the bishop's grave.

Now we sit in the brandy-colored light of late afternoon
Under the locust trees,
                    attended and small
From the monastery. Two nuns hop back and forth like grackles
Along the path. The light drips from the leaves.

Little signals of dust rise uninterpreted from the road.
The grass drones in its puddle of solitude.

The stillness is awful, as though from the inside of a root ...

—Time's sluice and the summer rains erode our hearts
                                    and carry our lives away.
We hold what we can in our two hands,
Sinking, each year, another inch in the earth ...

Mercy upon us,
            we who have learned to preach but not to pray.

The last line is a concession about the poem as a whole. It admits that, as
prayer, the poem is a failure. Despite the dazzling attentiveness of these
lines, Wright insists that they come closer to preaching than praying. He
deliberately diminishes himself and the poem for the sake of elevating our
conception of prayer. Prayer, perhaps, is the thing that, unlike time and the
summer rain, will not erode our hearts. Whatever prayer is, the concession
points to it as something beyond these lines.

In the end, by denying itself the status of prayer, Wright's beautiful
"The Monastery at Vršac" becomes an ode to prayer itself, and the conces-
sional structure is well suited for odes. Concessional poems often bestow
praise that is unlikely, but not, by the end, improbable. As the poems in
Supplemental Poems show, the subjects are sometimes common, everyday
things like an accordion or an old movie. But concessional poems also pay
tribute—often unexpected tribute—to more elevated subjects, including
saints, an infant's sublime perceptions in Larissa Szporluk's "Mare Incog-
nito," the weight of memory in Sophie Cabot Black's "In Light of All," and
even one's own sense of self in Deirdre O'Connor's "Translation." Though
their praise sometimes is spare and barely eked-out—as it is in both Emily
Wilson's "Undone," which hesitates to admit the thrill of "trouble"; and in
Kimberly Johnson's "Pater Noster," which ends by praising the process of
shearing away described in its concession's initial negations—the structure
provides poets ample opportunity to renovate the subjects they initially
disparage, diminish, expose, or otherwise play down. They are tributes, but
they are complex tributes. They don't simply restore or reinstate received
conceptions of their subjects. Rather, they renovate, and to renovate means
to refresh, to revive.

If we look up "concessions" in the index to Howard Raiffa's *The Art
and Science of Negotiation,* we are told "*See also* Strategic misrepresenta-
tions." Poets do use concessions in strategic ways, but the best concessional
poems don't simply "spin" the points they concede. The acknowledge-
ments are genuine acknowledgements, and the poems embrace the com-

plexity they provoke. In an age of spin, we need such poems more than ever. Not all argument is slick maneuvering that seeks to sell us something. Poems that employ the concessional structure can remind us that persuasive arguments and definitive points of view can be strengthened by acknowledging and even embracing complication.

In her book *The Language of Inquiry*, Lyn Hejinian urges poets to "undertake the preservation of otherness." The concessional structure offers one way of doing so. It allows "otherness" in, acknowledges it, and often unfolds *from* it. Not all poetry proceeds, as W.B. Yeats once suggested, as an argument with the self. Concessional poems show us that part of what can make a poem powerful is the way it reaches beyond the self, or beyond a former self, which may be exactly what Yeats meant. Yes, these poems concede, there are good reasons to withdraw; yes, they seem to commiserate, I understand why you've written off this person or thing; yes, I understand why you've given up on this ideal. "But—," they say. "Still—," they say. In a world weighed down by cynicism, the concessional structure can show us how to face real limitations without being defeated by them. As Kobayashi Issa told us many years ago:

> The world of dew
> is the world of dew.
> And yet, and yet—

SUPPLEMENTAL POEMS

In Light of All
Sophie Cabot Black

In light of all that has happened
Which you didn't want to have happen, remember
It was going to happen even as you believed

It could never happen
And as far as knowing what happens next,
Nothing can be done except whatever possible

To make what you want have happen,
To also be present while it is happening,
To be there and to be able to say you were,

And to write it down for someone else to know
They do not know what is happening
So they can say they know what happened

While the light in which all that has happened
Happened in so many ways that finally the light
Became what happened.

Saints
Amy Gerstler

Miracle mongers. Bedwetters. Hair-shirted wonder workers. Shirkers of the
soggy soggy earth. A bit touched, or wholly untouched living among us?
They shrug their bodies off and waft with clouds of celestial perfume. No
smooching for this crew, except for hems, and pictures of their mothers ...
their lips trespass only the very edges of succor. *Swarms of pious bees precede
her.* One young girl wakes up with a ring on her finger and a hole in her
throat. Another bled milk when her white thigh was punctured. All over the
world, a few humans are born each decade with a great talent for suffering.
They have gifts that enable them to sleep through their mistreatment: the
sleep of the uncomplaining just, the sleep of the incomplete. Our
relationship to them is the same as our relationship to trees: what they
exhale, we breathe.

On Sentimentality
Andrew Hudgins

The first time I saw *Limelight*, it didn't move me.
Tereza looks from side to side, her mouth
so far open it overwhelms her face;
she doesn't think to cover it, just stands
in the doorway, distraught, hands lost at her sides.
And then she screams. He's taken his posters,
leaving bright rectangles where they'd hung.
The room is as neat as other people's lives.
I thought the scream was too much, sentimental.
But life doesn't scruple at anything.
Coming home from work, I walked in the door
and fell to my knees. I didn't think to scream.

The pictures were gone and the room was eerily neat
except for a frantic woman who felt she had
to say good-by. And that was all she'd say.
The second time I saw Tereza there,
in the door, her body curved slightly forward in grief,
I felt his absence sinking into her
and thought, *Because she isn't real*
she'll do everything I did and do it better.
She finally understands he's gone. She screams.
We're real, we cannot do it for ourselves.

Pater Noster
Kimberly Johnson

This garden is a ruin. The female
lacrosse team cleat the turf all day,
swatting leaf from stalk, netted staves bent
on one white ball. They gulp and shrill

their rabble post to post—they do not
speak to me. At sundown, taxicabs
disgorge their laughing fares, the debutantes
pert and pranked for evening. As evening falls,

maidens shuck their pinafores,
swains unbreech, blanch, babble, and are claimed.
They pair and tread, tread and crush
the white, thin sprouts. Several shear to woodside,

to grapes stretching vine to soil. They clutch
at each cluster, stropping branch
to point, hands ablush and fumbling, chops
dripping, wide devouring eyes. They do not

look on me. They are so self-consumed.
They tangle in roots, titter and thrill,
shameless in the sweet, abundant fall,
in the necessary fall.

To His Coy Mistress

Andrew Marvell

Had we but world enough, and time,
This coyness, lady, were no crime.
We would sit down, and think which way
To walk, and pass our long love's day.
Thou by the Indian Ganges' side
Shouldst rubies find; I by the tide
Of Humber would complain. I would
Love you ten years before the flood,
And you should, if you please, refuse
Till the conversion of the Jews.
My vegetable love should grow
Vaster than empires and more slow;
An hundred years should go to praise
Thine eyes, and on they forehead gaze;
Two hundred to adore each breast,
But thirty thousand to the rest;
An age at least to every part,
And the last age should show your heart.
For, lady, you deserve this state;
Nor would I love at lower rate.
    But at my back I always hear
Time's winged chariot hurrying near;
And yonder all before us lie
Deserts of vast eternity.
Thy beauty shall no more be found,
Nor in the marble vault shall sound
My echoing song; then worms shall try
That long preserved virginity,
And your quaint honor turn to dust,
And into ashes all my lust:
The grave's a fine and private place,
But none, I think, do there embrace.
    Now therefore, while the youthful hue
Sits on thy skin like morning dew,
And while thy willing soul transpires
At every pore with instant fires,
Now let us sport us while we may,
And now, like amorous birds of prey,

Rather at once our time devour
Than languish in his slow-chapped power,
Let us roll all our strength and all
Our sweetness up into one ball,
And tear our pleasures with rough strife
Thorough the iron gates of life;
Thus, though we cannot make our sun
Stand still, yet we will make him run.

Translation
Deirdre O'Connor

Though there's no such thing as a "self," I missed it—
the fiction of it and how I felt believing in it mildly
like a book an old love sent with an inscription
in his hand, whatever it meant,
After such knowledge, what forgiveness ...

—the script of it like the way my self felt
learning German words by chance—*mitgefuhl,
unheimlichkeit*—and the trailing off that happened
because I knew only the feelings, abstract
and international, like ghosts or connotations
lacking a grammar, a place to go:

this was the way my self felt when it started
falling apart: each piece of it clipped
from a garden vaguely remembered
by somebody unrecognizable—
such a strange bouquet that somebody sent
to nobody else, a syntax of blossoms.

Mare Incognito
Larissa Szporluk

The moon makes my son go silent.
It sucks the fight from his mind,
leaving him hollow in my arms,
like a final piece of tunnel
diminished between lights.

I lose him to the brighter world;
the dark one vibrates with alarm,
as if the storm about to come
had sprung upon its axis.
Trees turn blue from drag;
leaves, like minnows, in reverse,
breaking for the shallows.
In human terms, in human terms,
their flesh is being stolen.
Long bone shadows slam into the ground.

His head is cold all over.
Its curves extend forever.
In the high winds, in the high key of heaven,
he is totally filled with God.

Undone
Emily Wilson

Trouble, sprung from the wish I spoke
from between the hawthorn and the bone
white apple boughs, braced like a harrow,
many-bladed, against the earth—
was that heaven?—the tourniquet of hands
and lips and dressed thorns?

Considering the Accordion
Al Zolynas

The idea is distasteful at best. Awkward box of wind, diminutive, misplaced
piano on one side, raised Braille buttons on the other. The bellows, like some
parody of breathing, like some medical apparatus from a Victorian
sick-ward. A grotesque poem in three dimensions, a rococo thing-am-a-bob.
I once strapped an accordion on my chest and right away I had to lean back
on my heels, my chin in the air, my back arched like a bullfighter or
flamenco dancer. I became an unheard-of contradiction: a gypsy in graduate
school. Ah, but for all that, we find evidence of the soul in the most unlikely
places. Once in a Czech restaurant in Long Beach, an ancient accordionist
came to our table and played the old favorites: "Lady of Spain," "The Sabre

Dance," "Dark Eyes," and through all the clichés his spirit sang clearly. It seems like the accordion floated in air, and he swayed weightlessly behind it, eyes closed, back in Prague or some lost village of his childhood. For a moment we all floated—the whole restaurant: the patrons, the knives and forks, the wine, the sacrificed fish on plates. Everything was pure and eternal, fragilely suspended like a stained-glass window in the one remaining wall of a bombed-out church.

CHAPTER FOUR

The Retrospective-Prospective Structure

MARK YAKICH

> *The past isn't dead. It isn't even past.*
> —William Faulkner

William Faulkner's enigmatic epigram is a wonderfully compact description of the retrospective-prospective structure, a two-part structure that begins with a retrospective consideration of the past and then concludes with a prospective look at the present, or even with a prediction or hope for the future. The first part of the structure deals with something that happened in the past or with memories of past events. Sometimes this first part reveals very private dilemmas, traumas, or feelings dear to the speaker's heart; sometimes it merely identifies past experiences. The second part of the structure expands on the first part by bringing the poem into the present moment. This involves some kind of revision, realization, or new action based on the past.

Almost always, the movement from the first to the second part is signaled by grammatical shifts. The movement, or "turn," can be marked by a change in verb tense; by key "time" words, such as "now," "today," "used to," "before"; or by conditional phrases such as "would," "should," "could," or the second part of "if/then." As we will see in the poems below, this "now" moment can be filled with a range of emotions, including resignation, epiphany, rejection, lament, self-consciousness, and foresight.

Here is a poem by the French poet Jean Follain that displays our structure simply:

Buying

She was buying an elixir
in a city

of bygone times
yet we should think of her
now when shoulders are as white
and wrists as fine
flesh as sweet
Oh, vertiginous life!

This poem expresses a moment of recognition, even strange joy, upon con-
sidering a past event. Notice the two-part movement. The poem begins
with a character doing something in the past: "She was buying an elixir."
Then there is a quick change to the present: "yet we should think of her /
now." The speaker asks the reader to re-envision the character. A woman
bought an elixir in a city long ago—a hundred years ago, perhaps a thou-
sand—but now we can conjure her in the mind as if she were right beside
us. The change in grammatical tense indicates the two-part movement in
our structure, from past ("was buying") to present ("shoulders are"). In
this little poem, there is a stunning moment of revelation in its second part,
which ties together past and present: "Oh, vertiginous life!" Time, in other
words, is inconstant and dizzying, even though it appears to be linear.

If the first part of the retrospective-prospective structure deals with the
past, it would seem obvious that our individual memories of past events
would offer much material for composition. From Web sites like MySpace
to talk shows like *Oprah*, we seem to be a society that enjoys talking about
itself as a means of self-promotion, self-obsession, catharsis, and penitence.
Indeed, twentieth-century literature is rife with confessions or pseudo-
confessions.

Historically, writers have not been so apt to use the details of their per-
sonal lives as literary material. Rather, this trend slowly developed in litera-
ture until it emerged fully over the course of the past two centuries. One of
the first writers to use his own biography as material for writing was the
Christian theologian Saint Augustine. In *The Confessions*, Augustine not
only recounts his sins of lust and pride and his transgressions of faith, but
he also presents his own personal discovery of peace and Christian divinity
as a potential conversion model for others. For Augustine, this notion of
"confession" entailed both admission of past wrongs and transformation
of present behavior. The next great "confessor" was the eighteenth-century
philosopher Jean-Jacques Rousseau, who wrote his own *Confessions* in
which he attempted to include all of his biography in astonishing detail,

ranging from stealing a silk ribbon as a boy to naming and renaming his pet dog in retirement.

The use of personal history as material for poetry, however, should mostly be credited to the Romantic poets of the nineteenth century. William Wordsworth was especially concerned with bringing autobiography into his poems. Wordsworth was the first poet in the English-speaking tradition to use his own experiences and memories as the raw materials for an epic poem. Up until that point, epic poetry was the province of war (in *The Iliad*), a quest (in *The Odyssey*), or both (in *The Aeneid*); or it was domestic but universal (Adam and Eve in John Milton's *Paradise Lost*). Wordsworth narrowed down his epic to the individual, and in doing so he opened up a new world. In *The Prelude*, a poem-project that he began in his twenties and continually went back to rework throughout his life, Wordsworth meditates on memory and on the self. Suitably, the poem is subtitled "Growth of a Poet's Mind." The individual, precisely the poet, traces not "the ways of God justified to man," as was Milton's aim in his epic *Paradise Lost*, but the development of the individual self through its own history and thought. At the end of *The Prelude*, which spans some thirteen long sections called "books," the poet comes to his great epiphany: redemption and restoration of the past lies in memory and in the sublimation of memory into poetry.

In the twentieth century, the confessional poets, including Robert Lowell, Sylvia Plath, John Berryman, and Anne Sexton, picked up where Wordsworth and the Romantics left off. The confessional poets brought their personal histories even further to the forefront of their poetry, often to a shocking or titillating extent. Over time critics, poets, and readers have defined "confessional" in a variety of ways—from a simple admission of impropriety, such as stealing a cookie from Mother's cookie jar, to measuring the depths of one's mind, such as recollecting a psychotic episode. Although the confessional poets are known for using "real-life" events and memories in their work, their poems often include examples and details that never *really* happened. In other words, their poems are as much about art and artifice as they are about authentic personal histories and revelations. Sylvia Plath, for instance, turns her father into a Nazi in her famous poem "Daddy," even though he emigrated from Germany years before Hitler and the Nazis came to power. Yet there is an element of "emotional truth" in Plath's equating the father in her poem with a Nazi.

Whether a poem relies on "factual truth" or "emotional truth," the retrospective-prospective structure provides a *strategy* for organizing these memories. Often our past self doesn't line up with our present self; the self has transformed from within or has been transformed from without. And, as we will see, just such moments of transformation have become the essence of many poems.

In his essay "My Grandfather's Tackle Box: The Limits of Memory-Driven Poetry," the poet Billy Collins points out that what's at stake in a good deal of contemporary poetry, especially poems that are "confessional" or "personal," is memory. But, he writes, "It is impossible to view the past . . . without also seeing the present and in it the mirror image of the self. The observer is an ingredient in the observed." Thus, according to Collins, for a memory-driven poem there should be "a sense of the poem's own present." The present is so vital for Collins because a memory-driven poem that merely recounts memories without any gesture to the present or future can be awfully dull or can run the risk of pure nostalgia. Obviously a poem can be set entirely in the past—that is not at issue—but if a poem intends to *reflect* on that past, it needs to do more than simply describe a memory. It is the poet's job to extend past experience into present experience. The penultimate stanza of one of Collins' poems, "This Much I Do Remember," emphasizes just this point:

> Then all of the moments of the past
> began to line up behind that moment
> and all of the moments to come
> assembled in front of it in a long row,
> giving me reason to believe
> that this was a moment I had rescued
> from millions that rush out of sight
> into a darkness behind the eyes.

This handful of lines sums up nicely that our memories of the past, and even our future memories, can be captured in the moment of a poem. Whether we want to call this kind of poem a "lyric," where the focus is on a particular moment, especially "the moment" of reading the poem, or whether we want to label it an "epiphany" poem, where the speaker has a realization or an insight, the poem is trying to come to terms with the past and not simply recounting it. The first part of the retrospective-prospective structure underscores the notion that our memories are powerful things, things that cannot and perhaps should not be easily escaped. But it is the second part of the structure that hones in on the lessons to be learned or regrets to be acknowledged. And more often than not, the "I," or the character in these kinds of poems, comes to the conclusion that a specific action needs to be taken or a certain idea needs to be practiced, if not in the present moment then in the near future.

Such is the case with William Butler Yeats' poem "The Circus Animals' Desertion." For most of his life Yeats wrote poems, plays, and prose that borrowed or expanded images and archetypes from Irish history and folk tales, and very often he let these images and archetypes stand in for real people he knew. Toward the end of his life, however, Yeats regretted many things, and these regrets were not limited to indiscreet love affairs or political failures. He felt significant remorse for putting more energy into his writing than into his "real life." In "The Circus Animals' Desertion," he examines his life as paralleled and denoted, stage by stage, in his poetry, and he considers what, if anything, is left for him besides regret:

I.

I sought a theme and sought for it in vain,
I sought it daily for six weeks or so.
Maybe at last, being but a broken man,
I must be satisfied with my heart, although
Winter and summer till old age began
My circus animals were all on show,
Those stilted boys, that burnished chariot,
Lion and woman and the Lord knows what.

II.

What can I but enumerate old themes,
First that sea-rider Oisin led by the nose
Through three enchanted islands, allegorical dreams,
Vain gaiety, vain battle, vain repose,
Themes of the embittered heart, or so it seems,
That might adorn old songs or courtly shows;
But what cared I that set him on to ride,
I, starved for the bosom of his faery bride.

And then a counter-truth filled out its play,
'The Countess Cathleen' was the name I gave it,
She, pity-crazed, had given her soul away
But masterful Heaven had intervened to save it.

I thought my dear must her own soul destroy
So did fanaticism and hate enslave it,
And this brought forth a dream and soon enough
This dream itself had all my thought and love.

And when the Fool and Blind Man stole the bread
Cuchulain fought the ungovernable sea;
Heart mysteries there, and yet when all is said
It was the dream itself enchanted me:
Character isolated by a deed
To engross the present and dominate memory.
Players and painted stage took all my love,
And not those things that they were emblems of.

III.

Those masterful images because complete
Grew in pure mind, but out of what began?
A mound of refuse or the sweepings of a street,
Old kettles, old bottles, and a broken can,
Old iron, old bones, old rags, that raving slut
Who keeps the till. Now that my ladder's gone,
I must lie down where all the ladders start
In the foul rag and bone shop of the heart.

Sections I and II contain the first part of our two-part structure. Using the images and characters he once used in his literary works to represent aspects of his life, Yeats re-views his past poetry and preoccupations, enumerating "old themes." For example, in stanza two, the poet focuses on the title character from his first major poem, "The Wanderings of Oisin," a poem that he went back to throughout his career, continually revising or commenting on it. Oisin is a figure from Irish mythology who, like Odysseus in some ways, travels across lands and seas in the name of love and has a variety of adventures along the way. As Yeats suggests at the end of the stanza ("I, starved for the bosom of his faery bride"), Oisin is a stand-in for his own longing for a beloved. And that beloved is alluded to in the very next stanza: the Countess Cathleen is a character from one of Yeats' plays who sells her soul to save the Irish people and who represents Maud Gonne, a woman Yeats pursued for thirty years. After recounting these and other characters, images, and allegories—figurative language that stands in for real-life people and events—Yeats concludes with great remorse in the last lines of Section II: "Players and painted stage took all my love, / And not those things that they were emblems of."

In the poem's final section, we see the second part of our structure. The speaker comes to terms with the past by reaching back to a deeper past ("Those masterful images . . . out of what began?") only to push the poem forward by declaring the action he must take in the present: "Now that my ladder's gone, / I must lie down where all the ladders start / In the foul rag and bone shop of the heart." The picture painted is not pretty ("old kettles, old bottles, and a broken can . . . that raving slut . . . ,") but it is, the speaker wants to claim, *real*. He realizes that he can no longer rely on figurative language, but must begin to grapple with the imperfections of lived life. Notice, too, how the image of the heart given at the beginning of the poem—"I must be satisfied with my heart"—is repeated in these last lines, bringing the poem full circle. Without reference to any other characters or figures from the past, the "I" acknowledges that his heart is all that is left him.

Rethinking one's past creative endeavors is a theme that many artists eventually explore. Like Yeats in the poem above, Muriel Rukeyser in "The Poem as Mask" attempts to come to terms with previously held ideas. Her poem is shorter than Yeats' and instead of covering decades of experience it centers on one specific creation—a poem that she had written years earlier:

The Poem as Mask

Orpheus

When I wrote of the women in their dances and wildness,
    it was a mask,
on their mountain, gold hunting, singing, in orgy,
it was a mask; when I wrote of the god,
fragmented, exiled from himself, his life, the love gone down with song,
it was myself, split open, unable to speak in exile from myself.

There is no mountain, there is no god, there is memory
of my torn life, myself split open in sleep, the rescued child
beside me among the doctors, and a word
of rescue from the great eyes.

No more masks! No more mythologies!

Now, for the first time, the god lifts his hand,
the fragments join in me with their own music.

If you are coming to this poem for the first time, you may be inclined to think that the italicized "Orpheus" underneath the title means that the poem is in the voice of Orpheus, the pied piper and poet of Greek legend. That is a possibility. Orpheus' songs charmed wild animals and beasts as well as stones and trees. He is famously known for going down to the underworld to retrieve his wife, Eurydice, and then losing her again because he looked back on their return trip to the world of the living. Later, as the myth goes, a group of Dionysus' devotees tear Orpheus apart limb from limb, leaving his head to float down the river still singing. There are phrases and allusions, such as "gold hunting, singing, in orgy" and "my torn life, myself split open," in the poem that support such a reading. However, this poem may also be a reexamination of an older Rukeyser poem, "Orpheus," in which the poet used Orpheus' life as allegory for her own. In this reading, the speaker in the first line is the poet talking about her previous poem: "When I wrote of the women in their dances and wildness, it was a mask." As in Yeats' poem, the poet is in a quarrel with herself. She once used Orpheus to discuss her own life but now realizes that was not only a pretense or disguise, but also a mistake. Myth was the wrong choice to illustrate her real-life anguish.

To examine the two-part movement of the retrospective-prospective structure, look to the grammatical tenses in the poem. Notice that the first stanza is in past tense: "I wrote" and "it was." This stanza describes previous events and perspectives in which the speaker tried to write her experiences through the voice of Orpheus. Whereas the speaker in the Yeats poem spends most of the time focusing on the past, the speaker here quickly transitions to the now. The second, third, and fourth stanzas are all in present tense: "There is," "god lifts," and "fragments join." The speaker—dispensing with her previous mask of Orpheus—struggles to understand how memory is as much a part of the present as it is of the past. While there is neither "mountain" nor "god" in the present moment, there certainly is "memory / of my torn life." With that second stanza begins the second part of our structure. The speaker begins to re-see the past by trying to tell what *really* happened, devoid of myth. As readers, we don't know exactly what has happened to the speaker though it seems to have something to do with a child and perhaps a hospital scene. (In fact, Rukeyser had undergone a dangerous Caesarean section.) But it doesn't matter exactly. The important point is that the speaker has come to a realization about the past. In the one-line third stanza, she emphatically declares that realization, a life of

"No more masks! No more mythologies!" She will live and write about her life differently from now on.

The most dramatic turn to the present comes at the end of the poem. There are two key words that signal this turn. As in the Yeats poem, the word "Now" appears, and for even more emphasis "Now" is followed closely with "first," setting up the final epiphany in the last line: "the fragments join in me with their own music." And there is yet another structural parallel with the Yeats poem. Notice how a concept from the first stanza returns here in the last stanza. The speaker initially talks of "the god, / fragmented," and here at the end "the fragments" have been transformed, coming together inside the speaker to create her own myth. Not all poems that employ the retrospective-prospective structure use this particular strategy of returning to a previous concept, but many do use it to register clearly how what once was has changed.

In Billy Collins' poem "Personal History," we again can see a two-part movement from past to present, but in this case, the speaker focuses on a relationship with another person and not one of his own creations:

> "I would love you ten years before the flood."
> —Andrew Marvell

A long time ago when cataclysms were common
as sneezes and land masses slid
around the globe looking for places
to settle down and become continents,
someone introduced us at a party.

Later on, as the Renaissance flowered,
I fell in love with you, egged on by the sonnet
and the idea of your individuality.

We married during the Industrial Revolution,
coughing on a brown lawn above a city
humming with flywheels and drive belts.
The ceremony went like clockwork.

When war rattled the world, we shut the blinds
and huddled under a table while sirens harmonized.
Everything but our affection was rationed.

Now we find ourselves in the post-modern age,

using one of its many Saturday nights
to drive to the movies in a Volkswagen.

"It doesn't seem we've been together that long,"
you say, looking at my profile,
contracting the past into the rearview mirror,
beaming the future into the tunneling of our headlights.

The first four stanzas of "Personal History" follow the past relationship between the speaker and the "you," from their first encounter at a party to a real and/or metaphorical war experience. Then in stanza five, the turn to the present moment is signaled by the word "Now" and by the shift from past- to present-tense verbs. The sixth stanza places the you and I squarely in the present moment. Not only does it offer an immediate scene, given some urgency with a piece of dialogue, but it also provides commentary on the present moment, where the past is seen in "the rearview mirror" and the future is seen in "the tunneling of our headlights."

In "Personal History," we have love, death, taxes, fashion, phobias, old saws that commingle in amusing ways, and outright silliness: after having catalogued all the things the couple has been through over the centuries, the "you" says, "'It doesn't seem we've been together that long.'" Here, memory is given a playful spin. With its humorous tone and its romantic content, Collins' poem is very different from Yeats' and Rukeyser's. Clearly, there is no restriction on the range of topics that a retrospective-prospective poem may address.

In the poems above, a line can literally be drawn between the stanzas that explore the past and the stanzas that turn to the present. "Her Door" by Mary Leader, however, cleaves the past and present in another way.

Her Door

There was a time her door was never closed.
Her music box played "Für Elise" in plinks.
Her crib new-bought—I drew her sleeping there.

The little drawing sits beside my chair.
These days, she ornaments her hands with rings.
She's seventeen. Her door is one I knock.

There was a time I daily brushed her hair
By window light—I bathed her, in the sink
In sunny water, in the kitchen, there.

I've bought her several thousand things to wear,
And now this boy buys her silver rings.
He goes inside her room and shuts the door.

Those days, to rock her was to say a prayer.
She'd gaze at me, and blink, and I would sing
Of bees and horses, in the pasture, there.

The drawing sits as still as nap-time air—
Her curled-up hand—that precious line, her cheek ...
Next year her door will stand, again, ajar
But she herself will not be living there.

The poem alternates between past and present, and the shifting tenses make the temporal oscillation very clear. The first stanza is in past tense; the speaker is recalling her daughter as a baby. The second stanza is in present tense; the daughter is now seventeen. The following stanzas continue this alternation until the final stanza, which begins in the present and then moves into the future: "Next year her door will stand ... But she herself will not be living there." Essentially, what this poem does is take our two-part structure and heighten it. The turn from past to present occurs over and over in Leader's poem, whereas in the previous poems the turn occurred only once and was the central event. Here again, an image/concept from the past becomes crucial to comprehending the past-present transformation. In fact, in "Her Door" there are two images that are revisited: the daughter's "door" and the speaker's "drawing." And while the door to the daughter's bedroom opens, closes, and then shall open again, the drawing that the speaker made of the daughter as a baby remains unchanged: "The little drawing sits beside my chair," and "The drawing sits as still as nap-time air."

"Her Door" is a variation on the villanelle, a conventional poetic form involving the intricate weaving of end-rhymes and refrains. Leader generally sticks to the villanelle's rhyme scheme, but she modifies lines that would otherwise be refrains, repeating only key words or terms. For example, the first refrain, "There was a time her door was never closed," is repeated as "She's seventeen. Her door is one I knock." In lines 12 and 18, just where one would expect refrains, the "door" image is kept alive but the entire line is not repeated. The second refrain, "Her crib new-bought—I drew her sleeping there," is repeated in a variety of ways that maintains a physical sense of "there": "In sunny water, in the kitchen, there"; "Of bees and horses, in the pasture, there"; and "But she herself will not be living there." With its alternating lines, the villanelle provides a perfect form for Leader's poem, allowing "Her Door" to flip back and forth between past and present, between how things used to be and how they are now. When, just as they would in a conventional villanelle, the two refrains meet in the concluding couplet, they mark the speaker's understanding not of the present but of the future:

> Next year her door will stand, again, ajar
> But she herself will not be living there.

In Leader's own words, "The villanelle does the work of handling survivor's guilt. It is akin to the broader structure of elegy which does, more generally, the work of grief." And guilt and grief certainly are two of the possible emotions we have when reflecting on our pasts, forging and re-forging our memories. As in our other examples, "Her Door" displays an effort to negotiate past and present into something more meaningful than mere recollection.

At the heart of the retrospective-prospective structure is a desire to give order to and come to terms with experience and memory. The movement of time is vital to how the structure works. The structure begins retrospectively in the past tense, telling or showing us past events or memories, and then, at some point, the poem moves prospectively into the present tense where the speaker acknowledges some kind of change. That acknowledgement may take a variety of expressions ranging from "negatives" of guilt, complicity, lament, or regret to "positives" of confession, epiphany, realization, or call to action.

As the work in this chapter and in Supplemental Poems shows, though the retrospective-prospective structure is itself fairly simple, the poems that employ it can be artful and complex. They can employ a variety of forms and styles, from the villanelle to the letter, as in Natasha Trethewey's "Letter Home" and James Galvin's "Dear May Eighth"; and they can use various controlling metaphors and extended comparisons, as in David Whyte's "Song for the Salmon" and Dunya Mikhail's "The Pomegranate Seeds."

Even larger variations are possible. In Terrance Hayes' "Tour Daufuskie," the speaker projects *someone else's* past into a present experience between him and his beloved. In Charles Wright's prose poem "The Poet Grows Older," the speaker conflates a past that is not his with a present that is: he dreams the dreams he wishes he'd had as a boy. Like Rukeyser's poem,

Brian Swann's "Exist" switches the structure's traditional hierarchy of emphasis, giving the majority of his poem over to the prospective. And in "This Room and Everything in It," Li-Young Lee consciously complicates the structure, shifting time frames from past-present to present-future, and engaging his speaker in the convoluted, though loving—and certainly *lovely*—effort at making future memory.

That the retrospective-prospective structure can involve so many and such various transformations, however, should not seem odd. It is a structure that at its heart is about just such transformation.

SUPPLEMENTAL POEMS

Dear May Eighth
James Galvin

Why was the last kiss May seventh
And so shy?

Your tongue was skittish.

Your clavicle—
Door-bolt, little key,
Tendril—
Was the world's crosstree—
Your collarbone was hot snow to touch.

I wanted to say commitment,
And so I was committed,
And so I did commit
Crimes against the immaculate.

Clavicle, clavichord,
Gold keys falling through me cold.

You explain
The sky I spent my life under,
The bottom of the ocean
That packed up and left.

You say it's the basin that makes the sky a bay.

The sunset plans its palette, its deployment.

It hasn't decided the denouement—
It's breathless. ...

Listen, Nobody's Business,
Why aren't you in love with me?

Is your overture over-subtle
Like this sunset—
White clavicle under gray thunderheads,
Cobalt throbs?

Streaky northern billows
And reds thrum into music—clavichord.

Then—get this—
Red cliff
Is palindromed,
Butterflied, flayed,
In strata of lenticulars.

Rain rains down
Blue-black on earth
And sends riders, striders,
Bruisy yellow,
Blood in a stream,
Back to the eastern horizon—
Where I kissed you.

If you would wake with me
I'd know how to die.

Yours, May eighth,
Sincerely,
Man under influence of sky.

Tour Daufuskie
Terrance Hayes

On that small island
during a tropical storm
in the last century

people tied to the necks
of pine trees drowned

when the wires and whips

and webs and ropes
of rain covered their bodies

so that when we moved
along the dirt back roads
and paused

to photo the AME church
and one room schoolhouse
and small shacks
of the black folk of Daufuskie

no voices trailed us
or floated out to greet us.

Sometimes now
the trunk of a tree
resembles the waist
of a black body;

sometimes your naked waist
still and rooted before me,
smells thick and sweet
as the freshly cut meat of a pine.

When I knock against you,
it is like swimming from the world

out to the small island of Daufuskie
in the witching hour of a storm,
like drowning in the arms of a tree.

This Room and Everything in It
Li-Young Lee

Lie still now
while I prepare for my future,
certain hard days ahead,
when I'll need what I know so clearly this moment.

I am making use
of the one thing I learned

of all the things my father tried to teach me:
the art of memory.

I am letting this room
and everything in it
stand for my ideas about love
and its difficulties.

I'll let your love-cries,
those spacious notes
of a moment ago,
stand for distance.

Your scent,
that scent
of spice and a wound,
I'll let stand for mystery.

Your sunken belly
is the daily cup
of milk I drank
as a boy before morning prayer.

The sun on the face
of the wall
is God, the face
I can't see, my soul,

and so on, each thing
standing for a separate idea,
and those ideas forming the constellation
of my greater idea.
And one day, when I need
to tell myself something intelligent
about love,

I'll close my eyes
and recall this room and everything in it:
My body is estrangement.
This desire, perfection.
Your closed eyes my extinction.
Now I've forgotten my
idea. The book

on the windowsill, riffled by the wind ...
the even-numbered pages are
the past, the odd-
numbered pages, the future.
The sun is
God, your body is milk ...

useless, useless ...
your cries are song, my body's not me ...
no good ... my idea
has evaporated ... your hair is time, your thighs are song ...
it had something to do
with death ... it had something
to do with love.

The Pomegranate Seeds
Dunya Mikhail

A long time has passed since we were first imprisoned
in the pomegranate.
In vain we rush and strike the interior surface with our heads,
hoping that a hole might open for us,
so that we could meet the air just once ...
Our losses increase each day.
Some of the seeds sacrificed their juice for freedom
as they ripped their way through the trenches.
I told my sisters, the pomegranate seeds:
the dents which begin to appear on the surface
prove the existence of a fist
which threatens our destiny and squeezes our hopes.
What are your suggestions for our liberation?
—Shall we stay close together?
—We will be smothered by the strain of togetherness.
—Shall we ask a higher power for help?
—No one will hear our shouts through this enveloping shell.
—Shall we wait for a savior?
—We will rot before anyone thinks of us.
—Then we should stand in circles, like impossible holes.
Before the circles were completed, a hole began to open by itself.
We wanted to dance a dabka,

but a worm reared its head over the terrified seeds.
The pomegranate began to shake,
a great crack appeared on the surface.
Some of the seeds trembled inside the human fist,
others were stripped off onto the ground ...
I am still suspended in the cavity
and the worm lies in ambush for me ...

Letter Home
Natasha Trethewey

       —New Orleans, November 1910

Four weeks have passed since I left, and still
I must write to you of no work. I've worn down
the soles and walked through the tightness
of my new shoes calling upon the merchants,
their offices bustling. All the while I kept thinking
my plain English and good writing would secure
for me some modest position. Though I dress each day
in my best, hands covered with the lace gloves
you crocheted—no one needs a *girl*. How flat
the word sounds, and heavy. My purse thins.
I spend foolishly to make an appearance of quiet
industry, to mask the desperation that tightens
my throat. I sit watching—

though I pretend not to notice—the dark maids
ambling by with their white charges. Do I deceive
anyone? Were they to see my hands, brown
as your dear face, they'd know I'm not quite
what I pretend to be. I walk these streets
a white woman, or so I think, until I catch the eyes
of some stranger upon me, and I must lower mine,
a *negress* again. There are enough things here
to remind me who I am. Mules lumbering through
the crowded streets send me into reverie, their footfall
the sound of a pointer and chalk hitting the blackboard
at school, only louder. Then there are women, clicking

their tongues in conversation, carrying their loads
on their heads. Their husky voices, the wash pots
and irons of the laundresses call to me. Here,

I thought not to do the work I once did, back bending
and domestic; my schooling a gift—even those half days
at picking time, listening to Miss J—. How
I'd come to know words, the recitations I practiced
to sound like her, lilting, my sentences curling up
or trailing off at the ends. I read my books until
I nearly broke their spines, and in the cotton field,
I repeated whole sections I'd learned by heart,
spelling each word in my head to make a picture
I could see, as well as a weight I could feel
in my mouth. So now, even as I write this
and think of you at home, *Good-bye*

is the waving map of your palm, is
a stone on my tongue.

Exist
Brian Swann

As a kid I never thought of "pain" as
    something I felt. What I felt I could not
name or share. Now out the window I watch
    a thin chemical yellow smear being
pushed down by gray rolls of night. Behind me
                the physics of the TV screen

Plays out plots and previews. Outside is shapes
    moving under neon like those who have
already moved on. Lighted windows stick
    in the sky, independent of stone or
brick. I can only exist in writing,
                when for a while I do not know

I "exist." I exist only when I
    don't exist? There I am at the window,
staring back at me, in glass, dependent
    on the dark. In a room beyond this one,

I see myself in replicas that come &
        go with light, most there when most dark.

The Poet Grows Older
Charles Wright

It seemed, at the time, so indifferent an age that I recall nothing of it except
an infinite tedium to be endured. I envied no one, nor dreamed of anything
in particular as, unwillingly, I enveloped myself in all of the various disguises
of a decent childhood. Nothing now comes to mind of ever embarking upon
famous voyages to the usual continents; of making, from the dark rooms and
empty houses of my imagination, brilliant escapes from unnatural enemies;
or, on rainy winter afternoons in an attic, of inventing one plot or
counterplot, against a prince or a beast ... . Instead, it must have been
otherwise.

I try to remember, nevertheless, something of all that time and place, sitting
alone here in a room in the middle of spring, hearing the sound of rain
which has fallen for most of April, concerned with such different things,
things done by others ... . I read of the aimless coups in the old dynasties
from Africa to Afghanistan, their new republics whose lists of war lords alone
are enough to distress the Aryan tongue; of intricate rockets in search of a
planet, soon, perhaps to land in a country somewhere outside the pedestrian
reach of reason; of the latest, old sailor's account of a water dragon seen
bathing off the grizzled coast of Scotland ... . It is at times such as this, and
without thinking, really, clothed in my goat's-wool robes, that I steal a camel
from an outlying Arabian stable, gather together my clansmen, and gallop
for days along the miraculous caravan trails to Asia.

Song for the Salmon
David Whyte

For too many days now I have not written of the sea,
not the rivers, nor the shifting currents
we find between the islands.

For too many nights now I have not imagined the salmon
threading the dark streams of reflected stars,
nor have I dreamt of his longing
nor the lithe swing of his tail toward dawn.

I have not given myself to the depth to which he goes,
to the cargoes of crystal water, cold with salt,
nor the enormous plains of ocean swaying beneath the moon.

I have not felt the lifted arms of the ocean
opening its white hands on the seashore,
nor the salted wind, whole and healthy
filling its chest with living air.

I have not heard those waves
fallen out of heaven onto earth,
nor the tumult of sounds and the satisfaction
of a thousand miles of ocean
giving up its strength on the sand.

But now I have spoken of that great sea,
the ocean of longing shifts through me,
the blessed inner star of navigation
moves in the dark sky above
and I am ready like the young salmon
to leave this river, blessed with hunger
for a great journey on the drawing tide.

CHAPTER FIVE

The Elegy's Structures

D.A. POWELL

When we think of the occasions of poetry, we think of love, triumph, and loss. Although the elegy is concerned primarily with loss, it is embedded with implied love and with an overwhelming need to triumph over death. Moving from consideration of the deceased to the concerns of the living, elegy mirrors the speaker's desire to rescue—not only from death but from transience as well—the person or thing that is either lost or in danger of being lost.

The structure of the elegy is difficult to pin down; in fact, the elegy is more a mode of thinking, or a complex set of conventions, than a single structure. An elegy often serves as an occasion for considering numerous issues, from the political to the deeply personal, apart from the mourning of the dead. Its turns can be multiple and various. Additionally, many of the elegy's conventions, including invocations and references to and calls for additional mourners, are structural. It is impossible to limit the elegiac mode to just one clear set of turns.

And yet, the elegy originates in an age-old desire: to bring the beloved back from obscurity, whether in a real or an imagined way. And this desire has an archetypal pattern of descent and ascent. One of the central devices of classical heroic poems is the descent into the Underworld. Odysseus descends in order to complete his journey; Aeneas, to find a new homeland. In both instances, the heroes revisit loved ones while they are immersed in the obscure chambers of hell. In Ovid's *Metamorphoses*, Orpheus makes his way into the gloom in order to reclaim his beloved Eurydice. By singing of his loss upon the lyre, Orpheus is able to move the ghosts, the Furies, and finally the king and queen of the Underworld themselves to tears. So moved are these beings that they release Eurydice from the bonds of death. The song Orpheus sings is born of emotion and recollection. After all, Orpheus' father is Apollo, god of the lyric poem; his grandmother is the goddess of memory. His songs fuse the powers of poetry with the device of remembrance, giving birth to the elegiac form. Ultimately, Orpheus fails in his quest, but his music nonetheless has power. Ovid describes how Orpheus' subsequent performances of poems move the trees to uproot themselves and to bend and drop their leaves. The mourning of the poems becomes wedded to the grieving that the Earth itself seems to enact in winter.

Three central elegiac structures stem from this mythic pattern. All three descend, but each emerges from the descent in a very different way. The elegy can succeed in salvaging victory from death by giving immortality to the object of mourning. The elegy can surrender to the experience of loss and forever resonate with sadness, refusing solace in a structure that signals the triumph of death but that also perhaps offers some consolation by displaying the ferocity of the elegist's love. Or the elegy can examine the disappearance of the dead and simply say "enough—I'll not continue down this path."

The elegy that turns toward immortality hopes to keep the dead present in the poem, creating in effect an imaginative resurrection that a poem's turn from hopeful grieving to established immortality can confirm. Such is the case in Edmund Spenser's *Astrophel*, an almost archetypal elegy that grieves the death of poet Philip Sidney. Sidney wrote, among other things, the sonnet cycle called *Astrophel and Stella*. This poem opens with an invocation, inviting an audience of fellow shepherd-poets to mourn:

> *Shepheards that wont on pipes of oaten reed,*
> *Oft times to plaine your loues concealed smart:*
> *And with your piteous layes haue learnd to breed*
> *Compassion in a countrey lasses hart.*
> *Hearken ye gentle shepheards to my song,*
> *And place my dolefull plaint your plaints emong.*

This invocation serves two significant purposes. First, it connects the poet, the poem, and so the poem's subject to the natural world, a world in which resurrection is commonplace, a world of seasons, of cycles, of both Fall and Spring. Second, calling to mind the pastoral tradition that gave rise to the elegy, it reinforces the notion of the elegy as an essentially communal act. Throughout *Astrophel* Spenser includes the figures of other mourners, giving voice to a sadness that exceeds the concerns of the poem's speaker. Spenser's is but one voice, enacting the grieving that is felt by all, rather like a professional mourner who has been asked to wail behind the coffin of the king.

After this invocation, which is an invitation for the participation of others and an effort, like Scheherazade's, to stave off death through a prolonged speech act, Spenser moves to memorializing the deceased. Talking against death, the poem continues—as a living entity—to inhabit the space once occupied by the beloved. Spenser provides an almost 200-line history of the life of the person being mourned: Astrophel, one of Sidney's creations, serves as a stand-in for the poet and as proof positive of Sidney's immortality. Astrophel's life is described in pastoral, mythic terms. He is a shepherd-poet in love with the fair maiden Stella until he is killed, like the god Adonis, by a thigh wound incurred during a hunting expedition. Spenser then describes the sadness of the characters in the poem, a sadness that for Stella is so great, so sympathetic, that she herself dies.

The poem's major turn occurs when the gods, having watched all that happened, take pity on the lovers and transform them so that they can be together forever, turning them into a flower, called an astrophel, or "star-lover," and a star, a stellar object. Though the elaborate *Astrophel* continues well beyond this event, the happy, even miraculous, immortality of Astrophel and Stella is, in the world of the poem, ultimate: it is guaranteed by the gods. And the couple's continued fame is further confirmed by the fact that each of the shepherd-poets who hears of the couple's death at once suffers "inward anguish and great griefe" but then works to devise the "meanes"—further poems?—"to shew [that is, show] his sorrow best." So wondrous are Astrophel and Stella, and thus Sidney, that poems will forever be written about them. Spenser writes: "can so divine a thing be dead? / Ah no, it is not dead, ne can it die."

Its forests populated with nymphs, maidens, gods of the wood, and lambs, *Astrophel*'s imagery is quite pagan in origin; however, the poem has strong echoes of biblical themes. With its emphasis on life everlasting, Christian theology certainly seems a natural twin to the "elegy as immortalization." But, whether pagan or Christian, what really matters is that, through Spenser's work, the beloved friend exists continually in a paradise of remembering.

This is the paradise—the paradise of remembering—that Thom Gunn creates in his thoroughly secular "In the Post Office":

> Saw someone yesterday looked like you did,
> Being short with long blond hair, a sturdy kid

Ahead of me in line. I gazed and gazed
At his good back, feeling again, amazed,
That almost envious sexual tension which
Rubbing at made the greater, like an itch,
An itch to steal or otherwise possess
The brilliant restive charm, the boyishness
That half-aware—and not aware enough—
Of what it did, eluded to hold off
The very push of interest it begot,
As if you'd been a tease, though you were not.
I hadn't felt it roused, to tell the truth,
In several years, that old man's greed for youth,
Like Pelias's that boiled him to a soup,
Not since I'd had the sense to cover up
My own particular seething can of worms,
And settle for a friendship on your terms.

Meanwhile I had to look: his errand done,
Without a glance at me or anyone,
The kid unlocked his bicycle outside,
Shrugging a backpack on. I watched him ride
Down 18th Street, rising above the saddle
For the long plunge he made with every pedal,
Expending far more energy than needed.
If only I could do whatever he did,
With him or as a part of him, if I
Could creep into his armpit like a fly,
Or like a crab cling to his golden crotch,
Instead of having to stand back and watch.
Oh complicated fantasy of intrusion
On that young sweaty body. My confusion
Led me at length to recollections of
Another's envy and his confused love.

That Fall after you died I went again
To where I had visited you in your pain
But this time for your—friend, roommate, or wooer?
I seek a neutral term where I'm unsure.
He lay there now. Figuring she knew best,
I came by at his mother's phoned request

To pick up one of your remembrances,
A piece of stained-glass you had made, now his,
I did not even remember, far less want.
To him I felt, likewise, indifferent.

"You can come in now," said the friend-as-nurse.
I did, and found him altered for the worse.
But when he saw me sitting by his bed,
He would not speak, and turned away his head.
I had not known he hated me until
He hated me this much, hated me still.
I thought that we had shared you more or less,
As if we shared what no one might possess,
Since in a net we sought to hold the wind.
There he lay on the pillow, mortally thinned,
Weaker than water, yet his gesture proving
As steady as an undertow. Unmoving
In the sustained though slight aversion, grim
In wordlessness. Nothing deflected him,
Nothing I did and nothing I could say.
And so I left. I heard he died next day.

I have imagined that he still could taste
That bitterness and anger to the last,
Against the roles he saw me in because
He had to: of victor, as he thought I was,
Of heir, as to the cherished property
His mother—who knows why?—was giving me,
And of survivor, as I am indeed,
Recording so that I may later read
Of what has happened, whether between sheets,
Or in post offices, or on the streets.

Gunn's poem incorporates another familiar tactic of the elegiac mode, used most often to bring the beloved back into the world: the reawakening of sexuality. Here, the speaker notes "feeling again, amazed, / That almost envious sexual tension which / Rubbing at made the greater, like an itch." He longs for the "young sweaty body" of a boy who reminds him of the lost lover, and he magnifies the boy's body by lovingly and even lustfully observing it—its "long blond hair," its "good back"—and by reducing himself to a perspective equal to that of an insect so he can be closer and see more:

"if I / Could creep into his armpit like a fly, / Or like a crab cling to his golden crotch." The memory of the beloved becomes even more sexually complicated as the speaker remembers a man who was his rival for the affections of the lost lover: "I thought that we had shared you more or less." And to compound the feelings of reemerging sexuality, the speaker remembers the rival in bed, but in the unsexual pose of dying. The rival is "mortally thinned" and "grim," and it is his body that lingers at the end of the poem, thereby unsexing a poem that began with such hope of new love that the very energy of the world seemed to rise in the pumping thighs of the boy on the bicycle.

The shift from the sexy boy to the dying rival would seem to defeat the speaker at his task of immortalizing were it not for the poem's final turn. Ultimately the speaker acquires a kind of triumph in his roles as "survivor" and as the one "Recording." And how Gunn records! Like so many of the great elegies, including *Astrophel*, Gunn's poem stretches beyond what would normally constitute a reasonable length, as if the breath implied by the poem's speech might somehow imbue the dead with life once more. For the older elegies, the length is manifested through a kind of "using up" of the world. A parade of natural imagery, forest figures, and mourners create a pageant not unlike a state funeral. With "In the Post Office," length—and breadth, *breath*—is attained by turning from the quick, to the self, to the dying, to the self, but always using these figures as a filter through which to consider the beloved. Though the poem is less populated than the classic elegies, it is nonetheless large in its scope, deftly moving through a world in which everyone seems to have his back or face averted from the speaker's gaze.

The speaker of the poem seems either to doubt or not to care about the communal nature of his memorializing, noting that he writes so that only he "may later read / Of what has happened." Such a drastic underestimation of the number of readers for the poem—which, after you, Dear Reader, have read it, is now at least two—seems strategic, a highlighting rather than a denial of community. And, in fact, the order of the three locations at poem's end emphasizes increased community: from the sheets of the poem, to dissemination at a post office, to the streets where the poem can be proclaimed.

Gunn's poem has mythological precedence. In Ovid's tale, Orpheus turned his attention to young boys, which Ovid called "those first flowers," and sang of Zeus' love for Ganymede and Apollo's love for Hyacinthus.

Orpheus' own reawakened sexuality was short-lived—like the gaze of long-ing that Gunn's speaker momentarily enjoys—as if to say that youth itself is fleeting, that life comes swiftly enough to a close, and that if we are to take our pleasures in the flesh, we need to take them in youth. But mostly Gunn's world is secular and sensual. In Gunn's poem, nobody is miracu-lously transformed into some everlasting thing of beauty, and immortality is consigned only to the acts of writing and reading more so than to some divine entity to whom the poet makes petition.

The solacing immortality in Gunn's poem, even if it provides only scant comfort, is great in contrast to the kind of elegy that refuses consola-tion. In this second kind of structure, the elegy gives in to grief and will not be consoled. One must think of the complex psychology of loss and re-member that anger and denial are the first steps of grieving. Certainly an elegy that refuses to turn toward contemplation of immortality—and thereby achieve some sense of solace—is still working through these first steps.

Of course, through elegy, poets cannot truly change the outcome of dying—they don't ever *really* win the chess game. Moreover, humans are powerless against the condition of loss, even to such extent as to not have a say in choosing the moment of remembering. In *The Past Recaptured*, Mar-cel Proust notes, "The truth is that for a long time after love for those who have died has left our hearts, their ashes, now of no further interest to us, continue to be mixed like an alloy with the incidents of the past. And though we love them no longer, it happens that, when we call to mind a room, a garden path, a road where they were at a certain hour, we are forced, in order to fill the space they occupied, to allude to them, even with-out longing for them or naming them or allowing anyone to know their identity."

Against such powerlessness, the poet seems justified in surrender; it is right, deeply fitting, to admit defeat, as does Hart Crane in "At Melville's Tomb":

> Often beneath the wave, wide from this ledge
> The dice of drowned men's bones he saw bequeath
> An embassy. Their numbers as he watched,
> Beat on the dusty shore and were obscured.
>
> And wrecks passed without sound of bells,
> The calyx of death's bounty giving back

A scattered chapter, livid hieroglyph,
The portent wound in corridors of shells.

Then in the circuit calm of one vast coil,
Its lashings charmed and malice reconciled,
Frosted eyes there were that lifted altars;
And silent answers crept across the stars.

Compass, quadrant and sextant contrive
No farther tides ... High in the azure steeps
Monody shall not wake the mariner.
This fabulous shadow only the sea keeps.

Crane's poem employs the elegiac mode's popular trope of sea imagery as a sign of loss. The drowned sailor is both a real and an imaginary figure who informs the poems of John Milton, Walt Whitman, Robert Lowell, T.S. Eliot, Derek Walcott, and a host of others, harkening back to the early English poems *The Seafarer* and *The Wanderer*, in which the sorrow of living is manifest through the brutal imagery of perils of the sea. But in Crane's poem the drowning is displaced. It is not Herman Melville's death; rather, the deaths of others are used to signify the death of Melville. So too, the poem itself is a kind of displaced elegy. Crane is mourning Melville's death as a way to mourn others, while at the same time, the very nature of poetry is being elegized. The pageantry of poems like Spenser's and Gunn's is turned into shadow. Although for an instant there seems to be some hope—beginning with "Then," the third stanza could signal a turn—ultimately even the stars, which once showered signs of immortality, now give only "silent answers." The world evoked by the poem is itself a world without poetry, where wrecks pass "without sound of bells."

The loss expressed in the poem's first three stanzas is confirmed with the turn to the final stanza. Though the fourth stanza's first line ("Compass, quadrant and sextant contrive") signals a new possibility for the poem by offering for the first time mention of instruments that can be used to measure the sea's vastness, they ultimately are powerless. They can make "No farther tides," that is, they cannot make any farther seas, a kind of afterlife where the dead actually might still live on. And just as these tools are of no use, neither is poetry: "Monody [lament] shall not wake the mariner." The poem's final line makes sure the reader is aware that the dead really are the possessions of the sea and nothing else—not memory, not poetry.

Still, while "At Melville's Tomb" makes a grand gesture of failure, saying that silence triumphs over the poet, it is of course a false failure because Melville's poems continue beyond his life. Crane's poem makes a fine music that sets itself squarely against the silence, and Crane, too, continues singing long past his own demise. In Ovid's version of the Orphic myth, Orpheus is eventually torn apart by nymphs who cannot bear his indifference to their seductions. And his voice, too, sings beyond the edge of living, as his disembodied head floats out to sea. The infinite is the first grace of the elegy; it is the vast wink of eternity toward which *all* poems aspire. None more so than the poems of loss.

In "Funeral Blues," W.H. Auden turns up the volume, crying out to the world, taking apart the heavens and the earth with his grief in an almost operatic performance:

> Stop all the clocks, cut off the telephone,
> Prevent the dog from barking with a juicy bone,
> Silence the pianos and with muffled drum
> Bring out the coffin, let the mourners come.
>
> Let aeroplanes circle moaning overhead
> Scribbling on the sky the message He is Dead.
> Put crêpe bows round the white necks of the public doves,
> Let the traffic policemen wear black cotton gloves.
>
> He was my North, my South, my East and West,
> My working week and my Sunday rest,
> My noon, my midnight, my talk, my song;
> I thought that love would last forever: I was wrong.
>
> The stars are not wanted now; put out every one,
> Pack up the moon and dismantle the sun,
> Pour away the ocean and sweep up the woods;
> For nothing now can ever come to any good.

At its outset "Funeral Blues" is filled with loss and saturated with grief. In the first two stanzas, regardless of all the alchemy of turning the world inside out through language, we still end up with nothing coming to life. The speaker of this poem not only wants to express his own suffering, he also wants everyone and everything to express it for him: stopped clocks, disconnected phones, muffled drums. The poem's grief song, its "blues," replaces all the sounds of the world.

The third stanza signals a shift in the speaker, who suddenly begins to recall the beloved, actually referring to him and to their relationship for the first time, but this brief turn toward consolation does not come to fruition. The beloved is remembered as *everything*, from the four cardinal directions, to the days and hours, to each syllable of the poem's song, which sets the poem up for an imaginative resurrection that is taken away almost as quickly as it was given: "I thought that love would last forever: I was wrong." Note especially how "song" is rhymed with "wrong," with its dull sound of finality. The fourth stanza confirms this finality, listing again —though this time in a despairing tone and on a cosmic level—all that should be done to signify the speaker's woe: pack up and throw away the world. In the final line of the poem the speaker starkly refuses the world of the living, "For nothing now can ever come to any good."

But "Funeral Blues" seems itself a good. This is, finally, a poem that still, regardless of its protestations, suggests that love *does* last. If it didn't, such passion would be unnecessary. It is precisely because love *hasn't* died that the speaker gets away with saying that it has: a richly paradoxical situation, this one, where the poem gets to be both outrageous and moving at the same time. Ultimately, though, in the space of his four stanzas, it seems that the speaker in "Funeral Blues" will not be comforted. If the heavens, the planets, and time are no givers of consolation, then nothing indeed can help right now to lift the speaker out of the well of sorrow. This is inconsolable grief at its finest, but not yet its most severe. For that we turn to the third elegiac structure.

Perhaps the most recent phenomenon in elegy is the refusal to continue grieving. In her poem "The End," Sharon Olds employs an objective, unemotional voice to talk of mortality, adding a chilling—and therefore perhaps even more moving—tone:

> We decided to have the abortion, became
> killers together. The period that came
> changed nothing. They were dead, that young couple
> who had been for life.
> As we talked of it in bed, the crash
> was not a surprise. We went to the window,
> looked at the crushed cars and the gleaming
> curved shears of glass as if we had
> done it. Cops pulled the bodies out
> bloody as births from the small, smoking
> aperture of the door, laid them

on the hill, covered them with blankets that soaked
through. Blood
began to pour
down my legs into my slippers. I stood
where I was until they shot the bound
form into the black hole
of the ambulance and stood the other one
up, a bandage covering its head,
stained where the eyes had been.
The next morning I had to kneel
an hour on that floor, to clean up my blood,
rubbing with wet cloths at those glittering
translucent spots, as one has to soak
a long time to deglaze the pan
when the feast is over.

In a careful avoidance of sentimentality, Olds describes how a young couple, faced with a possible pregnancy, move in glib tones from being "for life" to being spiritually and emotionally "dead." In a strange split-screen effect, the young couple is roused from bed by a "crash" so that they can watch versions of themselves reduced to "bodies" loaded into an ambulance. The imagery that ties together the still-living young couple and their dead versions is the imagery of blood: from menses, in the first case, from an accident in the latter. The speaker of the poem fuses the two worlds back into one by kneeling "to clean up my blood" as if it's another household chore. Though the tone of the poem is rather cold, the coldness reinforces the sense of loss, allowing the reader, rather than the poet, to provide the emotion. It's as if we've come to the end of a long party, a "feast" rather than a death, and instead of grief we get a "soak" and "a long time to deglaze." This is a complete turnabout compared to the older elegiac tradition in which the speaker, while shaping a sense of shared, participatory experience, bears the responsibility for mourning. Instead, the poem is drained of whatever hope or significance it could have held out for.

Like the elegies of Spenser, Gunn, Crane, Auden, and Olds, the work in Supplemental Poems also shows the elegy's three main structural possibilities. If a poem seeks immortality—turning from grieving back toward life—the elegy can seem to snatch victory from the jaws of defeat. Look, for example, at Gwendolyn Brooks' "the rites for Cousin Vit," in which the dead cousin gets to reinhabit the world, "the bars she knew," and to dance the "snake-hips with a hiss," and, at last, to be an "Is." Or examine John Berryman's comedo-tragic "Dream Song 29," in which, ultimately if darkly, "Nobody is ever missing."

If the poem surrenders to grief and does not move from the ground of sorrow, the elegy refuses consolation. Yuko Taniguchi's "Foreign Wife Elegy," for example, contains a speaker who imagines her death as a devastating event that bridges cultural barriers and causes her husband's voice to shake. The power of grief is so complete that it renders the husband both capable and incapable of speech.

And if the poet refuses even to grieve, the elegy is deflated, dismantled. Look, for example, at the matter-of-factness in Pablo Neruda's "My Dog Has Died," in which the old man who refuses to posit a heaven for humans imagines a heaven for dogs but then remembers the honesty of his relationship with the dog. We "never did lie to each other," says the old man, and he wipes his hands of grief as a sign of respect for the creature he buries. Or consider the complicated tonality of James Emanuel's "Emmett Till," in which the young man who was lynched refuses to "be still," even as the speaker refuses to acknowledge the noose, replacing it with a "coral toy" necklace.

Each of these elegiac structures can serve the poem. After all, there are no inappropriate responses to death; we cannot say that grieving is better than not grieving, or that faith in a life hereafter is better than no faith at all.

SUPPLEMENTAL POEMS

Dream Song 29
John Berryman

There sat down, once, a thing on Henry's heart
so heavy, if he had a hundred years
& more, & weeping, sleepless, in all them time
Henry could not make good.
Starts again always in Henry's ears
the little cough somewhere, an odour, a chime.

And there is another thing he has in mind
like a grave Sienese face a thousand years
would fail to blur the still profiled reproach of. Ghastly,
with open eyes, he attends, blind.

All the bells say: too late. This is not for tears;
thinking.

But never did Henry, as he thought he did,
end anyone and hacks her body up
and hide the pieces, where they may be found.
He knows: he went over everyone, & nobody's missing.
Often he reckons, in the dawn, them up.
Nobody is ever missing.

the rites for Cousin Vit
Gwendolyn Brooks

Carried her unprotesting out the door
Kicked back the casket-stand. But it can't hold her,
That stuff and satin aiming to enfold her,
The lid's contrition nor the bolts before.
Oh oh. Too much. Too much. Even now, surmise,
She rises in sunshine. There she goes
Back to the bars she knew and the repose
In love-rooms and the things in people's eyes.
Too vital and too squeaking. Must emerge.
Even now, she does the snake-hips with a hiss,
Slaps the bad wine across her shantung, talks
Of pregnancy, guitars and bridgework, walks
In parks or alleys, comes haply on the verge
Of happiness, haply hysterics. Is.

Emmett Till
James Emanuel

I hear a whistling
Through the water.
Little Emmett
Won't be still.
He keeps floating
Round the darkness,
Edging through
The silent chill.

Tell me, please,
That bedtime story
Of the fairy
River Boy
Who swims forever,
Deep in treasures,
Necklaced in
A coral toy.

A Dog Has Died
Pablo Neruda

My dog has died.
I buried him in the garden
next to a rusted old machine.

Some day I'll join him right there,
but now he's gone with his shaggy coat,
his bad manners and his cold nose,
and I, the materialist, who never believed
in any promised heaven in the sky
for any human being,
I believe in a heaven I'll never enter.
Yes, I believe in a heaven for all dogdom
where my dog waits for my arrival
waving his fan-like tail in friendship.

Ai, I'll not speak of sadness here on earth,
of having lost a companion
who was never servile.
His friendship for me, like that of a porcupine
withholding its authority,
was the friendship of a star, aloof,
with no more intimacy than was called for,
with no exaggerations:
he never climbed all over my clothes
filling me full of his hair or his mange,
he never rubbed up against my knee
like other dogs obsessed with sex.

No, my dog used to gaze at me,

paying me the attention I need,
the attention required
to make a vain person like me understand
that, being a dog, he was wasting time,
but, with those eyes so much purer than mine,
he'd keep on gazing at me
with a look that reserved for me alone
all his sweet and shaggy life,
always near me, never troubling me,
and asking nothing.

Ai, how many times have I envied his tail
as we walked together on the shores of the sea
in the lonely winter of Isla Negra
where the wintering birds filled the sky
and my hairy dog was jumping about
full of the voltage of the sea's movement:
my wandering dog, sniffing away
with his golden tail held high,
face to face with the ocean's spray.

Joyful, joyful, joyful,
as only dogs know how to be happy
with only the autonomy
of their shameless spirit.

There are no good-byes for my dog who has died,
and we don't now and never did lie to each other.

So now he's gone and I buried him,
and that's all there is to it.

Foreign Wife Elegy
Yuko Taniguchi

My language has its own world
where he doesn't know how to live,
but he should learn my language;
then he can call my mother to say
that I am dead. I drive too fast
and someone else drives too fast

and we crash on the icy road.
The death sweeps me away.
He can tell this to my mother
if he learns my language.
Her large yellow voice travels
and hits his body, but at least she knows
that I am dead, and if I die,
I want him to tell my mother
with his deep voice shaking.

CHAPTER SIX

The Dialectical Argument Structure

JOHN BEER

"When Shakespeare writes, 'Two loves have I,' reader, he is not kidding," John Berryman once remarked. Poetry often powerfully expresses the situation of the divided mind, the self caught between various incompatible options: an experience that has analogues in the loftiest philosophic reflection and the most mundane trip to the grocery store. A potent resource for exploring such internal divisions is the dialectical argument, in which the speaker or speakers of the poem inhabit by turns the perspectives of two or more partial and unsatisfying positions before finding a resolution that transcends their limitations. The two opposing positions are drawn into a larger conceptualization that contains elements of each. In its most famous formulation, the dialectical argument structure is a three-part structure that turns, according to philosopher Johann Fichte, from thesis to antithesis to synthesis.

Dialectical argument, which is derived from the Greek *dialektikos* (pertaining to conversation), may sound like a term only a dorm-room Marxist could love. But it describes a pattern of argument encountered every day. Suppose you call up your friend Turner to invite her to see the big rigs next weekend. Turner would much rather visit Sprezzatura, the lavish new restaurant in town. Even given your allergy to garlic and Turner's antipathy to monster trucks, the situation need not end in tears. Rather, in discussing your respective rationales behind your planned excursions, you might discover that the premiere of *Tosca* at the local opera can satisfy both your own desire for large objects in dramatic confrontation and Turner's yen for Italian culture. Your conversation has satisfied the dialectical argument structure. You didn't just compromise by going to a mutually agreeable alternative, like staying in and raking your sand garden. Rather, your resolution preserves some aspects of each of the incompatible alternatives.

To be sure, dialectical argument has a rich history. Greek tragedies provide exemplary dialectical encounters, though the resolutions tend to be less happy than that of our previous example. In *Antigone*, for instance, Antigone's desire to bury her brother Polynices collides with Creon's law forbidding his burial. The values represented by family and state are in this context absolutely incompatible. This conflict is not really resolved but rather ends tragically in Antigone's death and Creon's terrible suffering.

The Western philosophical tradition develops dialectical argument to the fullest degree. Such argument provides the principle behind Socratic dialogue. Socrates pushes his interlocutors to resolve the inescapable contradictions between their practice and the ideals by which they profess to be guided. For instance, in the *Euthyphro*, Euthyphro claims to be guided by piety in pressing a lawsuit against his own father, but under the pressure of Socrates' questioning he admits that his grasp on the concept of piety is nowhere near as sure as his action suggests. To Euthyphro's thesis that a pious action is one that is loved by the gods, Socrates offers the antithesis that the gods love an action *because* of its piety, so that piety must be a feature existing prior to divine favor. Characteristically, this Socratic dialogue ends without a final resolution.

For our purposes, the highest development of the concept of dialectical argument is found in the philosophy of G.W.F. Hegel. In Hegel's *Phenomenology of Spirit*, proposed norms for thinking and acting repeatedly break down because of their internal contradictions. At the same time, these norms become progressively more adequate by incorporating elements from previous attempts. Most famously, in Hegel's master/slave dialectic, the master fails inevitably in his quest for recognition. The master views the slave as a free source of recognition: the slave's obedience to the master's commands will prove an infinite confirmation of the master's value, and the master need not do anything in return. But the master's plan is self-undermining. Because the master sees the slave as essentially valueless, the slave's obedience can't count for anything. In the end (omitting an even more complex dialectic from the slave's perspective), the master-slave relationship produces its own contradiction, leading to an understanding that the desire for recognition can only be satisfied within a relationship of mutual equality. Hegel notes in his preface that dialectical procedure itself fails when it is reduced to "a lifeless schema, a mere shadow, and when scientific organization is degraded into a table of terms." This observation has serious consequences for the poet.

A poem by the classical Chinese poet T'ao Ch'ien beautifully exemplifies the dialectical argument structure. In it, T'ao Ch'ien confronts that largest of all poetic and philosophical themes: death.

Substance, Shadow, and Spirit

I
Substance to Shadow

Earth and heaven endure forever,
Streams and mountains never change,
Plants observe a constant rhythm,
Withered by frost, by dew restored.
But man, most sentient being of all,
In this is not their equal.
He is present here in the world today,
Then leaves abruptly, to return no more.
No one marks there's one man less—
Not even friends and family think of him;
The things that he once used are all that's left
To catch their eye and move them to grief.
I have no way to transcend change,
That it must be, I no longer doubt.
I hope you will take my advice:
When wine is offered, don't refuse.

II
Shadow to Substance

No use discussing immortality
When just to keep alive is hard enough.
Of course I want to roam in paradise,
But it's a long way there and the road is lost.
In all the time since I met up with you
We never differed in our grief and joy.
In shade we may have parted for a time,
But sunshine always brings us close again.
Still this union cannot last forever—
Together we will vanish into darkness.
The body goes; that fame should also end
Is a thought that makes me burn inside.
Do good, and your love will outlive you;

Surely this is worth your every effort.
While it is true, wine may dissolve care
That is not so good a way as this.

III
Spirit's Solution

The Great Potter cannot intervene—
All creation thrives of itself.
That Man ranks with Earth and Heaven
Is it not because of me?
Though we belong to different orders,
Being alive, I am joined to you.
Bound together for good or ill
I cannot refuse to tell you what I know:
The Three August Ones were great saints
But where are they living today?
Though P'eng-tsu lasted a long time
He still had to go before he was ready.
Die old or die young, the death is the same,
Wise or stupid, there is no difference.
Drunk every day, you may forget,
But won't it shorten your life span?
Doing good is always a joyous thing
But no one has to praise you for it.
Too much thinking harms my life;
Just surrender to the cycle of things,
Give yourself to the waves of the Great Change
Neither happy nor yet afraid.
And when it is time to go, then simply go
Without any unnecessary fuss.

The dialectical movement here is clear. T'ao Ch'ien's first two speakers, Substance and Shadow, each recommend a course of action for resisting the pull of death, but the two prescriptions—surrender to bodily desires or practice restraint in the hope of eternal fame—are mutually incompatible. The third speaker, Spirit (the universal principle within each individual), resolves the dilemma by dissolving it. Each earlier recommendation is based on trying to escape mortality; the wisest course is to accept it.

In general, a dialectical argument poem has three features. First, it inhabits each of the partial perspectives and makes each perspective compelling. Second, it effectively dramatizes the clash between the various perspectives. Finally, the closing resolution should be both satisfying and surprising—a genuine revelation of a broader point of view. T'ao Ch'ien's poem manages to meet all these conditions.

The arguments made by Substance and Shadow make the case for their prescriptions and at the same time express their varying forms of life. Consider the different ways in which the two arguments evolve. Substance moves from a consideration of the natural world through a complaint about human mortality to a final recommendation of drunkenness as consolation. Throughout, the bodily nature of Substance's existence is emphasized in the attention to natural detail and the final recommendation of physical pleasure. While Substance's section remains impersonal, Shadow's contribution engages directly with Substance. It not only addresses Substance's argument, but it also continually draws attention to Substance and Shadow's interlocking natures. Notice that, while Substance's speech only employs the pronouns "I" and "you" in the closing lines, barely acknowledging the conversational context of the poem, Shadow repeatedly addresses remarks to Substance. This concern for mutuality highlights the centrality of ethics for Shadow and at the same time brings into sharp relief the incompatibility of their perspectives: Shadow directly repudiates Substance's recommendation of drunkenness.

Employing both the more impersonal style characteristic of Substance and the liberal use of personal pronouns characteristic of Shadow, Spirit's speech also suggests a broader perspective than either. Spirit refers to specific religious and cultural figures and events: the Great Potter, the Three August Ones, P'eng-tsu, the Great Change. Spirit thereby situates the individual worries over death raised by Substance and Shadow within traditions of thinking that transcend the merely individual. Spirit's rhetoric displays a concern for balance and skepticism about ultimate knowledge that prepares us for the poem's resolution. For example, each claim within Spirit's speech is deftly paired with another, and most of these couplets disavow any final insight into the meaning of life's end: "Die old or die young, the death is the same, / Wise or stupid, there is no difference." These skeptical couplets make Spirit's ultimate claim persuasive, rejecting the underlying premise of both Substance and Shadow that death is an evil to be feared and combated. Spirit's position resolves the conflict even as it reveals a possibility we had not yet considered.

T'ao Ch'ien's poem, in its dialectical structure, draws upon central themes of classical Chinese thought; its conclusion is a recommendation of passivity in the face of eternity that is rather at odds with the individualism and rationalism of much of the West's traditions. But the dialectical argument structure can accommodate thought and experience arising from diverse times and cultures. It also need not take the explicitly argumentative form of "Substance, Shadow, and Spirit." Here, for instance, is the contemporary American poet William Bronk's "Duplicity":

> Order, our order, is to deny
> our nature; yet order is not to be denied:
> we want an order. We want to respect our wants:
> what else do we want?
>   Well, the something else we want
> is that our nature is orderless; that want,
> itself, is our want for an order: one we can feel.
>
> We mistrust an unfelt order, strange to us,
> though it is ours.
>   Complex, we wish for things
> more simple and, infinite, we want the things
> which are finite, contrary things. Acknowledging both,
> we wish our nature were not the doubleness
> we are coupled with, with which we have to live.
>
> There are no accidents, unnatural acts;
> the horror of human doings is the nature of us:
> our impossibility; our need to destroy
> ourselves, all finite things; our helpless loves
> for our half, our helpless half, the half we destroy,
> helplessly, with that intent; and the grief
> of that intent, of that finite order's loss
> our infinite intention's nature it is to lose.

The thrust of Bronk's knotty poem is signaled by the pun of his title. "Duplicity," which we usually think means "deception," can also refer simply to the condition of being double. Bronk argues that our discomfort with our double condition, as beings who feel the pull both of order and disorder, of law and exception, leads to a pervasive self-deception. In a manner much less methodical than T'ao Ch'ien, Bronk nevertheless pursues a similar aim. He gives voice to both the orderly and the disorderly aspect within us before finally recommending that the urge to side with one or the other is itself a denial of the reality of our lives.

On the one hand, according to Bronk, we all feel intuitively a desire for an orderly world of norms. In his sublime pun, "we want an order" (that is, we both desire and lack one). On the other hand, our peculiar human nature is shot through with contingency, with passionate resistance to rule: "that want, / itself, is our want for an order." Angels, after all, don't want order; they simply embody it. Bronk's dualism here recalls Immanuel Kant's famous distinction between the imperatives of duty and the impetuous urges of human nature. We all can recognize the desirability of an objective state in which Jessie's best friend keeps his hands off of Jessie's girl; at the same time, in that best friend's position, we'd like to have a woman like that (*mutatis mutandis*). For Bronk, the resolution is to be found in rejecting the identification of human nature with a perfect order: our nature *is* just to be torn between desire and law, and accepting that torn state without self-deception is the best that we can do. The horror of human doings is the nature of us.

In "Duplicity," the two perspectives—of human life as intrinsically ordered and as wanting order—are inhabited as much in the way the poem itself develops as in explicit statements made within the poem. If we rely solely on the statements of the poem, "Duplicity" can seem like a rather lifeless and abstract philosophical exercise. Consider three statements made early on in the poem:

- "Order, our order, is to deny / our nature"
- "order is not to be denied: / we want an order"
- "the something else we want / is that our nature is orderless"

Taken as a group, these statements certainly fulfill the dialectical argument's requirement for a clash of perspectives. On the one hand, we want to recognize the order that structures our lives; and on the other hand, we want to deny the actual ordering of our lives, to see ourselves as spontaneous and radically free.

But to see the actual drama of this confrontation, we need to attend to the poetic resources Bronk deploys. Look, for example, at how the repetition of "order" and "want" throughout the first several lines serves to highlight the double meanings of the words themselves—"order" as structure or command, "want" as desire or lack—while threatening to hollow them of meaning completely. Then compare the intellectual gamesmanship of this early use of repetition to the repetition of "helpless" and "half" in the poem's final stanza. Here, repetition is not an expression of cleverness, but of desolation. The poem itself, in its combination of dazzling syntactical and verbal play and deep pathos, replicates the argument of order and disorder. Bronk reconfigures this as a dualism of thinking and feeling; he reverses ordinary polarities by suggesting that idiosyncratic thinking is an ultimately ineffectual device for escaping the underlying order of emotional drives. The poem then offers itself as a model for the integration of these seemingly irreconcilable perspectives, an integration that might evade the disastrous losses to which, as its last line warns, our drives to find and to deny our order lead us.

Both T'ao Ch'ien and William Bronk use the dialectical structure to investigate fundamental philosophical issues. The language of both poems remains relatively remote from daily life. But the dialectical argument structure can also encompass familiar domestic scenes, as in this poem by Sharon Olds:

35/10

Brushing out our daughter's brown
silken hair before the mirror
I see the grey gleaming on my head,
the silver-haired servant behind her. Why is it
just as we begin to go
they begin to arrive, the fold in my neck
clarifying as the fine bones of her
hips sharpen? As my skin shows
its dry pitting, she opens like a moist
precise flower on the tip of a cactus;
as my last chances to bear a child
are falling through my body, the duds among them,
her full purse of eggs, round and
firm as hard-boiled yolks, is about
to snap its clasp. I brush her tangled
fragrant hair at bedtime. It's an old
story—the oldest we have on our planet—
the story of replacement.

In "35/10," unlike the poems we've seen so far, a single speaker articulates her divided point of view within a clearly delineated dramatic scene.

Brushing her daughter's hair, the speaker opposes her own perspective as she moves into middle age with her daughter's youth. The dialectical argument in this case doesn't operate as an explicit confrontation of the two points of view; instead, each is developed in parallel. Implicitly, the poem works by finding a way to bring these opposed ideas into relation with one another. The speaker, suddenly struck in the mirror by the thought that her daughter represents her negation, will find in the end a different, more satisfying way of thinking.

Olds develops the dialectical opposition in easily comprehensible terms. The slackness of the speaker's skin contrasts with the sharpness of the daughter's bone. The speaker presents a desert background against which the daughter's moist sexuality stands out. The end of the speaker's fertility coincides with the beginning of her daughter's. The subtlety of the poem comes in the way Olds offers a tentative reconciliation. By framing the scene as she does, the two females looking into the mirror, Olds prepares us to see, and to expect the speaker to see, her daughter as not simply a competitor, but also as a reflection. In the penultimate line, when Olds writes "It's an old / story—the oldest we have," she acknowledges that the daughter's inevitable replacement of her mother represents a continuation of the Olds story, rather than a simple negation of her own existence.

The basic form of the dialectical argument allows for a good deal of variation, as we've seen already. While the two English poems we've looked at present their reflections in free verse, more regular verse forms, and particularly the sonnet, lend themselves to the presentation of dialectical argument. Look at the structure of Edna St. Vincent Millay's "Sonnet XXX" from *Fatal Interview*:

Love is not all: it is not meat or drink
Nor slumber nor a roof against the rain;
Nor yet a floating spar to men that sink
And rise and sink and rise and sink again;
Love can not fill the thickened lung with breath,
Nor clean the blood, nor set the fractured bone;
Yet many a man is making friends with death
Even as I speak, for lack of love alone.
It well may be that in a difficult hour,
Pinned down by pain and moaning for release,
Or nagged by want past resolution's power,
I might be driven to sell your love for peace,

Or trade the memory of this night for food.
It well may be. I do not think I would.

Millay plays the dialectical structure of her poem against the sonnet form here. Traditionally, the turn from the octave to the sestet of a sonnet signals a turn in the argument. Most often, the sonneteer will use the sestet to resolve the difficulty posed in the octave. Millay follows this pattern to a degree, using the octave to set up the dialectical opposition between the inadequacies of love, seen from a pragmatic perspective (you can't eat it, float on it, set bones with it), and the overpowering claims of love seen from the lover's perspective. But Millay then torques the argument by personalizing it in the sestet. Rather than simply seeking a resolution, the speaker revisits the initial dilemma, but this time directly addresses the beloved: "I might be driven to sell your love for peace." In the end, the speaker remains one of love's partisans, but with a slightly chilly distance suggested by the repeated impersonal "It well may be." If the lovers of the octave are blind, here in the sestet the speaker's eyes stay at least half-open.

A striking feature of modern poems, demonstrated in Millay's concluding sestet, is a lack of confidence in the resolvability of essential conflicts. Accordingly, one increasingly prominent variant of the poem of dialectical argument is what we might call the poem of negative dialectics. Introduced by the theorist Theodor Adorno, negative dialectics affirms the essential conflict in thinking that Hegel relied upon while denying, at least within current social conditions, that such conflicts are resolvable. The poem of negative dialectics sets up an opposition, as in the poems we've already seen, but refuses to find a higher resolution. In fact, the absence of a final reconciliation is the point of the poem. Consider Joshua Clover's "Radiant City":

> First it was one thing then it was
> one thing after another. We
> tend to think of fused flowers
>
> as igniting outward from a
> central *place* as in sex as in
> Haussmann's Radiant City. I
>
> saw it live on TV.
> From overhead it's possible
> to speak of *the whole thing*. First day

of the riots but before that
I was near home when S—this is
just a personal incident—

passed by in an old red shirt. They
weren't letting people out of
the stations as of the early

rumors of lootings. This after
Eastern Europe. Buildings burning
to the south as in parables

as in what punk rock promised. I
found this exciting. "He was
in control of the whole thing."

The word is S doesn't do men
anyway. A few shopping bags
came into the City via

the last trains before the curfew.
We saw the 81 seconds
on TV maybe a thousand

times. Enough house-burnings for night
visions in Los Angeles but
still the helicopters busy

not really looking just humming
overhead. A car rocked side
to side as in a carnival

ride then rolled it ignited as in
an excellent carnival ride. No
clear argument—the whole thing was

interruption. She was naked
the one time we met she was in
a friend's bed to be delicate

in a state of some *déshabille*.
Radiant as in for example
1700 infrared

poppies blooming in the over-

head footage of south central. The
second night of riots. As in

Berlin years back—we have all seen
this footage—when the Wall came down
the main thing was chocolate also

blue jeans. "He kept trying to get
back up." We would not be allowed
to leave the station the police would

put us right back on the train. We
would not be allowed to leave ... the
stations lacquered sanitary

eggshell tones. Architecture as in
a floral pattern of faint veins
radiating from her pubic

cup across her hips & down her
thighs. We like to think we would get
on our knees only for love. An

older woman bearing her purse
into the City 60 feet
below the broken glass bolted

across the platform from our
train to the opposite track. Hours
passed after S until I loved

the looters. In homes we watched
the ether as in shopkeepers
shooting into a crowd. To the

opposite track—hours where the
walled city of *I wanted*
was hidden by the bright city

of *had need* as in being blown
away from that place in fractures
of reflective rubble. I had

planned to practice the compliance

position with my hands on my
head not trying to rise but was

interrupted—as in fantasies
of S in riot gear. This was
the poppy vision. I admit

I found the whole thing exciting.
We have all seen this footage

Clover's poem announces its immense argumentative stakes in its opening lines: "First it was one thing then it was / one thing after another." The opposition between synchronic unity and diachronic difference is illustrated most visibly in our changing experience of the city—from a harmoniously planned pattern to a series of events on television. But rather than seek a perspective from which these two views of experience could find an overarching synthesis, Clover's stuttering narrative ("the whole thing was / interruption") winds up allowing each point of view its partiality. Without some ideal of "the whole thing," experience decomposes into one damn thing after another, but the hubristic urge to subordinate reality to an ideal pattern leads to the unrest of Los Angeles in 1991 or Berlin in 1989. Is the poet on the side of the ideal or the real that incessantly interrupts it? As Clover himself notes, there's "No / clear argument." The truth of the poem lies not in its reconciliation of these warring elements but in its simultaneous sympathy for and attention to each.

As the poems included in this chapter and in Supplemental Poems show, the dialectical argument structure can enable a poet to investigate virtually any topic. Some poets take up enduring philosophical questions about the relationship of chaos and order, universal and particular (as in A.R. Ammons' "Hymn"), subjective and objective (as in Wallace Stevens' "Bouquet of Roses in Sunlight"), or mind and body (as in Andrew Marvell's "A Dialogue Between the Soul and the Body"). D.H. Lawrence uses the structure to playfully consider the relation of self and other (in "To Be Superior"), while Robert Penn Warren employs it for serious meditation on the difference between reality and deception (in "Picnic Remembered"). In Elizabeth Bishop's "Santarém," the political, cultural, and commercial terrain of a Brazilian city occasions the unsettling enactment of negative dialectics. If people or even people and *houses*, as is the case in Bernadette Mayer's "House & Bernadette," can disagree about a topic, that topic can serve as the basis for a dialectical argument poem or a poem of negative dialectics.

The particular topic of a poem employing the dialectical argument structure, in the end, is less important than the investment a poet brings to the various perspectives involved. Each of the points of view represented in the poem truly must be shown to have something at stake. A rich sense of the perspectives involved helps the poet develop their interplay elegantly and imaginatively. A dialectical argument poem should never grind its way mechanically through its two perspectives to a predetermined conclusion. Writing one, like reading one, is a process of discovery.

The true poem of dialectical argument embodies John Keats' idea of negative capability. For Keats, negative capability, the imaginative capacity that Keats thought Shakespeare exemplified, indicates the ability to occupy an infinity of partial positions without plumping for any particular one. A successful dialectical argument poem requires that a poet really take up and inhabit incompatible points of view. Maybe each point of view is one the poet can identify with in a certain mood, maybe not. But these poems provide an exercise in building negative capability, in leaving one's own particularized perspective behind to imagine what the world might look like from another vantage point. This imaginative engagement is at the heart of dialectical argument. Without it, as Hegel observed, we are left with just a lifeless schema, a mere shadow. With it, the poem of dialectical argument becomes a field on which the inevitable conflicts of history and life can play, finding by turns new possibilities of reconciliation and tragedy's stubborn pull.

SUPPLEMENTAL POEMS

Hymn
A.R. Ammons

I know if I find you I will have to leave the earth
and go on out
    over the sea marshes and the brant in bays
and over the hills of tall hickory
and over the crater lakes and canyons
and on up through the spheres of diminishing air
past the blackset noctilucent clouds
        where one wants to stop and look
way past all the light diffusions and bombardments

up farther than the loss of sight
   into the unseasonal undifferentiated empty stark

And I know if I find you I will have to stay with the earth
inspecting with thin tools and ground eyes
trusting the microvilli sporangia and simplest
   coelenterates
and praying for a nerve cell
with all the soul of my chemical reactions
and going right on down where the eye sees only traces

You are everywhere partial and entire
You are on the inside of everything and on the outside

I walk down the path down the hill where the sweetgum
has begun to ooze spring sap at the cut
and I see how the bark cracks and winds like no other bark
chasmal to my ant-soul running up and down
and if I find you I must go out deep into your
   far resolutions
and if I find you I must stay here with the separate leaves

Santarém
Elizabeth Bishop

Of course I may be remembering it all wrong
after, after—how many years?

That golden evening I really wanted to go no farther;
more than anything else I wanted to stay awhile
in that conflux of two great rivers, Tapajós, Amazon,
grandly, silently flowing, flowing east.
Suddenly there'd been houses, people, and lots of mongrel
riverboats skittering back and forth
under a sky of gorgeous, under-lit clouds,
with everything gilded, burnished along one side,
and everything bright, cheerful, casual—or so it looked.
I liked the place; I liked the idea of the place.
Two rivers. Hadn't two rivers sprung
from the Garden of Eden? No, that was four
and they'd diverged. Here only two

and coming together. Even if one were tempted
to literary interpretations
such as: life/death, right/wrong, male/female
—such notions would have resolved, dissolved, straight off
in that watery, dazzling dialectic.

In front of the church, the Cathedral, rather,
there was a modest promenade and a belvedere
about to fall into the river,
stubby palms, flamboyants like pans of embers,
buildings one story high, stucco, blue or yellow,
and one house faced with *azulejos*, buttercup yellow.
The street was deep in dark-gold river sand
damp from the ritual afternoon rain,
and teams of zebus plodded, gentle, proud,
and *blue*, with down-curved horns and hanging ears,
pulling carts with solid wheels.
The zebus' hooves, the people's feet
waded in golden sand,
dampered by golden sand,
so that almost the only sounds
were creaks and *shush, shush, shush.*

Two rivers full of crazy shipping—people
all apparently changing their minds, embarking,
disembarking, rowing clumsy dories.
(After the Civil War some Southern families
came here; here they could still own slaves.
They left occasional blue eyes, English names,
and *oars*. No other place, no one
on all the Amazon's four thousand miles
does anything but paddle.)
A dozen or so young nuns, white-habited,
waved gaily from an old stern-wheeler
getting up steam, already hung with hammocks
—off to their mission, days and days away
up God knows what lost tributary.
Side-wheelers, countless wobbling dugouts ...
A cow stood up in one, quite calm,
chewing her cud while being ferried,

tipping, wobbling, somewhere, to be married.
A river schooner with raked masts
and violet-colored sails tacked in so close
her bowsprit seemed to touch the church

(Cathedral, rather!). A week or so before
there'd been a thunderstorm and the Cathedral'd
been struck by lightning. One tower had
a widening zigzag crack all the way down.
It was a miracle. The priest's house right next door
had been struck, too, and his brass bed
(the only one in town) galvanized black.
Graças a deus—he'd been in Belém.

In the blue pharmacy the pharmacist
had hung an empty wasps' nest from a shelf:
small, exquisite, clean matte white,
and hard as stucco. I admired it
so much he gave it to me.
Then—my ship's whistle blew. I couldn't stay.
Back on board, a fellow-passenger, Mr. Swan,
Dutch, the retiring head of Philips Electric,
really a very nice old man,
who wanted to see the Amazon before he died,
asked, "What's that ugly thing?"

To Be Superior
D.H. Lawrence

How nice it is to be superior!
Because, really, it's no use pretending, one *is* superior, isn't one?
I mean people like you and me.—

Quite! I quite agree.
The trouble is, everybody thinks they're just as superior
as we are; just as superior.—

That's what's so boring! people are so boring.
But they can't really think it, do you think?
At the bottom, they must *know* we are really superior
don't you think?

don't you think, *really*, they *know* we're their superiors?—
I couldn't say.
I've never got to the bottom of superiority.
I should like to.

A Dialogue Between the Soul and the Body
Andrew Marvell

Soul
O, who shall from this dungeon raise
A soul, enslaved so many ways,
With bolts of bones, that fettered stands
In feet, and manacled in hands.
Here blinded with an eye; and there
Deaf with the drumming of an ear.
A soul hung up, as 'twere, in chains
Of nerves, and arteries, and veins.
Tortured, besides each other part,
In a vain head, and double heart?

Body
O, who shall me deliver whole,
From bonds of this tyrannic soul?
Which, stretched upright, impales me so,
That mine own precipice I go;
And warms and moves this needless frame,
(A fever could but do the same),
And, wanting where its spite to try,
Has made me live to let me die.
A body that could never rest,
Since this ill spirit is possessed.

Soul
What magic could me thus confine
Within another's grief to pine,
Where, whatsoever it complain,
I feel, that cannot feel, the pain.
And all my care itself employs,
That to preserve, which me destroys:
Constrained not only to endure

Diseases, but, what's worse, the cure:
And ready oft the port to gain,
And shipwrecked into health again?

Body
But physic yet could never reach
The maladies thou me dost teach:
Whom first the cramp of hope does tear,
And then the palsy shakes of fear;
The pestilence of love does heat,
Or hatred's hidden ulcer eat;
Joy's cheerful madness does perplex,
Or sorrow's other madness vex;
Which knowledge forces me to know,
And memory will not forego.
What but a soul could have the wit
To build me up for sin so fit?
So architects do square and hew,
Green trees that in the forest grew.

House & Bernadette
Bernadette Mayer

B: House are you anyone who could be doing anything at this moment?
    Are you a boy watching train tracks in the past standing in a big yellow
    field?

H: I am not a house. I am an apartment on the 9th floor of an inhospitable
    building in a similar city. I enclose you in a series of rectangles. And
    what thanks do I get, I am cluttered with the clothing and poems of chil-
    dren and poets

B: House I have been wanting to repaint your rectangular walls but what do
    I do with all these things?

H: First get rid of the poems, they pile up. And all the mail that's connected
    to them, you can throw that out too. Sometimes I can even hear it in my
    potentially beautiful porous walls. And the phone calls ...

B: Wait the phone calls are also another thing, do you want to get rid of the
    people, the children also? Would you prefer to be empty like the place
    next door? Belonging to a dead person!

H: Emptiness insults me but I have my limits and you have exceeded them, you even make too much noise and the neighbors are complaining.

B: House do you take it personally? If the landlord evicts us you will be sold instead of rented, before that you will be renovated—would you prefer that? It would be like going to the dentist, your walls would be scraped and evened and perfected by harsh hands, even machines.

H: Maybe I wouldn't mind.

B: You would not be called house anymore, no one would even address you on leaving and entering, you'd be thought of as an inanimate thing.

H: OK I get the point but what is this confusing me with a boy near a train track, I think you ask too much of my understanding.

B: House you must be fooling—after twelve years you understand all, I was just thinking while I was in you of all the other places people can be and be doing things in, I didn't mean to offend your immobility.

H: Oh now I see, after playing up to me, all you wanna do is leave, go elsewhere, desert me to the sales, the renovations, the heartless newcomers, well you certainly have that freedom—as you point out I can't go anywhere

B: But house I've been faithful to you for over a decade and my children want to keep you forever.

H: Yeah what about Max?

B: How did you know that?

H: Sister, I can hear.

B: Well, Max has never moved, at least in his remembering and he loves to move, to change, to ...

H: Yes, I've heard this before. Do you realize that before you invaders appeared, I had encountered few other humans since my birth? In 1939!

B: When you call me sister, does that mean you are a male? or maybe a feminist of either sex?

H: I want you to repaint my walls, my plaster is starving to absorb, parts of my ceiling hate their current condition.

B: But you didn't answer my question.

H: As you call me House, I will not answer on the grounds I might incriminate myself.

B: House have you ever been party to a crime?

H: Only the crimes of your noisy parties and of your overcrowding me with poetry and children and your secrets.

B: So you don't like the children. Is there anything you want to admit?

H: You act like a prosecuting attorney; it's not my fault I'm falling apart; I wish you had more money; I am like a poor person's teeth; I like the children; I even like the Muses never knowing if my windows are open or not though I hate the way you let the moths come in to fly to my already deteriorating ceiling fixtures.

B: House, what is your crime?

H: I admit I was designed in blatant rectangles and even my windows contain 12 rectangles each a bitch to clean.

B: Should we move out of you?

H: I am gracious, I surround you, I have three exits, I will accommodate you but don't tell me any more secrets till you repaint my walls and ceilings.

B: House you have too many but not enough doors.

H: And cease to drop the telephone on the floors, I have to sleep now you ought to go to bed too and by the way all those books make me seem smaller.

B: House, I am gay.

H: And I am too.

Bouquet of Roses in Sunlight
Wallace Stevens

Say that it is a crude effect, black reds,
Pink yellows, orange whites, too much as they are
To be anything else in the sunlight of the room,

Too much as they are to be changed by metaphor,
Too actual, things that in being real
Make any imaginings of them lesser things.

And yet this effect is a consequence of the way
We feel and, therefore, it is not real, except
In our sense of it, our sense of the fertilest red,

Of yellow as first color and of white,
In which the sense lies still, as a man lies,
Enormous, in a completing of his truth.

Our sense of these things changes and they change,
Not as in metaphor, but in our sense
Of them. So sense exceeds all metaphor.

It exceeds the heavy changes of the light.
It is like a flow of meanings with no speech
And of as many meanings as of men.

We are two that use these roses as we are,
In seeing them. This is what makes them seem
So far beyond the rhetorician's touch.

Picnic Remembered
Robert Penn Warren

That day, so innocent appeared
The leaf, the hill, the sky, to us,
Their structures so harmonious
And pure, that all we had endured
Seemed the quaint disaster of a child,
Now cupboarded, and all the wild
Grief canceled; so with what we feared.

We stood among the painted trees:
The amber light laved them, and us;
Or light then so untremulous,
So steady, that our substances,
Twin flies, were as in amber tamed
With our perfections stilled and framed
To mock Time's marveling after-spies.

Joy, strongest medium, then buoyed
Us when we moved, as swimmers, who,
Relaxed, resign them to the flow
And pause of their unstained flood.
Thus wrapped, sustained, we did not know
How darkness darker staired below;
Or knowing, but half understood.

The bright deception of that day!
When we so readily could gloze
All pages opened to expose
The trust we never would betray;
But darkness on the landscape grew
As in our bosoms, darkness, too;
And that was what we took away.

And it abides, and may abide:
Though ebbed from the region happier mapped,
Our hearts, like hollow stones, have trapped
A corner of that brackish tide.
The jaguar breath, the secret wrong,
The curse that curls the sudden tongue,
We know; for fears have fructified.

Or are we dead, that we, unmanned,
Are vacant, and our clearest souls
Are sped where each with each patrols,
In still society, hand in hand,
That scene where we, too, wandered once
Who now inherit a new province:
Love's limbo, this lost under-land?

The then, the now: each cenotaph
Of the other, and proclaims it dead.
Or is the soul a hawk that, fled
On glimmering wings past vision's path,
Reflects the last gleam to us here
Though sun is sunk and darkness near
—Uncharted Truth's high heliograph?

CHAPTER SEVEN

The Descriptive-Meditative Structure

COREY MARKS

The descriptive-meditative structure, as its name suggests, links description and meditation. But the term "descriptive-meditative" is imperfect; it names only two parts in what is essentially a three-part structure: description, meditation, and re-description. M.H. Abrams coins the term in his definitive essay, "Structure and Style in the Greater Romantic Lyric," and describes how such poems move:

> The speaker begins with a description of the landscape; an aspect or change of aspect in the landscape evokes a varied but integral process of memory, thought, anticipation, and feeling which remains closely intervolved with the outer scene. In the course of this meditation the lyric speaker achieves an insight, faces up to a tragic loss, comes to a moral decision, or resolves an emotional problem. Often the poem rounds upon itself to end where it began, at the outer scene, but with an altered mood and deepened understanding which is the result of the intervening meditation.

Poems that rely on this structure use the descriptive frame as a way to create the particular circumstances for a poem's meditation, and to demonstrate a change in the speaker when the outer scene is re-described at the poem's end. The movement between outer and inner states allows the structure to dramatize a moment of realization, of changing thought.

The descriptive-meditative poem stands as one of the significant lyric inventions of the Romantic period, but it has even earlier roots in religious devotion and the poems that grow out of that devotion. Abrams writes that "The Romantic meditations, then, though secular, often turn on crises—alienation, dejection, the loss of a 'celestial light' or 'glory' in experiencing the created world—which are closely akin to the spiritual crises of the earlier religious poets." As Abrams points out in the final section of his essay, the descriptive-meditative poem grows out of a three-part structure for religious devotional practice: "composition of place," "meditation," and "colloquy." Poets such as John Donne, George Herbert, and Henry Vaughn began using this three-part structure in their religious poetry, and the Romantics later adapted it.

The Romantics use this structure to show the power not of confession and prayer, but of memory and imagination. And not until the Romantic period does this structure marry a detailed and specific descriptive frame with a sustained and involved meditation that imitates the winding motions of human consciousness. Abrams finds examples of the descriptive-meditative structure in the works of such major Romantic figures as William Wordsworth, Samuel Taylor Coleridge, Percy Bysshe Shelley, John Keats, and their successors—Matthew Arnold, Walt Whitman, Wallace Stevens, and W.H. Auden.

In one of the great Romantic examples of the descriptive-meditative structure, "Lines Composed a Few Miles Above Tintern Abbey on Revisiting the Banks of the Wye During a Tour. July 13, 1798," William Wordsworth's speaker describes a familiar landscape he revisits after a five-year absence. The title alone emphatically calls attention to a particular place and time. The poem begins with a twenty-two-line description of the springs feeding the river, the cliffs and woods, the cottages and orchards. He then shifts into overt meditation, considering how frequently he has recalled this landscape while living in the city, relying on the memory for pleasure, solace, and restorative grace.

But with "somewhat of a sad perplexity" he registers a difference between the memory he has carried of the place and what he now sees. When he superimposes the picture held in memory over the actual scene, he finds they are mismatched. Wordsworth referred to this device of aligning memory with immediate perception as the "two consciousnesses." Imagine looking through a View-Master, that childhood toy that layers two images over each other to create a 3-D scene. You expect to see a single sharply defined landscape but instead see two pictures, one hovering over the other, their differences disconcertingly apparent.

Wordsworth's View-Master mishap sets the central question of the poem in motion: why the difference between memory and perception? What are the implications of this difference? Clearly, the speaker has changed; nature is no longer "all in all" to him as it was in his boyhood. He has fallen from a state of "thoughtless" communion with nature. Age has transformed him into a creature of thought, attuned to the "still, sad music of humanity." The poem reckons with his loss of immediate ease and connection with nature and comes to a newfound understanding of the "abundant recompense" he receives for his loss. He recognizes "A presence that disturbs me with the joy / Of elevated thoughts; a sense sublime / Of something far more deeply interfused." That sublime sense arrives by way of eye and ear, "both what they half create, / And what perceive." Memory—initially the source of his dilemma—proves to be "a dwelling place / For all sweet sounds and harmonies." In fact, the poem ends by viewing the landscape as a source for future memories that will provide solace for both the speaker and his younger sister, Dorothy, whom the poem finally addresses. He sees the landscape anew; the meditation has allowed him to perceive the scene in terms of this powerful potential rather than solely in terms of loss.

Though Wordsworth's "Tintern Abbey" enlarged the scope and range of the descriptive-meditative poem, it was Samuel Taylor Coleridge who initiated the Romantic approach to the structure. His so-called "conversation poems"—a label coined by critic G.M. Harper, borrowing from Coleridge's description of his poem "The Nightingale"—begin the pattern. Harper's name for this famous group of poems underscores another element common to the descriptive-meditative poem: the quality of address. More often than not, these poems speak to a specific listener.

Coleridge's own "This Lime-Tree Bower My Prison" addresses his friend and fellow writer, Charles Lamb, and clearly relies on the descriptive-meditative structure Wordsworth also used. It begins by locating the speaker in his cottage garden, and moves from feelings of dejection and isolation to a joy born from the speaker's feelings of friendship and generosity toward Lamb. The poem records an incident when Lamb and William and Dorothy Wordsworth came to visit Coleridge. An injury—a skillet of boiling milk had spilled on his foot—prevents Coleridge from accompanying his friends on a walk, and it is his being left behind in his garden while his friends wander the wider natural world that troubles him into meditation. And that is how he does follow his friends; the meditation takes the form of an imagined walk:

This Lime-Tree Bower My Prison
[Addressed to Charles Lamb of the India House, London]

Well, they are gone, and here must I remain,
This lime-tree bower my prison! I have lost

Beauties and feelings, such as would have been
Most sweet to my remembrance, even when age
Had dimm'd mine eyes to blindness! They, meanwhile,
Friends, whom I never more may meet again,
On springy heath, along the hill-top edge,
Wander in gladness, and wind down, perchance,
To that still roaring dell, of which I told;
The roaring dell, o'erwooded, narrow, deep,
And only speckled by the mid-day sun;
Where its slim trunk the ash from rock to rock
Flings arching like a bridge; —that branchless ash,
Unsunn'd and damp, whose few poor yellow leaves
Ne'er tremble in the gale, yet tremble still,
Fann'd by the water-fall! and there my friends
Behold the dark green file of long lank weeds,
That all at once (a most fantastic sight!)
Still nod and drip beneath the dripping edge
Of the blue clay-stone.
                    Now, my friends emerge
Beneath the wide wide Heaven—and view again
The many-steepled tract magnificent
Of hilly fields and meadows, and the sea,
With some fair bark, perhaps, whose sails light up
The slip of smooth clear blue betwixt two Isles
Of purple shadow! Yes! they wander on
In gladness all; but thou, methinks, most glad,
My gentle-hearted Charles! For thou hast pined
And hunger'd after Nature, many a year,
In the great City pent, winning thy way
With sad yet patient soul, through evil and pain
And strange calamity! Ah! slowly sink
Behind the western ridge, thou glorious Sun!
Shine in the slant beams of the sinking orb,
Ye purple heath-flowers! richlier burn, ye clouds!
Live in the yellow light, ye distant groves!
And kindle, thou blue Ocean! So my friend,
Struck with deep joy may stand, as I have stood,
Silent with swimming sense; yea, gazing round
On the wide landscape, gaze till all doth seem

Less gross than bodily; and of such hues
As veil the Almighty Spirit, when he makes
Spirits perceive his presence.
                                A delight
Comes sudden on my heart, and I am glad
As I myself were there! Nor in this bower,
This little lime-tree bower, have I not mark'd
Much that has sooth'd me. Pale beneath the blaze
Hung the transparent foliage; and I watch'd
Some broad and sunny leaf, and lov'd to see
The shadow of the leaf and stem above
Dappling its sunshine! And that walnut-tree
Was richly ting'd, and a deep radiance lay
Full on the ancient ivy, which usurps
Those fronting elms, and now, with blackest mass
Makes their dark branches gleam a lighter hue
Through the late twilight: and though now the bat
Wheels silent by, and not a swallow twitters,
Yet still the solitary humble-bee
Sings in the bean-flower! Henceforth I shall know
That Nature ne'er deserts the wise and pure;
No plot so narrow, be but Nature there
No waste so vacant, but may well employ
Each faculty of sense, and keep the heart
Awake to Love and Beauty! and sometimes
'Tis well to be bereft of promis'd good,
That we may lift the soul, and contemplate
With lively joy the joys we cannot share.
My gentle-hearted Charles! when the last rook
Beat its straight path along the dusky air
Homewards, I blessed it! deeming its black wing
(Now a dim speck, now vanishing in light)
Had cross'd the mighty Orb's dilated glory
While thou stood'st gazing; or, when all was still,
Flew creaking o'er thy head, and had a charm
For thee, my gentle-hearted Charles, to whom
No sound is dissonant which tells of Life.

The poem establishes its setting immediately, but more briefly than
Wordsworth's poem, locating the speaker in his garden. The poem's quick

description of the garden wall allows us to see little beyond a general impression of the speaker's surroundings, as though the speaker is blind to detail and withdraws in the bower that encloses him. We quickly come to understand that he feels held captive, forced into solitude and withheld from experience: "Well, they are gone, and here must I remain, / This lime-tree bower my prison!" The image of the bower as prison conveys the intense feelings of isolation, loss, and even punishment that wrack the speaker, underscoring the speaker's desire to leave the garden and follow his friends.

By the poem's end, however, the speaker notices what he couldn't before. The poem's return to the garden is richly detailed and joyous, the place transformed by a reawakened sense of nature:

> And that walnut-tree
> Was richly ting'd, and a deep radiance lay
> Full on the ancient ivy, which usurps
> Those fronting elms, and now with blackest mass
> Makes their dark branches gleam a lighter hue

The poem's movement from the early lack of description to this later overflow of detail conveys the speaker's powerful change. The speaker comes to see his former prison with a new attentiveness and generosity, realizing that there is "No plot so narrow, be but Nature there."

How does the poem arrive at this change? Through the meditation. Abrams tells us that the strongest descriptive-meditative poems "manifest a transaction between subject and object in which the thought incorporates and makes explicit what was already implicit in the outer scene." Coleridge's brief descriptive opening, through the force of its metaphor, sets the scene for the meditation that follows, a meditation that escapes from and ultimately transforms the prison.

Relying on a rich memory of the landscape, the speaker imagines following his friends until he comes to stand next to them, a journey that takes him from dejection to joy. In fact, the welling of joy in the poem yields an almost magical sense of transformation. At first, the speaker feels at odds with his friends' pleasure, and worries over his own losses—loss of "Beauties and feelings," loss of future memories, and loss of companionship. But his meditation allows him to imagine the sights and sensations his friends encounter with such vividness that his dour mood evaporates:

> Now, my friends emerge
> Beneath the wide wide Heaven—and view again

The many-steepled tract magnificent
Of hilly fields and meadows, and the sea,
With some fair bark, perhaps, whose sails light up
The slip of smooth clear blue betwixt two Isles
Of purple shadow! Yes! they wander on
In gladness all . . .

The speaker's long, detailed meditation draws the reader into the journey. We are so immersed, so captivated, that we almost forget that the speaker only imagines the walk.

Of his companions, the speaker most powerfully empathizes with Lamb. Lamb has also been imprisoned in a city away from nature for too long: "For thou hast pined /And hunger'd after Nature, many a year, / In the great City pent." By living in the city, Lamb has, in fact, suffered worse losses and has longed more powerfully than the speaker—though a foot-bath of boiling milk sounds pretty bad. Still, Lamb sees at last what has so long been denied to him, and that recognition draws the speaker from his melancholy: "A delight / Comes sudden on my heart, and I am glad / As I myself were there!" The shared delight makes him attentive to the details that had been dark to him in his moment of dejection. The meditation leads the speaker to see anew with his physical eye, to recognize that the natural glory the distant Lamb views exists in his own narrow plot as well.

The assurances uncovered in both "Tintern Abbey" and "This Lime-Tree Bower My Prison" are harder to come by for many contemporary poets who employ the descriptive-meditative structure. Skepticism has worried away faith in religion, nature, and imagination that earlier generations possessed, though longings for those earlier convictions still make their way into the poems. Charles Wright's brief "Clear Night" articulates such a longing:

Clear night, thumb-top of a moon, a back-lit sky.
Moon-fingers lay down their same routine
On the side deck and the threshold, the white keys and the black keys.
Bird hush and bird song. A cassia flower falls.

I want to be bruised by God.
I want to be strung up in a strong light and singled out.
I want to be stretched, like music wrung from a dropped seed.
I want to be entered and picked clean.

And the wind says "What?" to me.
And the castor beans, with their little earrings of death, say
   "What?" to me.
And the stars start out on their cold slide through the dark.
And the gears notch and the engines wheel.

The poem functions as a condensed version of the descriptive-meditative structure. Because the poem is so brief, the device of framing meditation with description stands out sharply. In fact, the stanzas themselves formally reinforce the structural elements. Stanza one sets forth the particular landscape, stanza two initiates the meditation, and stanza three offers a direct transaction between meditation and landscape.

The poem begins with a vividly concise description of its setting, focusing on details that become essential to the meditation that follows: the clear sky, the moon as thumb, the play of light as fingers moving over the piano-like slats of the deck, the silence and song of birds. Then the poem abruptly shifts from a quiet act of description to an ecstatic cry; a flower softly falls and is answered with the force of the speaker's longing. The meditation enters with a suddenness that startles us with its intensity and directness. Even so, we realize that the description triggers and shapes the meditation; the first stanza's images resonate through the second stanza. The falling flower itself is an intimation of death. And when the speaker says, "I want to be bruised by God," it is easy to imagine the thumb-top of the moon bearing down on him. The four lines of the middle stanza play out rich variations of the earlier images of fingers, light, song, and even birds (the dropped seed picked clean).

The anaphora in the second stanza (the repetition of "I want" at the start of each sentence) raises the intensity and formality of the meditation. The speaker pleads by way of prayer to be touched and transformed by God, even if that touch comes as damage. A God that bruises and picks him clean is still a God that exists, that listens and answers.

And yet, notice that his prayer does not address God; rather, the speaker seems to speak to the landscape in which he hopes he has found signs of divine presence. Here, then, we see how the descriptive-meditative poem need not address only an absent or present auditor. It can even address the scene itself.

In the final stanza, the scene that initiated the meditation now responds to the speaker: "And the wind says 'What?' to me. / And the castor beans, with their little earrings of death, say 'What?' to me." The yard speaks, and the speaker's attention shifts to overt images of change and death. The wind, which is perhaps what causes the cassia flower to fall in the first stanza, offers an image of transformation, but it is a more severe transformation than the speaker had in mind. The castor beans—which contain ricin, a devastating natural toxin—directly introduce death into the poem even as they echo earlier imagery. The picked-clean seed the speaker wants to become prefigures them and even implies that there is something poisonous in the human.

With their questions, the wind and beans suggest nature cannot even understand the speaker's cry. The speaker comes to face the stark presence not of God but of death, and this hard lesson changes the way he describes the landscape. From the smallest embodiments of death fallen in his yard, the speaker's attention sweeps to the vast sky where the stars "start out on their cold slide through the dark." His gaze moves beyond the moon to the larger sky behind it, beyond the fingerprints of a divine presence to a cold and mechanized emptiness lubricated by death. The poem's power and intensity come in great part from condensing the descriptive-meditative structure, moving with the force of surprise from the initial domestic scene to the meditation's plea for reassurance to the harsher nature that answers, riveting the speaker's attention.

Louise Glück's "Mock Orange" also employs the descriptive-meditative structure in a condensed manner. Like Coleridge's poem, it establishes its scene quickly, focusing in on an aspect of the landscape:

> It is not the moon, I tell you.
> It is these flowers
> lighting the yard.
>
> I hate them.
> I hate them as I hate sex,
> the man's mouth
> sealing my mouth, the man's
> paralyzing body—
>
> and the cry that always escapes,
> the low, humiliating
> premise of union—
>
> In my mind tonight
> I hear the question and pursuing answer
> fused in one sound

that mounts and mounts and then
is split into the old selves,
the tired antagonisms. Do you see?
We were made fools of.
And the scent of mock orange
drifts through the window.

How can I rest?
How can I be content
when there is still
that odor in the world?

Like Coleridge and Wright, Glück looks into the domesticated land-
scape. But rather than viewing it from the yard itself, or from a doorway,
the speaker looks through an open window. Her attention falls to the mock
orange in her yard, a plant whose flowers smell like citrus but do not pro-
duce oranges. As in Wright's poem, the meditation begins abruptly, with
an escalation of language and intensity. While there is an air of insistence in
the speaker's address—"It is not the moon, I tell you"—that quality does
not prepare us for the emotional force of her declaration: "I hate them. / I
hate them as I hate sex." With these lines a new emotional register, one of
anger and shame, suddenly enters the poem, dramatizing the moment of
recognition and insight.

The meditation itself explores the fierce emotional association forged
between the mock orange and the myth of sexual union. The speaker as-
serts her feeling, recalls the stifling and humiliating act itself, and then ana-
lyzes and dismantles the erotic myth. The "premise of union" taunts her,
promises a false transformation—an escape from selfhood—that inevita-
bly collapses into "the old selves, / the tired antagonisms." Moving from
hatred to shame—"We were made fools of"—the meditation leaves the
speaker without the kind of resolution Wordsworth and Coleridge achieve.
The landscape continues to unsettle her, now with an aspect that enters her
space: the odor drifts through the window. In fact, the shift from sight to
smell is an important change in the poem's re-description. More invasive
than the sight of the flowers, the smell amplifies what she initially registered
with her eyes, permeating her space and making what she came to realize in
the meditation feel even more inescapable. The flowers' smell promises
something that it cannot produce, and its echo becomes a form of mockery.
The association the speaker makes at the start of the meditation is now

inextricably fused to the landscape, as though the taunting odor of sex lingers in the world.

As evidenced in the poems by Coleridge, Wright, and Glück, the descriptive-meditative structure is capable of delivering poems of great variety; however, the descriptive-meditative structure has also given rise to an important, related structural variant: the meditative-descriptive poem, in which the structure turns inside out. Marianne Moore's "A Grave" is perhaps the most famous example of this structural variant. Her poem begins with a meditation on the desire to possess a natural scene—here a seascape rather than a landscape—through describing and imagining it in human terms. The poem then presents a series of descriptions that slowly strip away those human terms before closing at last with a brief return to meditation.

Like Coleridge's, Moore's poem is rooted in a particular experience. When Moore and her mother once watched the surf on Monhegan Island after a storm, a man came and stood directly between them and the water. The meditation begins with the force of indignation:

A Grave

Man looking into the sea,
taking the view from those who have as much right to it as you have to
   it yourself,
it is human nature to stand in the middle of a thing,
but you cannot stand in the middle of this;
the sea has nothing to give but a well excavated grave.
The firs stand in a procession, each with an emerald turkey foot at the
   top,
reserved as their contours, saying nothing;
repression, however, is not the most obvious characteristic of the sea;
the sea is a collector, quick to return a rapacious look.
There are others besides you who have worn that look—
whose expression is no longer a protest; the fish no longer investigate
   them
for their bones have not lasted:
men lower nets, unconscious of the fact that they are desecrating a
   grave,
and row quickly away—the blades of the oars
moving together like the feet of water-spiders as if there were no such
   thing as death.

The wrinkles progress among themselves in a phalanx—beautiful
    under networks of foam,
and fade breathlessly while the sea rustles in and out of the seaweed;
the birds swim through the air at top speed, emitting catcalls as
    heretofore—
the tortoise-shell scourges about the feet of the cliffs, in motion
    beneath them;
and the ocean, under the pulsation of lighthouses and noise of
    bellbuoys,
advances as usual, looking as if it were not that ocean in which dropped
    things are bound to sink—
in which if they turn and twist, it is neither with volition nor
    consciousness.

"A Grave" creates a meditative frame around a long descriptive pas-
sage; the proportions are reversed. The meditation begins with a proposi-
tion: "it is human nature to stand in the middle of a thing, / but you cannot
stand in the middle of this." It then begins to explore one of the common
ways we imagine the sea, calling it a grave. Most of this examination occurs
in the description, and we have the sense that the human presence recedes
as the description moves forward. After the passage of description, the
poem returns briefly to meditation, ending again with assertion; the ocean
depths are devoid of "volition" and "consciousness." The moment of re-
meditation—to turn our own terms inside-out—has moved from the sur-
face, from the confines of human imagination, to the vast depths beyond
human perception and definition. It is now meditation that is altered by
the intervening description.

"A Grave" considers the very act the descriptive-meditative poem un-
dertakes, questioning the way human imagination and understanding are
projected onto landscape. Moore's speaker is a secondary observer; she
addresses the man who tries to "stand in the middle of a thing." The man
who stands in the way, between the speaker and the sea, claims the view for
himself. It is "human nature" that we try to "take the view" by imagining
the landscape in a particular way, by containing it in a frame, transforming
it into symbol. But no one can own the view. There are others who "have as
much right to it," and, anyway, the sea will exceed these moments of own-
ership, outlasting each human viewer:

There are others besides you who have worn that look—

whose expression is no longer a protest; the fish no longer investigate
them
for their bones have not lasted

The man will die, the speaker will die, and the sea will continue, indifferent
at last to the human gaze. As in Wright's poem, we encounter a sense of na-
ture's terrifying disinterest in the human.

Early in the poem, the sea is described through figurative language that
evokes the sense of ceremony we associate with graves and burial: the fir
trees "stand in a procession," the waves "progress among themselves in a
phalanx." But by the poem's end, the figurative language recedes, stripping
away the human projections (they "fade breathlessly") to reveal the sea's
cold and inhuman reality that exceeds and overwhelms human perception.
Below our demarcations—the "pulsation of lighthouses and noise of bell-
buoys"—exists a place devoid of human life, a true grave. We are left with
the sense that the sea, now called ocean, has made us aware of the limits of
human imagination. And yet, we cannot help but bring imagination to bear
on the world.

The poem doesn't argue against the impulse behind the descriptive-
meditative act; rather, it places it in a more skeptical register and in so doing
prefigures the uncertainties and rebukes of later descriptive-meditative po-
ems like "Clear Night" and "Mock Orange." It is our nature to engage the
world imaginatively even if we recognize our limitations. And by acknowl-
edging those limitations, poetry can examine how we create our sense of
the world and our place in it. In the end, "A Grave" revitalizes the
descriptive-meditative poem by using it to question the very Romantic cer-
tainties that generated the structure.

One of the reasons the descriptive-meditative poem continues to be re-
newed by poets writing after the Romantic era is that its simple three-part
structure allows enormous variety and complexity. As shown in this chap-
ter's poems and in Supplemental Poems, the success of a descriptive-
meditative poem doesn't depend as much on *what* is described as on *how*
it's described, and on how the poem establishes a descriptive frame for a
meditation that moves between outward and inward landscapes, drama-
tizing a mind in the process of change. And the structure itself has flexibil-
ity, as Moore's poem and Tom Andrews' "At Burt Lake" show. Each begins
with an idea that is then dramatized by the setting described.

The descriptive-meditative structure comes from a tradition that
values nature, so wild vistas often provide sources for contemplation:

mountains, forests, rivers, oceans. But someone wanting to write a descriptive-meditative poem need not pack up the laptop and head for the countryside to contemplate wind-tossed trees and sun-flared cataracts. Wright's speaker remains in his own yard. A parking lot stirs the speaker in Olena Kalytiak Davis' "Resolutions in a Parked Car," while Tony Hoagland's speaker in "A Color of the Sky" watches a changing landscape through the window of a moving car. And the speaker in Philip Larkin's "Church Going" turns his attention to the inside of a church.

The descriptive-meditative structure can begin slowly, with a detailed evocation of setting that allows the particular crisis of the poem to burble to the surface, as in "Tintern Abbey." Or like Coleridge's "This Lime-Tree Bower My Prison," it can begin with the force of a single image that abruptly launches the speaker into meditation. It can be brief and concise like Glück's "Mock Orange," or sprawling and rangy like Susan Mitchell's "Wave."

Of course, what gives these poems their power is the meditation. The meditation can be abstract discourse, argument, complaint, ecstatic cry. It can come to a tidy resolution, lead to an unwanted realization, or remain unresolved, still troubling the poet. It can be hopeful, skeptical, indignant, visionary, wild, resigned, joyous, reasoned, angry, dejected. But it must have energy, a movement impelled by the emotional situation. If it feels too pat, too flatly explanatory, too static, the meditation will lose the reader's interest or, worse, come off as lecture.

These poems are dramatic lyrics. Even though they rely on first-person speakers who may sound a great deal like the poets writing the poems, they still create a sense of character, of someone actually speaking, thinking, and feeling. As the poems here demonstrate, descriptive-meditative poems surprise and convince us when they seem—when they are—dynamically alive in the world to which they respond.

SUPPLEMENTAL POEMS

At Burt Lake
Tom Andrews

To disappear into the right words
and to be their meanings ...

October dusk.
Pink scraps of clouds, a plum-colored sky.
The sycamore tree spills a few leaves.
The cold focuses like a lens ...

Now night falls, its hair
caught in the lake's eye.

Such clarity of things. Already
I've said too much ...

         Lord,
language must happen to you
the way this black pane of water,
chipped and blistered with stars,
happens to me.

Frost at Midnight
Samuel Taylor Coleridge

   The Frost performs its secret ministry,
Unhelped by any wind. The owlet's cry
Came loud—hark, again! loud as before.
The inmates of my cottage, all at rest,
Have left me to that solitude, which suits
Abstruser musings: save that at my side
My cradled infant slumbers peacefully.
'Tis calm indeed! so calm, that it disturbs
And vexes meditation with its strange
And extreme silentness. Sea, hill, and wood,
This populous village! Sea, and hill, and wood,
With all the numberless goings-on of life,
Inaudible as dreams! the thin blue flame
Lies on my low-burnt fire, and quivers not;
Only that film, which fluttered on the grate,
Still flutters there, the sole unquiet thing.
Methinks, its motion in this hush of nature
Gives it dim sympathies with me who live,
Making it a companionable form,
Whose puny flaps and freaks the idling Spirit
By its own moods interprets, every where

Echo or mirror seeking of itself,
And makes a toy of Thought.

                    But O! how oft,
How oft, at school, with most believing mind,
Presageful, have I gazed upon the bars,
To watch that fluttering *stranger*! and as oft
With unclosed lids, already had I dreamt
Of my sweet birth-place, and the old church-tower,
Whose bells, the poor man's only music, rang
From morn to evening, all the hot Fair-day,
So sweetly, that they stirred and haunted me
With a wild pleasure, falling on mine ear
Most like articulate sounds of things to come!
So gazed I, till the soothing things, I dreamt,
Lulled me to sleep, and sleep prolonged my dreams!
And so I brooded all the following morn,
Awed by the stern preceptor's face, mine eye
Fixed with mock study on my swimming book:
Save if the door half opened, and I snatched
A hasty glance, and still my heart leaped up,
For still I hoped to see the *stranger's* face,
Townsman, or aunt, or sister more beloved,
My play-mate when we both were clothed alike!

   Dear Babe, that sleepest cradled by my side,
Whose gentle breathings, heard in this deep calm,
Fill up the interspersèd vacancies
And momentary pauses of the thought!
My babe so beautiful! it thrills my heart
With tender gladness, thus to look at thee,
And think that thou shall learn far other lore,
And in far other scenes! For I was reared
In the great city, pent 'mid cloisters dim,
And saw nought lovely but the sky and stars.
But *thou*, my babe! shalt wander like a breeze
By lakes and sandy shores, beneath the crags
Of ancient mountain, and beneath the clouds,
Which image in their bulk both lakes and shores
And mountain crags: so shalt thou see and hear

The lovely shapes and sounds intelligible
Of that eternal language, which thy God
Utters, who from eternity doth teach
Himself in all, and all things in himself.
Great universal Teacher! he shall mould
Thy spirit, and by giving make it ask.

   Therefore all seasons shall be sweet to thee,
Whether the summer clothe the general earth
With greenness, or the redbreast sit and sing
Betwixt the tufts of snow on the bare branch
Of mossy apple-tree, while the nigh thatch
Smokes in the sun-thaw; whether the eave-drops fall
Heard only in the trances of the blast,
Or if the secret ministry of frost
Shall hang them up in silent icicles,
Quietly shining to the quiet Moon.

Resolutions in a Parked Car
Olena Kalytiak Davis

After I'm done pleading with the steering wheel,
after I'm done screaming at the white doors
of the Friendship Inn, no, even while I'm spitting

and howling, I know, yes, this is the way
we find out about ourselves: crying in rental cars
in parking lots in strange cities that are already

too familiar. The huge ship in front of you,
don't you hope it will soon disembark? Don't you
hate hotels? Don't you hate to travel

just to see the same pockmarks and limps,
the weight carried just below the waist
and above? Just look at what we have done

to ourselves, and topped it off with a club sandwich,
a scribble of neon. I'm wailing
like some foreigner in a foreign country

we don't give a shit about because how could we

understand something as subtle as the mutilation
of ears and lips? Please, I beg you,

perform some crazy rite over me so things can either
finally dissolve or finally become solid.
Please, I need something primitive and complex

to relieve me of this world subdivided into better
and better ways to avoid life. Sicker
and sicker ways. Someone is brewing

their own beer. Someone knows why he is
the best candidate for the job. Death cruising
down 90. Laughing, Sweetheart, Death is the least of it.

I'm in a parking lot in Spokane reintroducing myself
to myself. I'm feeling like throwing up.
In a parking lot in Spokane I am resolving

to read Nietzsche, to pierce and tattoo myself,
in a parking lot I'm determining things
about my labia and nose and heart.

A Color of the Sky
Tony Hoagland

Windy today and I feel less than brilliant,
driving over the hills from work.
There are the dark parts on the road
                when you pass through clumps of wood
and the bright spots where you have a view of the ocean,
but that doesn't make the road an allegory.

I should call Marie and apologize
for being so boring at dinner last night,
but can I really promise not to be that way again?
And anyway, I'd rather watch the trees, tossing
in what certainly looks like sexual arousal.

Otherwise it's spring, and everything looks frail;
the sky is baby blue, and the just-unfurling leaves
are full of infant chlorophyll,
the very tint of inexperience.

Last summer's song is making a comeback on the radio,
and on the highway overpass,
the only metaphysical vandal in America has written
MEMORY LOVES TIME
in big black spraypaint letters,

which makes us wonder if Time loves Memory back.

Last night I dreamed of X again.
She's like a stain on my subconscious sheets.
Years ago she penetrated me
but though I scrubbed and scrubbed and scrubbed,
I never got her out,
but now I'm glad.

What I thought was an end turned out to be a middle.
What I thought was a brick wall turned out to be a tunnel.
What I thought was an injustice
turned out to be a color of the sky.

Outside the youth center, between the liquor store
and the police station,
a little dogwood tree is losing its mind;

overflowing with blossomfoam,
like a sudsy mug of beer;
like a bride ripping off her clothes,

dropping snow white petals to the ground in clouds,

so Nature's wastefulness seems quietly obscene.
It's been doing that all week:
making beauty,
and throwing it away,
and making more.

Church Going
Phillip Larkin

Once I am sure there's nothing going on
I step inside, letting the door thud shut.
Another church: matting, seats, and stone,
And little books; sprawlings of flowers, cut

For Sunday, brownish now; some brass and stuff
Up at the holy end; the small neat organ;
And a tense, musty, unignorable silence,
Brewed God knows how long. Hatless, I take off
My cycle-clips in awkward reverence.

Move forward, run my hand around the font.
From where I stand, the roof looks almost new—
Cleaned, or restored? Someone would know: I don't.
Mounting the lectern, I peruse a few
Hectoring large-scale verses, and pronounce
'Here endeth' much more loudly than I'd meant.
The echoes snigger briefly. Back at the door
I sign the book, donate an Irish sixpence,
Reflect the place was not worth stopping for.

Yet stop I did: in fact I often do,
And always end much at a loss like this,
Wondering what to look for; wondering, too,
When churches will fall completely out of use
What we shall turn them into, if we shall keep
A few cathedrals chronically on show,
Their parchment, plate and pyx in locked cases,
And let the rest rent-free to rain and sheep.
Shall we avoid them as unlucky places?

Or, after dark, will dubious women come
To make their children touch a particular stone;
Pick simples for a cancer; or on some
Advised night see walking a dead one?
Power of some sort or other will go on
In games, in riddles, seemingly at random;
But superstition, like belief, must die,
And what remains when disbelief has gone?
Grass, weedy pavement, brambles, buttress, sky,

A shape less recognisable each week,
A purpose more obscure. I wonder who
Will be the last, the very last, to seek
This place for what it was; one of the crew
That tap and jot and know what rood-lofts were?

Some ruin-bibber, randy for antique,
Or Christmas-addict, counting on a whiff
Of gown-and-bands and organ-pipes and myrrh?
Or will he be my representative,

Bored, uninformed, knowing the ghostly silt
Dispersed, yet tending to this cross of ground
Through suburb scrub because it held unspilt
So long and equably what since is found
Only in separation—marriage, and birth,
And death, and thoughts of these—for which was built
This special shell? For, though I've no idea
What this accoutred frowsty barn is worth,
It pleases me to stand in silence here;

A serious house on serious earth it is,
In whose blent air all our compulsions meet,
Are recognized, and robed as destinies.
And that much never can be obsolete,
Since someone will forever be surprising
A hunger in himself to be more serious,
And gravitating with it to this ground,
Which, he once heard, was proper to grow wise in,
If only that so many dead lie round.

Wave
Susan Mitchell

I don't mean this as a command, though
if you want to wave to someone
there's no reason why you shouldn't.
I'll go on looking out this window, pretending
you're not here, not doing something
as ridiculous as jerking your hand
up and down. I'm devoted
to an enormous expanse of violet
which is how the Atlantic wants to be today.
Cutting across the violet are gigantic
stripes of green and within
the green stripes

which are swelling, breathing deeply, the sun
encaged like a canary.
If that's too difficult to visualize,
think of a green grape inside
lime Jell-O, the frigid
cafeteria air, the iced celery,
the chartreuse translucency
you are about to take into your mouth.
Its palpitations.
On the horizon is a freighter and maybe
this is what you have been waving at,
a very complicated rig
resembling the skyline of a major city
with smokestacks and fire escapes.
It reminds me of those complex
apparatuses Freud's patients dreamed about—
ingenous metaphors for the urinary tract
or genitals. There is even something red
on the rig like the wattles of a turkey.
But if you are not waving
at the freighter, then maybe
it's that sparkle jumping about
like batons, like rhinestone drumsticks.
My Atlantic is cat's-paw, a purpurate
empurpling into which I yearn
violently to be dipped,
rubbed against the many ink pads
of the ocean. But since the water
is violetted only from this distance, its methyls
dissolving as one gets close enough
to feel the scratch of floating sargasso
my appetite is impossible to gratify.
To come up close on such purples,
such spangles, we'd have to find some cheap
bazaar, a flea market where the heaps
of scarves, the gauzy, flimsy
costumes have been steeped
in Tyre, though once real kings and queens
went everywhere in such frieze and panelwork

with cloaks of night-sky and constellations.
I envy birds of prey, how they don't
waver as they come in close,
how they undress the tassels and pom-poms,
the nosegay heads, the lacework
of the little birds, how
they ankle and beak in furbelows
of blood. But hush. Here it comes, what
I've been waiting for, the smash
and loops of wave on wave,
this crested cobra
towering above. What membrane
keeps that transparency
from dispersing into the air the way
the juices of citrus,
tangelo or tangerine resist momentarily
the teeth, that holding back
to make it linger,
the pillow play of lip,
all that plumping before
it breaks?

The Astronomer's Prayer to the Andromeda Galaxy
Kevin Prufer

Spinning dime, torque in the hubcap, catherine wheel:
You are a speck burning in the corner
Of my astronomer's eye—the lens' ghost and the sky's ghost.

I want to explain your silence.
I want to stretch a piano wire from here to there, and play.
I want to catch you as I would a fish or a whispered name.
I want to get you in my net.

But the white dustmoths call: "Look here!"
And the grass with its million thin fingers tells me: "Look, look here!"
And the owl wails and the cat cries,
And I can't see for the moon's glare.

                              (after Charles Wright)

CHAPTER EIGHT

The Mid-course Turn

JERRY HARP

As the whole of *Structure & Surprise* emphasizes, a powerful structural dynamic in many poems is the shift in tone or reorientation of thought, known as the *volta* or turn. Much associated with the Petrarchan sonnet form—which shifts, or turns, in the movement from the octave to the sestet—the turn can occur in a variety of places in a variety of poems. For example, as literary critic Hugh Holman explains, a turn sometimes occurs in the Shakespearean sonnet in the shift from the three quatrains that introduce, develop, and complicate the argument, to the final, rhymed couplet; and the Miltonic sonnet is distinctive for the appearance of the turn in no fixed position.

At times the strength of the turn, whether it appears in a sonnet or another kind of poem, can be extreme. In his book of essays, *Poetry as Persuasion,* poet-critic Carl Dennis discusses the kind of radical shift in a poem that he calls a "mid-course correction." The kind of shift that Dennis focuses on is radical because it constitutes, as he puts it, "a shift in genre"; this shift is one strong enough to suggest that the poem's speaker has in the course of the poem changed her or his mind about what kind of poem is under way. As an example of this kind of shift, Dennis examines Horace's ode commemorating Octavian's victory over Cleopatra, a poem that "seems to begin as a joyous public celebration of the triumph of the imperial order and ends in private brooding over the heroic death of Cleopatra." This movement from a public to a private voice is one that Dennis then finds reversed in Robert Lowell's "For the Union Dead," which begins with the speaker's personal expression of lamentation and loss but then shifts into a public voice that calls the city of Boston to accounts for "its estrangement from the best ideals of its own culture."

While a poem that effectively shifts genres in the course of its development is one instance of the dynamic of what I am referring to as the "midcourse turn," this kind of shift is at least similar to the less radical kinds of turns often found in the traditional sonnet. Even if the turn does not always constitute a shift in genre, it is nevertheless one worth considering along with the more radical "corrections" that Dennis emphasizes. One helpful example of a borderline case, a poem whose turn comes close to shifting genre without quite fully doing so, is the anonymous sixteenth-century poem "Western Wind," a poem that I have long thought of as a primal cry of English literary tradition:

> Western wind, when wilt thou blow,
>   The small rain down can rain?
> Christ, if my love were in my arms
>   And I in my bed again!

As literary critic Robert Wallace points out, the opening two lines address the natural forces of wind and rain personified, the first of which is addressed as a kind of deity. The poem's third line then shifts into a much different kind of cognitive and spiritual world, the language of which is more tonally complex than that of the first two lines. Much of this tonal complexity is created by the ambiguity of the opening cry of "Christ," which functions as both angry expletive and prayerful invocation. This tonal complexity is similar to that encountered in many poems of the biblical book of Psalms. The cry partakes of both expletive and invocation as the painful longing and crying out for help carry over from the opening two lines. This cry of "Christ" also gestures toward something of the longing for intimacy, in this case intimacy with the Divine, voiced in the poem's latter two lines. Of course, the scene of intimacy in bed with the speaker's beloved is closeness of a more carnal kind than the stance of prayer might initially imply, but I take it that what he longs for is an intimacy, a feeling of belonging, that integrates every part of his experience, from the greatest heights of spiritual harmony to the greatest depths of physical union. Further, the incomplete conditional of the closing line suggests that what the speaker longs for finally exceeds his capacity to speak. Thus, while this poem features a strong turn, from an address to the west wind to a more tonally complex and finally incomplete address to Christ, the poem remains throughout a cry of lamentation and an invocation. There is no shift of genre, strictly speaking, though there is a dramatic shift in the poem's implied world.

There are precedents for the mid-course turn in the history of much European discourse. One practice in European educational tradition that encouraged a kind of verbal dexterity was that of arguing multiple sides of a given dispute, as the chapters on the concessional and the dialectical argument structures in *Structure & Surprise* note. Arguing different sides of a dispute occurs in Plato's *Dialogues*, and such argument was also a part of the *disputationes de quolibet*, the ritual debates of the medieval universities that functioned not only as intellectual exercise, but also as public entertainment. Perhaps a kind of mid-course turn occurs nowhere as conspicuously as in the *Summa Theologiae* by Saint Thomas Aquinas (1225–1274), each article of which begins with a proposal that is in some sense counter to what the article finally will conclude. After a series of arguments in favor of this opening position, there appears the *Sed contra* (usually translated, "But on the contrary") clause, which changes the direction of the thought; it is this *Sed contra* clause that parallels the mid-course turn. The *Sed contra* is usually followed by an explanation of the counter position, which then leads to a series of replies to the preceding arguments. Thus, Article Nine of the First Question of the *Summa* addresses the issue of "whether Holy Scripture should use metaphors." Aquinas then provides three objections to the use of metaphors in Scripture, the general force of which is that metaphor is either inappropriate to or obscurantist of matters of divine revelation. He then follows up with the *Sed contra*:

> On the contrary, It is written (Osee xii. 10): *I have multiplied visions, and I have used similitudes by the ministry of the prophets.* But to put forward anything by means of similitudes is to use metaphors. Therefore this sacred science may use metaphors.

The explanatory passage then sets out why metaphor may be used in theology: because "God provides for everything according to the capacity of its nature," and because all human knowledge begins with sensory experience, it is appropriate for spiritual truths to be expressed in material terms, such as one finds in sacred Scripture's use of metaphor. The article then ends with replies to the arguments with which it began.

Debates similar to the medieval *disputationes de quolibet* continued in many educational practices of the Renaissance; thus, the poetry of the age also shows the enactment of turns of argument in such a poem as "Western Wind." Among Renaissance poets John Donne makes extensive use of the turn. His poem "The Dissolution" provides a striking example of a mid-

course turn that occurs in an unexpected moment of the poem, which be-
gins with a meditation on the death of the speaker's beloved:

> She is dead; and all which die
> To their first elements resolve;
> And we were mutual elements to us,
> And made of one another.
> My body then doth hers involve,
> And those things whereof I consist, hereby
> In me abundant grow, and burdenous,
> And nourish not, but smother.
> My fire of passion, sighs of air,
> Water of tears, and earthy sad despair,
> Which my materials be,
> But near worn out by love's security,
> She, to my loss, doth by her death repair,
> And I might live long wretched so
> But that my fire doth with my fuel grow.
> Now as those active kings
> Whose foreign conquest treasure brings,
> Receive more, and spend more, and soonest break:
> This (which I am amazed that I can speak)
> This death, hath with my store
> My use increased
> And so my soul more earnestly released,
> Will outstrip hers; as bullets flown before
> A latter bullet may o'ertake, the powder being more.

Because the two lovers were composed of each other, her dissolution at
death means that the material of which she was made is resolving back into
him. Because of the lovers' mutual composition, at her death his body
"involves"—that is, enfolds—hers. This act of enfolding means that he is
now composed of an abundance of material, both that which makes up his
own body and that which formerly made up hers. As literary critic A.J.
Smith points out, the ancient physician Galen asserts that an overabun-
dance of being can be as dangerous as a deficit. Thus, the speaker's enfold-
ing of the material of his beloved's body puts him in a precarious position,
for he is himself resolving back into the earth, air, fire, and water that he
catalogues in relation to his own existence—that is, he is resolving back
into the four elements of which, going back to the conceptions of antiquity,

the material world is made. In the speaker these elements are associated with his passions (fire), sighs (air), tears (water), and despair (earth). The wretchedness of the speaker's existence is to live in the midst of this abundance of being, an abundance ironically brought on by his beloved's death. But it is this very abundance of being that, rather unexpectedly, leads to his own quickly approaching death. For his abundance of being functions as a faster-burning fuel. Thus, he will overtake her in death.

While it is often the case that the turn occurs at the beginning of a sentence, the turn in "The Dissolution" occurs at a sentence's end. This turn is marked by the beginning of a new line, though it is the final line of a seven-line sentence: "But that my fire doth with my fuel grow." This turn signals a shift into a new realization: the speaker's newly and sadly acquired abundance of being will not lead to the speaker's life burning on longer because of his abundance of fuel; rather, this abundance will function as faster-burning fuel. The turn is then reinforced by the word "Now," which signals an explanation of the speaker's current state. The wit of this turn is of an especially striking and ingenious kind, one that plays an unexpected variation on the imagery thus far established in the poem. While an elegy often takes an unexpected turn—for example, by refusing the consolation that it seemed to be moving toward—Donne's "The Dissolution" stands out for the way it takes up the ideas of "store" (abundance) and "use" to create the image of one bullet being overtaken by another because the latter was fired with a greater charge. After the turn the speaker articulates his realization that rather than having to wait through his sojourn on earth to be reunited with his beloved, he will already be there to meet her when she arrives. Like a victorious king grown profligate with the treasure gathered from his conquests, the speaker will the sooner run out of his own treasure, the "store" of his being, because his life is now burning away more quickly than before. Thus will the speaker outstrip his beloved on their way to their final destination hereafter precisely because he has gained from her a double charge of being. Because of the poem's powerful turn, the speaker will arrive in the hereafter sooner than the very beloved whose death he laments.

One of the poems that Carl Dennis analyzes is Robert Lowell's "For the Union Dead," which shifts from personal recollection to social commentary. A similar, if tonally distinct, movement occurs in Lowell's "Memories of West Street and Lepke":

Only teaching on Tuesdays, book-worming
in pajamas fresh from the washer each morning,

I hog a whole house on Boston's
"hardly passionate Marlborough Street,"
where even the man
scavenging filth in the back alley trash cans,
has two children, a beach wagon, a helpmate,
and is a "young Republican."
I have a nine months' daughter,
young enough to be my granddaughter.
Like the sun she rises in her flame-flamingo infants' wear.

These are the tranquilized *Fifties,*
and I am forty. Ought I to regret my seedtime?
I was a fire-breathing Catholic C.O.,
and made my manic statement,
telling off the state and president, and then
sat waiting sentence in the bull pen
beside a Negro boy with curlicues
of marijuana in his hair.

Given a year,
I walked on the roof of the West Street jail, a short
enclosure like my school soccer court,
and saw the Hudson River once a day
through sooty clothesline entanglements
and bleaching khaki tenements.
Strolling, I yammered metaphysics with Abramowitz,
a jaundice-yellow ("it's really tan")
and fly-weight pacifist,
so vegetarian,
he wore rope shoes and preferred fallen fruit.
He tried to convert Bioff and Brown,
the Hollywood pimps, to his diet.
Hairy, muscular, suburban,
wearing chocolate, double-breasted suits,
they blew their tops and beat him black and blue.

I was so out of things, I'd never heard
of the Jehovah's Witnesses.
"Are you a C.O.?" I asked a fellow jailbird.
"No," he answered, "I'm a J.W."
He taught me the "hospital tuck,"

and pointed out the T-shirted back
of Murder Incorporated's Czar Lepke,
there piling towels on a rack,
or dawdling off to his little segregated cell full
of things forbidden the common man:
a portable radio, a dresser, two toy American
flags tied together with a ribbon of Easter palm.
Flabby, bald, lobotomized,
he drifted in a sheepish calm,
where no agonizing reappraisal
jarred his concentration on the electric chair—
hanging like an oasis in his air
of lost connections …

The poem begins with what is in many ways a comfortable and de-
tached, disengaged existence, portraying the speaker as a leisured aca-
demic, teaching but once a week and spending much of his time at home
reading. The reference to "book-worming" suggests a kind of burrowing in
that, while it might provide sustenance, it also works to isolate the speaker
from the world outside his house, which he "hogs"—the animal imagery is
telling with regard to his state of mind—on "Boston's / 'hardly passionate
Marlborough Street'." Even the beach-wagon-owning young Republican
"scavenging filth" suggests a kind of detachment from the political con-
cerns that the speaker is soon to recollect. Further, the evident delight that
the speaker has with his daughter—one sign of deep engagement in the
opening verse paragraph—is undercut by the intrusion of the archaic po-
etic diction of "Like the sun she rises," as well as by the oddly detached tone
of "her flame-flamingo infants' wear," phrasing that sounds more like ad-
vertising copy than fond description. These are indeed tranquilized days, as
the speaker emphasizes: "These are the tranquilized *Fifties*, / and I am forty.
Ought I to regret my seedtime?" While the life in which the speaker finds
himself is not necessarily a bad one, it is nevertheless rather conspicuously
detached and disengaged from the kind of political involvement to which
the poem abruptly turns.

The poem's turn marks a shift into the past as the speaker recalls his
public statement against the war. As a matter of fact, Lowell wrote Presi-
dent Franklin D. Roosevelt a letter, dated 7 September 1943, informing the
nation's leader that the poet would not be participating in the war effort
and setting out the reasons for his refusal. The poem turns to these days of

political protest, markedly different from the poem's opening notes of domestic isolation. As a result of his protest, Lowell was sentenced to a year and a day in a federal correctional facility in Danbury, Connecticut, but before he was taken there, he had to spend several days in the West Street Jail in New York. The poem thus continues with Lowell in jail, spending his time in leisure of a very different sort from that with which the poem begins.

The speaker's condition at this point, confined and yet outdoors, walking on the roof of the jail, shows up in sharp contrast to the poem's opening verse paragraph, in which the speaker is at liberty and yet burrowed indoors. As the "sooty clothesline entanglements" provide details of the world that he witnesses, they also provide an image of his own entanglement in the world of politics and human suffering. And yet his involvement in this world also occasions his own confrontation with defeat. This defeat is shown not only emblematically by the violent world of the jail, where Bioff and Brown blow their tops and beat Abramowitz black and blue, but also by the irony that Lowell and other pacifists, because of their unwillingness to fight, are jailed along with violent criminals.

The unofficial head of this criminal population is Louis Lepke, often identified as the head of the criminal organization Murder, Inc., which as the name implies supplied murders for hire. Strictly speaking, Lepke was not the organization's head, but rather its most persistent client, making him a kind of de facto czar. Either way, it is this figure much associated with murder who lives as the jail's aristocrat. In possession of "things forbidden the common man," Lepke holds quiet sway. Even in the jail, the signs of social stratification—reminiscent of those that the speaker gently satirizes before the poem's turn—show up again, though in transmuted form. Of the things that Lepke possesses, the most frustrating for the speaker would seem to be those that serve as emblems of the failure of his own patriotic stand against the war, a stand fired by his Catholic faith. The "two toy American / flags tied together with a ribbon of Easter palm" quietly mock his pacifist and religious stance.

The shift, in "Memories of West Street and Lepke," from present-tense description to recollections of a strikingly different place and time is a move familiar from the descriptive-meditative structure, which generally includes another movement also. This second move typically returns the poem, albeit in transformed and even renewed terms, to where it began. Part of what is striking about "Memories of West Street and Lepke," part of what contributes to the extremity of its single turn, is that there is no final return at all. Rather, the poem trails off after Lepke's "lost connections." The speaker's life hangs in suspension as the poem leaves off with the past, providing no renewed or renewing return to the speaker's present life, which remains very much in question.

The final example of the mid-course turn that I should like to consider, Debora Greger's "Head, Perhaps of an Angel," begins with an intimate scene in which, ironically, communication is almost impossible. The poem then ironically turns toward a moment of communication not with a deepening of intimacy, but rather with a movement into the relative detachment of metaphysical and theological considerations. The poem opens with a group taking a meditative walk along the beach:

> Point Dume was the point
> he said, but we never came close,
> no matter how far we walked the shale
>   broken from California.
>
>   Someone's garden
> had slipped, hanging itself by a vine
> from the cliffs of some new Babylon
>   past Malibu.
>
>   Drowning the words
> the wind didn't fling back in our faces,
> the Pacific washed up a shell:
>   around an alabastron
>
> of salt water for the dead,
> seaweed rustled its papers, drying them out,
> until it died. Waves kept crashing
>   into the heart
>
>   of each shell
> I held to my ear like a phone,
> but they were just the waves of my blood.

Although the poem begins with the recollection of a statement—"Point Dume was the point / he said"—the world of this journey up the beach is one that frustrates communication as words are either flung back in the faces of the walkers or drowned in the waves. The speaker's gestures of holding shells like telephones to her ear suggest attempts at some further communication. However, the poem does not hold out much promise for a connection, for what the speaker hears are "just the waves of my blood." Nevertheless, it is precisely these "waves" of her blood, resonant with the ocean waves crashing beside the walkers, and "crashing / into the heart / of each shell," that hold out the promise of some elemental connection.

In fact, the poem's turn signals a point of connection at once more elemental and more conceptual, more metaphysical than the everyday connection of conversation. In the midst of these connections, there also echoes a human voice:

> And through it all
>
> I heard him say,
> how could it be nine months ago
> his grandson had taken his own life,
>   somewhere back east?
>
> He was fifteen.
> O Pacific, what good is our grief?
> Something screamed at the sandy child
>   who poured seawater
>
> into a hole.
> *Child, you will never empty the ocean,*
> Augustine said. *How can I believe?*
>   The wet fist of a wave
>
> dissolved in sand.
> Like a saint, a seagull flapped down the beach
> in search of something raw—an angel
>   with an empty pail?
>
> No, a teenage boy,
> hands as big as a man's, held a sea slug
> quaking like an aspic. Under a rock, another one
>   drew into its body
>
> a sea creature
> larger than itself. Live, said Death
> to child and childless alike, indifferently.
>   *I am coming.*

Because the walkers' words are either flung back at them or drowned, words that the speaker recalls "him" saying about his grandson's suicide, words that remain outside of quotation marks, must be recalled from earlier, before the walk began. Unable to communicate with her companions on the walk, the speaker turns to address the ocean itself with the question, "O Pacific, what good is our grief?" The imagery of the ocean befits the concern of the question, for the ocean remains a powerful force and image of both life and death, with its constant motion teeming with living creatures even as it threatens death to any land dweller who would enter it unprepared. In an even more primal sense, the ocean's salt water recalls the source of all life even as these same waters call to mind the all-enveloping force of death. These associations are both powerful and commonplace; thus, the poem does well simply to present the images, which do their work without overstating the case.

But there remains the question of how to respond to personal grief. After the turn ("And through it all / I heard him say"), the poem responds in large part with its elemental ocean imagery, but it then also alludes to a story famous in the history of Christian theology, and thus invokes one of the central mysteries of this theological tradition. After the speaker apostrophizes the ocean, the poem responds with an allusion to a story of St. Augustine confronting the impossibility of explaining in human language the doctrine of the Trinity, the doctrine that the one living God is three divine persons in one divine nature. St. Augustine did indeed write a book on the Trinity, though the story to which Greger alludes comes from a letter attributed to St. Cyril of Jerusalem. According to the story, Augustine, while walking along the beach contemplating the mystery of the Trinity, encounters a child with a spoon. When the saint asks the child what he is doing, the latter responds that he is trying to ladle out the ocean. Augustine tells him that this is impossible to do, to which the child replies that it is no more impossible than explaining the doctrine of the Trinity. This exchange implies that the Trinity, however hard one might work at ladling out explanations, remains a mystery surpassing human understanding.

As a response to the speaker's question, the allusion to the St. Augustine episode implies that death remains a similar mystery. Thus, the answer to the grandfather's heartbroken question about his grandson's suicide is not to be a discursive proposition, but rather an action that engages the whole person. The strength of the poem is its rather ritualistic sense and scene—walking beside the ocean as a makeshift sacrament. But in the world of this poem, no St. Augustine or mysterious child appears to offer consolation; rather, a seagull flaps "Like a saint" down the beach, leading to the ambiguous image of the sea slug. On the one hand, this image emphasizes the sheer force of survival by showing how a living thing can assimilate something larger than itself; the image functions as a reminder that one can assimilate even as large a grief as that for the death of a beloved person. On the other hand, looking at the scene with an emphasis on the sea creature under the rock functions to remind one of ultimate defeat, for everyone and everything living is ultimately swallowed in death. What comfort the image provides is cold comfort.

Fittingly, the poem ends with the personification of death—at once an elemental part of all earthly existence and a profound preoccupation of both philosophy and theology. The poem's ultimate refusal to turn away from death is the gesture of allowing Death the final word, "I am coming." Living with an awareness of the inevitability of one's death delivers a sense of personal finitude, the awareness that one's own being is utterly contingent. Living with awareness of such contingency holds the promise of delivering one into a more authentic mode of existence because this awareness means embracing contingency as the condition of one's being. The sheer radiance and givenness of the moment, which precisely because it is a moment cannot recur, open one to the responsibility held for each moment of one's being. When, at the end of Greger's poem, Death utters the active declaration "I am coming," Death thus also calls upon the addressee to respond in similarly active terms, to respond in terms of what philosopher Jacques Derrida calls the singularity and responsibility of personhood. While the poem begins with a kind of despair over the possibilities of communication, the poem's turn opens it toward deeper, though disturbing—because of death's remembrances—possibilities of call and response. Death calls out its command to live; the poem sets out the conditions of a deeply human response.

As can be seen in the poems by Donne, Lowell, and Greger, and in the Supplemental Poems, what often makes the mid-course turn striking is the strength or severity of the shift. For example, the turn in Samuel Taylor Coleridge's "Kubla Khan" shifts the poem from the third-person, epic-style voice of the opening to the first-person visionary proclamation that ends the poem. Similarly radical are the two turns in Jason Sommer's "Other People's Troubles," which shifts from parable to personal anecdote to family story—the latter of which, a recollection of the Holocaust, bears on historical narrative. Like the poems by Donne and Greger, Alan Shapiro's "The Accident" and Mary Szybist's "Heaven in Miniature" are elegies marked by strong turns. William Logan's "The Shadow-Line" begins as nature meditation, then the perspective widens both spatially and temporally, though the poem ends on a note not so much of resolution as of resignation.

Poems often do well to end differently from the way they begin. Even if, as many excellent poems do, a poem returns to the same time and place as its opening line, it should do so with a difference. The poem should do something unexpected, go somewhere unexpected in terms of tone, syntax, image, diction, locution, location, voice, stance, rhythm, etc. The structure of the mid-course turn remains a strong device to take a poem onto unexpected terrain.

SUPPLEMENTAL POEMS

Kubla Khan; Or a Vision in a Dream. A Fragment
Samuel Taylor Coleridge

In Xanadu did KUBLA KHAN
A stately pleasure-dome decree:
Where ALPH, the sacred river, ran
Through caverns measureless to man
    Down to a sunless sea.
So twice five miles of fertile ground
With walls and towers were girdled round:
And there were gardens bright with sinuous rills,
Where blossom'd many an incense-bearing tree;
And here were forests ancient as the hills,
And folding sunny spots of greenery.

But oh that deep romantic chasm which slanted
Down the green hill athwart a cedarn cover!
A savage place as holy and inchanted
As e'er beneath a waning moon was haunted
By woman wailing for her demon-lover!
And from this chasm, with ceaseless turmoil seething,
As if this earth in fast thick pants were breathing,
A mighty fountain momently was forced:
Amid whose swift half-intermitted burst

Huge fragments vaulted like rebounding hail,
Or chaffy grain beneath the thresher's flail:
And 'mid these dancing rocks at once and ever
It flung up momently the sacred river.
Five miles meandering with a mazy motion
Through wood and dale the sacred river ran,
Then reached the caverns measureless to man,
And sank in tumult to a lifeless ocean:
And 'mid this tumult Kubla heard from far
Ancestral voices prophesying war!
    The shadow of the dome of pleasure
    Floated midway on the waves;
    Where was heard the mingled measure
    From the fountain and the caves.
It was a miracle of rare device,
A sunny pleasure-dome with caves of ice!

    A damsel with a dulcimer
    In a vision once I saw:
    It was an Abyssinian maid,
    And on her dulcimer she play'd,
    Singing of Mount Abora.
    Could I revive within me
    Her symphony and song,
    To such a deep delight 'twould win me,
That with music loud and long,
I would build that dome in air,
That sunny dome! those caves of ice!
And all who heard should see them there,
And all should cry, Beware! Beware!
His flashing eyes, his floating hair!
Weave a circle round him thrice,
And close your eyes with holy dread,
For he on honey-dew hath fed,
And drank the milk of Paradise.

The Shadow-Line
William Logan

A shadow loon flies from the glassy lake
over mangroves and the freshwater pond
where a lone canoeist casts between the fronds
lying along the shore like broken rakes.

He shatters the inky lacquer where the stars
are scattered like a pinch of cooking salt
in the old recipes. It's no one's fault.
The red dot on the tree line must be Mars,

or just a radio tower blinking, blinking
messages two lovers might overlook.
Night fish are rising to the maggoty hook.
I can't tell any longer what you are thinking.

The shadow of the loon will soon embrace
the shallows of the continental shelf
as night becomes a shadow of itself.
Another shadow passes over your face.

We used to spend summer nights listening to jazz—
rude subtleties of the horn! Now we discuss
surrendering to what will happen to us,
or ought to, or perhaps already has.

The Accident
Alan Shapiro

While it was happening,
    the absolute
not me of it, the all
    of a sudden see-
through whir of wings beside me
    that the late sun
just as I looked up
    turned to a hovering
flash, a watery gray—
    green iridescence
as the beak dipped into

a funnel of blossom,
dipped and was gone, and not even
    the blossom's white
tip bent in its going,
    or shivered—

While this, which could have happened
    without me, here
or elsewhere, happened the way
    it did, and would
continue happening
    for others, for no one,
for nothing but the blind urge
    of its happening,
this ever-transient
    accidental
crossing of momentums
    that was, in this case,
beautiful but could
    have not been and so
seemed all the more consoling
    for the thought—

even the thought of death,
    just then, consoling,
shaping itself inside me
    as the now there
now not there hovering
    of bird, flower, late
sun iridescences—
    beloved singers,
you who in the aftermath
    surged from the shadows
to sing in your different voices
    the same song, Route
of evanescence, Mother
    of beauty, It
avails not, time nor place,
    distance avails not,

if you had known, just then,
    three hundred miles
away, in another state,
    that one of the nurses
getting my brother up
    from the commode
and back to bed, the one
    who held him on
his left side, the dead side,
    all of a sudden
lost hold of him and, as
    he fell hard, grabbed
for the loose papery gown
    and ripped it off,
so that he lay there naked,
    utterly exposed—

beloved singers, tricksters
    of solace, if
you had known this, seen
    this, as I did not,
you would have offered him
    no sumptuous
destitution, no fire-
    fangled feathers,
or blab about death as being
    luckier than one
supposes. You would have bowed
    your heads, you would
have silently slipped back
    into the shadows
out of which you surged forth,
    singing to me.

Other People's Troubles
Jason Sommer

The Jewish parable goes
that in the waiting room
where all souls come, they leave

a bundle of their troubles
on hooks. At their return,
emerging from interviews,
they eye the parcels hung
in hundreds on the walls
with care, and take their own.

*

Trash night, curbside sits
a little sofa meant
for the taking, no one around
even to see our need.
A few speculatable stains,
though in the abstract forest
on its cover, shadows turn out
to be not impeded streetlight
but the body's unguent,
armrests oiled by arms.
We leave the sofa there,
sturdy and recoverable,
life in it yet.

*

Lilly said that on
the rim of Birkenau,
before the women heard
the name or saw the chimneys'
fires and long shadows
of ash, but after stripping,
herding, shearing, searching,
the unhinged laughter at this,
the only nakedness of its kind
in their lives, a minute
of dribbled shower, the slap
of disinfectant—scalp
crotch and underarms—
the mad clothes thrown at them
without regard for fit,
rag remnants of gowns,
tattered cocktail dresses'

satin, tulle, and crepe
put on—more laughter then:
*Who are these scarecrows who
are us?* But not one of them—
the heavy woman choked
inside the sheath skirt
with the slender girl tenting
in a gown with a train; not
the tall woman bound
in the arms of the short dress,
pulling it down to cover
her thighs, with the small woman
hiking up folds—no one
would trade with anyone.

Heaven in Miniature

for Tina Wang (1984–2001)

Mary Szybist

After the crash, I tried imagining:

After they lift you out of the car—(I begin)
you wake beneath a cypress-flooded sky,
etcetera. Or, in a field, sunlit
immense, where a white-haired, white-robed shepherd
calls out to you, unbuckles your sandaled feet.
Etcetera, etcetera, I try.

———

After the oarsmen lift Odysseus
out of the hollow hull, after they set
him down asleep on the sand and leave him there,
he wakes beneath an olive tree spreading
its leaves in a mist. It's not what he was promised.
The land looks strange, unearthly strange
and unforgivable. He's sick for home
and doesn't recognize the way the thick
low mist sticks to the sea-raged, ragged shore.
Hardly recognizes the treasure that sits

around him like spilled confetti. He begins,
therefore, to count. It's all he can think to do:
to count up what is there; to stack gold coin
on coin. Everything he remembers is there,
but then, he can't remember. So he counts;
he counts and does not see the shepherd boy
approaching (disguised Athena—his Athena),
ready to give him a new body; doesn't
see he's about to recognize the skyline,
about to find all who are dear to him
unharmed. He's weeping, kneeling on the shore
of his own country, trying to figure
what's lost. Along the sand he lays out each
bright piece of woven clothing, polished bronze,
each surpassingly beautiful ornament
and counts and counts and finds that he lacks nothing.

CHAPTER NINE

Substructure

PRAGEETA SHARMA and MICHAEL THEUNE

Today's contemporary poems, with their disparate sense-making and fragmentation, often appear befuddling. Seemingly more exploratory than structural, they come across as random reactions to stimuli rather than participants in and practitioners of poetry's traditional patterns. Yet in many cases, a rigorous structure guides these strange and "difficult" poems. Though engaging contemporary social and political discourses, their "free verse" frequently is grounded in traditional structures. More and more, we encounter poems that develop a subtle configuration; rather than an obvious poetic structure, they possess a substructure hidden from plain view.

"Substructure," to coin a phrase for discussion, is a term that we can use to isolate some aspects that initially may seem very new in the contemporary poem. Simply put, substructure is the subtle, underlying structure that helps to pattern a poem. As the name implies, substructure is like the foundational beams in the basement that hold up a house. It could also be thought of as a trellis, a lattice that backs a complex floral arrangement, or as the skeleton and musculature that give a body shape and movement. These metaphors are imperfect, but they are helpful insofar as they emphasize that substructure is subtle—often, it seems, invisible. However, though subtle, once seen, substructure is a clear support, a governing element of the way the poem works, of what the poem means. Recognizing a poem's substructure is an important part of understanding the fuller meaning, of entering into the larger experience, of the poem.

Unlike the structures in the first seven chapters of this book, "substructure" does not name a specific structure; rather, it is a reminder that all writing is organized, arranged. Even the most paratactic—that is, associative or list-like—writing offers a structure for its content. Moving from beginning to end, it at least provides "shapes of content" (to borrow a phrase from the painter and photographer Ben Shahn). This organization, this structure, is not neutral but rather a vital part of the poem's meaning and effects.

The word substructure is an expansion of the concept *sottonarrativa*, or "subnarrative," formulated by poet Charles Wright. When asked in an interview with J.D. McClatchy to explain what he means by subnarrative, a term he used briefly in a previous response to mean "a story line but one not always in evidence," Wright responded, "I'm not sure I can, actually," but then he continued:

> Undernarrative, *sottonarrativa*, is about as close as I can get. The smaller current in a larger river. The story line that runs just under the surface. It's broken, interrupted, circuitous, and even invisible at times, but always there. Which is to say, it's not a "logic of image," or a balancing of blocks, or a "logic of the irrational," or whatever. It's a continuous story line by someone who can't tell a story. Subnarrative. Its logic is narrative but its effects are imagistic.

Pressed a bit further, Wright compares subnarrative to a train ride he took by a river and among mountains, a ride that involved "many, many tunnels," a ride that thus created strange, contradictory effects. On the one hand, when it could be seen, the "colors and patterns and design" of the landscape were "twice as luminous as they would have been had they remained constant and usual," and so "each time the landscape appeared, it was unusual." On the other hand, "it was basically that same landscape all the way down the river, a constant thread that you sometimes saw and sometimes didn't, but was always there." According to Wright, "I would hope that subnarrative, *sottonarrativa*, would work somewhat in this fashion."

Wright's concept is helpful, but it is limited by focusing only on narrative and image in poetry. As has been shown in the previous chapters, narrative is not the only guiding force behind poetry; many structures are at work in poetry that are not primarily narrative. And images are not the only elements that a structure can connect. Conceptual bytes, bits of grammatical, linguistic play, and all manner of allusive sampling can be joined. Still, Wright's initial insights have provided a way to begin to explore some seemingly more difficult contemporary poems, a way taken up by Stephen Burt in his essay "Close Calls with Nonsense."

The subtitle of Burt's essay supplies its goal: it hopes to teach the contemporary reader "How To Read, and Perhaps Enjoy, Very New Poetry."

According to Burt, the poems that interest him and that he's going to discuss share "a surface difficulty," which he explains by noting that "they tease or demand or frustrate, they're hard or impossible to paraphrase, and they try not to tell stories." What Burt describes as "a surface difficulty," however, may, in fact, be deep. According to Burt, these difficulties really have changed the nature of what a poem is. In a section of his essay called "What I Miss in What I Like," Burt notes that "in pursuing certain virtues—colorful local effects, persona and personality, juxtaposition, close calls with nonsense, uncertainty, critiques of ordinary language—the current crop of American poets necessarily sacrifices others." According to Burt, the sacrificed virtues he misses in contemporary poetry are "the arguments, the extended rhetorical passages and essayistic digressions I enjoy in the poems of the seventeenth and eighteenth centuries (and in W.H. Auden, and in Marianne Moore)." In short, though he recognizes that "American poetry also harbors a few new-ish poets devoted more straightforwardly to argument and wit," Burt now mostly misses the kind of writing focused on in this book—he misses structured poetry.

But, as has been shown throughout the chapters of *Structure & Surprise*, it is not the case that just a "few" contemporary poets employ argument and wit—many do. And, in fact, Burt himself suggests that identifying a poem's structure is a vital step in understanding difficult, contemporary poetry. Recognizing the need for a certain kind of decoding in order to make sense of the "nonsense" of contemporary American poetry, Burt suggests specific tactics for the reader to access the "difficult" poem. As one tactic, Burt gives his readers questions to ponder when embarking on the task of reading a difficult poem: "Ask what kind of non-poetic speech or text a given line evokes: does the poem seem to quote, or remind you of, an adventure story? A tell-all memoir? A bureaucrat's memo?" These "kinds" of speech, as much as they imply certain kinds of content, tone, and style, often also imply structures. For example, many adventure stories are written using German author Gustav Fretyag's pyramid of building and descending action. And Burt is very interested in the arrangement of the poem; according to him, another tactic is to ask, "why place the phrases in this, and no other, array?"

Burt's questions provide a useful entry into a poem by John Ashbery, whose name is virtually synonymous with poetic difficulty. Deeply influenced by the French Surrealists and Wallace Stevens, Ashbery is a poet of wild juxtaposition, one who tries to follow all the strange contours of the moving mind, combining sense and nonsense, as in his poem "Late Echo":

Alone with our madness and favorite flower
We see that there really is nothing left to write about.
Or rather, it is necessary to write about the same old things
In the same way, repeating the same things over and over
For love to continue and be gradually different.

Beehives and ants have to be re-examined eternally
And the color of the day put in
Hundreds of times and varied from summer to winter
For it to get slowed down to the pace of an authentic
Saraband and huddle there, alive and resting.

Only then can the chronic inattention
Of our lives drape itself around us, conciliatory
And with one eye on those long tan plush shadows
That speak so deeply into our unprepared knowledge
Of ourselves, the talking engines of our day.

A chatty poem, Ashbery's "Late Echo" is itself a kind of "talking engine" that breezily incorporates many seeming ambivalences and contradictions: "madness and favorite flower"; "to continue and be gradually different"; "alive and resting"; "conciliatory" but wary, with "one eye" open. However, though it may seem languorously lavish, "Late Echo" is also structured. This short lyric is very much like a "non-poetic" short essay. A contemplative poem about the practice of art-making, it opens with the first stanza's thesis statement about how poems should be made, suggesting that the process of making a poem is like kissing a lot of frogs until you find the prince; that is, one must keep rewriting the same poem, covering the same ground, until new ground is broken. The second stanza turns to provide detailed instructions for how to accomplish this process. The speaker suggests that one continuously restate timeless themes of art and philosophy—landscape, seasons, colors, still life, futility, and truth—until the continual retracing of such matter gives way to visionary knowledge. The third stanza then turns to offer the results of such an enterprise, letting readers know what to expect from such an undertaking. Additionally, this stanza itself serves as an example of what might be created by such a process. After Ashbery himself talks about ants and bees and the seasons, something new—the wild and strange third stanza itself—in fact does seem to emerge from his poem and so the poem enacts its own ideas, remaking itself. Ashbery's poem is thus both trellis and flower.

Or trellises. The brief essay of "Late Echo" also employs concessional strategies. The opening gambit of the poem is to claim that "there really is nothing left to write about." And what a gambit!—anything could come after this concession. Ashbery has found a way to turn a bald statement of poetic ennui—the feeling that everything has been done before in poetry—into a real advantage. Building from this negation, he constructs a kind of argument for cathartic experience from some apparent void. From out of nothing, repetition arises until finally the "talking engines" take over, delivering or revealing a new kind of knowledge. The poem's opening concession ultimately allows Ashbery to clear a way for his strangeness. Certainly there is plenty of madness here, but to see this poem clearly is to see that this madness also is arranged, enacting the emergent organization of a blossoming flower.

Organization slowly emerges, too, from the following poem by Thomas Sayers Ellis:

Or,

Or Oreo, or
worse. Or ordinary.
Or your choice
of category

    or
    Color

or any color
other than Colored
or Colored Only.
Or "Of Color"

    or
    Other

or theory or discourse
or oral territory.
Oregon or Georgia
or Florida Zora

                or
                Opportunity

        or born poor
        or Corporate. Or Moor.
        Or a Noir Orpheus
        or Senghor

                or
                Diaspora

        or a horrendous
        and tore-up journey.
        Or performance. Or allegory's armor
        of ignorant comfort

                or
                Worship

        or reform or a sore chorus.
        Or Electoral Corruption
        or important ports
        of Yoruba or worry

                or
                Neighbor

        or fear of ...
        of terror or border.
        Or all organized
        minorities.

There is much about "Or," that asks a reader to ignore its structural underpinnings. The title itself—"Or," with its comma followed by blank space—encourages the reader to look at the poem as a totality. That is, anything and all that follows is simply one alternative to be put into the blank implied by the title. And, in fact, it is tempting to read the poem as a heap of options. At first glance, "Or," seems a wild assemblage, a loose list poem, and the words in this list seem selected largely only for their "or" sounds—the conjunctive "or" peeks its head in almost every other word so that the poem seems connected like a potentially infinite daisy chain.

This poetic technique is vital. It helps to make the poem resonant and incantatory, and it illustrates how, like connotation itself, ideas often form from the materiality of words themselves. However, this technique is only part of the meaning-making capacity of the poem. Looking at more than the incantatory, one can see that the various elements of "Or," are not at all random but organized around important ideas of and issues in African and African-American culture in an attempt to come to terms with a Eurocentric and white American bias. For example, an "Oreo" is slang for a black person who thinks and behaves in ways stereotypically believed more common for a white person. "Florida Zora" and "Senghor" allude to author Zora Neale Hurston's Florida, which is not the Florida of the 2000 U.S. presidential election that denied so many African Americans their votes, and to poet and Senegalese President Léopold Sédar Senghor, a leader in the black intellectual movement called Negritude.

If "Or," is about the African-American experience, then it also seems as though the poem, most directly, is written as a kind of response to some questionnaire—perhaps an application form for a job, for voting, for immigration—that asks applicants to register their race. Not itself a "bureaucrat's memo," although by being a list it reads very much like one, "Or," is a response to such a bureaucratic form, one that registers an imaginary applicant's experience with exclusionary terms and language. It is an angry fantasia. This is a poem ticked off at having to tick off a definitive race, often a designation with racist implications. For example, though the designation "Other" likely was an effort to neutralize the application process, it is not really neutral—if one's race is not in fact listed, then "Other" is exclusionary. "Or," suggests that terms and categories inherently misrepresent, and even those terms created to render more accurate definitions sometimes make more problems.

Against this bureaucratic befuddlement, "Or," provides active, charged, and charging language. It is constructed with idiosyncratic associations. In fact, this poem leaps so much that almost every included detail could be considered a turn. To use Ashbery's language, "Or," is a "talking engine" that tries to say something between the lines provided by official political and economic discourse, and as such, "Or," goes beyond explicating the problem of race in America to initiating an experience. In doing so, it churns up associations that begin to supply readers with "unprepared knowledge / Of [them]selves."

However, this engine, though on the move, is not aimless. For all its leaping, "Or," includes some key structural moves that make it a strong poem "organized" to pack a tactful punch. Key among these moves is that the poem's first twelve lines, through "or / Other," serve to establish the context of the poem. These lines let readers know they are dealing with issues of race, with "choice[s] / of category." They clearly problematize the normalization of race through its representation via bureaucratic means, pointing to the terrible marginalization of the "other" represented ultimately through names and overt or covert name-calling—those features of "oral territory" that can be hiding in plain view, like a conjunction in a noun.

From its established context, the poem turns into an angry dream sequence. It considers a wide range of unique and often preposterous options and categories: it offers options like "born poor," which is real for so many, and options like "Electoral Corruption," which isn't an option but a truth. This portion of the poem takes pains to show that efforts at normalizing race are not themselves normal but rather fraught with significant exclusions and subtle, derogatory implications.

With "or / Neighbor," the poem reaches a conciliatory moment, but then the poem turns to its conclusion, its simmering last stanza that names the consequences of such systematic racism: terror and borders. The final two lines—"Or all organized / minorities"—present a deep, rigorous ambiguity. For some, "organized minorities" pose a grave threat, while for so many others these lines hold out a great hope: organizing—perhaps unionizing, putting into a politically efficacious shape—all minorities is what will bring about real and lasting change. This poem would read much differently if the last stanza were chopped up and included somewhere in the poem's middle, where it could go if the poem were truly a random list. But this poem has a point, a hope, a dream, and though some difficult poetry poses as anti-closural, "Or," clearly has a strong finish, driving home its point.

This also is true of Sarah Gambito's "Paloma's Church in America":

> Across the street a beautiful asian was burning. I took my
> sandals off. Seven times hotter the fire remembered babies. And
> canals of babies burning it back. I took off your sandals, and your
> sandals, too. Sometimes we waited for stone tablets. Most often we
> brewed what tea we could of the desert. Silicate, mica, a mysterious
> formica. We drank and became practiced. We missed our mothers.
> Our mothers couldn't call. We called in dreams. We dreamed
> illnesses on our new bodies. The bodies clung to covenants. The
> covenants, in turn, drove to scholarship. (Stewardship,
> pharmacists like to say. Star Connection, my Tanenbaum makes to

say.) So many babies, the asian said. Across the street a beautiful
iconoclast was burning. I do remember that dream more than
all—that I did not doubt. Your Honor, I saw the future.

"Paloma's Church in America" resists easy investigation: who is
Paloma? who is the "we"? what is "Star Connection"? While some of these
questions are answered in the course of Gambito's book *Matadora*, which
explores similar themes and characters throughout its various poems,
much also can be determined by recognizing and then examining this
strange poem's familiar structural shift from dream to waking, from insight
to action.

Although the poem's speaker uses a kind of peculiar, estranged lan-
guage—perhaps the result of traumatic experience or a respectful formal-
ism—the poem rather clearly opens with a vision. The speaker sees what is
at once a religious experience and an act of political witnessing. References
to the biblical burning bush—Moses had to remove his sandals when he
was near it—are juxtaposed with images of burning (napalmed?) children
and the Buddhist monk who famously set himself on fire to protest the
Vietnam War. What exactly this vision means is not immediately apparent,
even to the poem's speaker. Whereas Moses' experience of the burning
bush led to the receiving of the Ten Commandments, inscribed on stone
tablets, the poem's speaker is given only bits of sand—silicate and mica
—that she is forced to prepare herself to become knowledgeable, "prac-
ticed."

But this preparation has an effect. The middle part of the poem reads
like a dawning revelation: from dreams to bodies, from bodies to cove-
nants, from covenants to scholarship, a kind of stewardship, and finally to
an understanding of what "the asian" was saying with his iconoclastic act of
self-sacrifice. The end of the poem turns into an awakening: the speaker can
remember her dream and know without a doubt that it was significant. In
fact, the speaker is so confident of the vision that she gives testimony to its
authenticity, and even its continuing relevance.

"Paloma's Church in America" is a contemporary example of a time-
honored structure in poetry, the dream-vision. Employed in poems such as
Samuel Taylor Coleridge's "Kubla Khan" and John Keats' "Ode to a Night-
ingale," it clearly employs that structure's turn from dream to wakefulness.
Seen with that tradition behind it, some details of the poem emerge. For
example, unlike many dream-vision poems, in which the speaker startles
awake, Gambito's speaker describes the step-by-step process of awakening,

portraying it as work, as conscious effort. Gambito's poem isn't only about having visions and epiphanies; it is also about working to make such visions real. And, in fact, in the poem this effort has its rewards: at the end of such effort, one attains certainty. Whereas after his experience of the nightingale's song Keats' speaker asks, "Do I wake or sleep?," Gambito's speaker proclaims: I am awake, I have seen something profound, and I am prepared to tell about it. Similarly, a reader of this poem, prepared with a knowledge of poetic structures, can see more deeply into the details of the working of the poem and can register more fully the poem's significance.

However much the poetic statements of our day imply an endless openness to poems, we must turn again and again to the poems to see how they are making their meanings, to see what they ultimately are saying. Structure plays a central role in this sense-making. While the poems by Ashbery, Ellis, and Gambito might be seen as abstract art or as soundscape, they also have much in common with essay and lecture. They're not messes, nor are they pure abstractions. Though these poems' various difficulties invite active, diverse engagement, the poems also clearly are organized to help deliver and even enact meanings.

To read such poems fully and completely, one must be able to see and account for the poetic structure at work in the poems. This can be, but isn't necessarily, difficult. For example, Charles Simic's "The Initiate" (in Supplemental Poems) is, in fact, a subnarrative, employing a day's wandering to organize its wild encounters and images. Francis Ponge's "The Lizard" actually provides its substructure in its prefatory "Argument," while Wislawa Szymborska's "Evaluation of an Unwritten Poem" is supposedly constructed as a running commentary on an already existing poem. While employing the choppy style of a telegram, Kevin Young's "Urgent Telegram to Jean-Michel Basquiat," a poem written to the spirit of the deceased artist, employs the kinds of turns familiar in letter-writing or prayer: initial act of salutation, followed by praise, followed by pleas for intercession. And for any reader of *Structure & Surprise* it should be clear that section XVII from Major Jackson's "Urban Renewal" incorporates a mid-course turn, shifting from the poem's initial, surreal story in order to "look at these signs from a different view."

However difficult such poems seem—and Stephen Burt is right, such poems simply do seem much less difficult when approached with an eye toward deciphering their structure—these poems in no way leave structure behind. Though often subtle or hidden, with careful inspection structure

and, with it, the fuller significance of the poem, emerge—and so does a
sense of the continuing significance of structure itself.

SUPPLEMENTAL POEMS

From **Urban Renewal**
Major Jackson

XVII

What of my fourth grade teacher at Reynolds Elementary,
who weary after failed attempts to set to memory
names strange and meaningless as the grains of dirt around
the mouthless, mountain caves at Bahrain Karai:
Tarik, Shanequa, Amari, Aisha, nicknames the entire class
after French painters whether boy or girl. Behold
the beginning of sentient formless life. And so,
my best friend Darnell became Marcel, and Tee-tee
was Braque, and Stacy James was Fragonard,
and I, Eduard Charlemont. The time has come to look
at these signs from other points of view. Days passed
in inactivity before I corrected her, for Eduard was
Austrian and painted the black chief in a palace in 1878
to the question whether intelligence exists. All of Europe
swooned to Venus of Willendorf. Outside her tongue,
yet of it, in textbooks Herodotus tells us of the legend
of Seworset, Egyptian, colonizer of Greece,
founder of Athens. What's in a name? Sagas rise and
fall in the orbs of jumpropes, Hannibal grasps a Roman
monkeybar on history's rung, and the mighty heroes at recess
lay dead in woe on the imagined battlefields of HALO.

The Lizard
Francis Ponge (*translated by Margaret Guiton*)

Argument

This unpretentious little text perhaps shows how the mind forms an
allegory and then likes to resorb it.

A few characteristics of the object first appear, then develop and intertwine through the spontaneous movement of the mind thus leading to the theme, which no sooner stated produces a brief side reflection from which there at once emerges, unmistakably, the abstract theme, and during the course of its formulation (towards the end) the object automatically disappears.

When the wall of prehistory develops cracks, this wall at the end of the garden (it's the garden of present generations, father and son)—a little animal emerges, very sharply delineated, like a Chinese dragon, abrupt but, as we all know, harmless and therefore thoroughly likable. A masterpiece of prehistoric jewelry, in a metal halfway between verdigris and quicksilver. Only its belly is fluid, bulges like a drop of mercury. What style! A reptile with feet! Is this a step forward or a relapse? Nobody knows, silly. Little saurian.

This wall encloses us very imperfectly. Imprisoned as we may be we are the mercy of *the outside*, which throws, which sends, this little dagger under the garden door. Both as a threat and a bad joke.

This little dagger that wiggles through our minds in an absurdly baroque style.

Sudden halt. On the hottest stone. An ambush? or an automatic "at ease!"? It goes on. Let's take advantage of this and shift our point of view.

In the world of words there is good reason for the LIZARD'S wiggly *zed* or *zeal*, its *ard* ending, like *coward, sluggard, bastard, haggard*. It appears, disappears, reappears. But is never familiar. Always a bit disoriented, always furtively seeking its way. These insinuations are not too familiar. Or venomous. No malice: not a sign of any complicity with humans.

A sort of little locomotive. A little train of hasty allegations, colorless, slightly monstrous, familiar and at the same time preposterous—which moves along with the fatal precipitation of a mechanical toy, skimming over the ground, as they do, for short distances but much less awkward, less obstinate. It doesn't crash into a piece of furniture or a wall—on the contrary very silent and supple. When it has run out of steam, of arguments, of dialectical resilience, it always manages to disappear into some crack or fissure in the masonry where it pursues its quarry … .

Sometimes it leaves the tip of its tail between your fingers.

… A mere chromatic scale? A mere arpeggio? All in all, a good surprise, even if it gave you a start. We'll get back to that stone.

Or else we suddenly see it, plastered to the wall: there it was, motionless.

Silhouetted like this, there's something a bit threatening about it. It's that over-delineated side, that little dragon, or dagger, side.

But we are quickly reassured: it's not at all aimed at you (like snakes). It's giving you, far better than a bird, time to consider it: it naturally pauses like this on the hottest stone ... Indecision? Anxiety? Stupor? Indolence? An ambush?

An enemy of flies on the ground! We can't say it wouldn't hurt a fly as it feeds on them. You have to feed on something if you're a little oviparous bibelot responsible for your own perpetuation. As though a candlestick for instance, or a little bronze on the doctor's mantelpiece, indulged in a spasm, exhibited its characteristic quick contortion. It then darts out its little tongue like a flame. Yet this isn't fire, these aren't flames coming out of its mouth, but actually a tongue, a very long forked tongue that goes in as fast as it came out—that quivers at its own audacity. And why are they so fond of the surfaces of masonry constructions? Because of the glaring whiteness (and dull expanse) of this kind of beach which attracts flies—the flies they waylay and harpoon with the tip of their pointed tongues.

The LIZARD thus presupposes a masonry construction, or a rock that is white enough to approximate this. Very well lit and hot.

And a crack on this surface through which it communicates with (let's be brief) prehistory ... from which the lizard *s'alcive* (had to invent this word).

So here, for you can never be too accurate about these things, here are the necessary and sufficient conditions ... in practical terms, here is a way of arranging things that will guarantee the appearance of a lizard.

First, some sort of masonry construction with a glaring surface and fairly well heated by the sun. Then a crack in this construction through which its surface communicates with the obscurity and freshness inside it or on the other side. As an added touch let a fly come and settle on it as evidence that no disturbing movement is visible on the horizon ... Through this crack, on this surface, a lizard will then appear (and immediately swallow the fly).

And now, why not be honest *a posteriori*? Why not try to understand? Why let the poem stand as a trap for the reader and myself? Am I so eager to leave a poem, a trap? Instead of allowing my mind to take a forward step or two? What does this glaring surface of the rock, or of the masonry barrier that I previously evoked, resemble if not a page—lit up and brought to a white heat by a passionate desire to inscribe an observation on it? So here, then, is the way things are transmuted.

When the following conditions have been combined:
A page lit up and brought to a white heat by a passionate desire to inscribe

an observation on it. A crack through which it communicates with the obscurity and freshness inside the mind. As an added touch let a word or several words settle on it. On this page, through this crack, there will inevitably come ... (immediately swallowing all the previous words) ... a little train of colorless thoughts—which skims over the ground and likes to go back into the tunnels of the mind.

The Initiate
Charles Simic

St. John of the Cross wore dark glasses
As he passed me on the street.
St. Theresa of Avila, beautiful and grave,
Turned her back on me.

"Soulmate," they hissed. "It's high time."

I was a blind child, a wind-up toy.
I was one of death's juggling red balls
On a certain street corner
Where they peddle things out of suitcases.

The city like a huge cinema
With lights dimmed.
The performance already started.

So many blurred faces in a complicated plot.

The great secret which kept eluding me:
    knowing who I am ...

The Redeemer and the Virgin,
Their eyes wide open in the empty church
Where the killer came to hide himself ...

The new snow on the sidewalk bore footprints
That could have been made by bare feet.
Some unknown penitent guiding me.

In truth, I didn't know where I was going.
My feet were frozen,
My stomach growled.

Four young hoods blocking my way.
Three deadpan, one smiling crazily.

I let them have my black raincoat.

Thinking constantly of the Divine Love and
    the Absolute had disfigured me.
People mistook me for someone else.
I heard voices after me calling out unknown names.

"I'm searching for someone to sell my soul to,"
The drunk who followed me whispered,
While appraising me from head to foot.

At the address I had been given,
The building had large X's over its windows.
I knocked but no one came to open.
By and by a black girl joined me on the steps.
She banged at the door till her fist hurt.

Her name was Alma, a propitious sign.
She knew someone who solved life's riddles
In a voice of an ancient Sumerian queen.
We had a long talk about that
While shivering and stamping our wet feet.

It was necessary to stay calm, I explained,
Even with the earth trembling,
And to continue to watch oneself
As if one were a complete stranger.

Once in a hotel room in Chicago
I caught sight of a man in a shaving mirror
Who had my naked shoulders and face,
But whose eyes terrified me!

Two hard staring, all-knowing eyes!

Alma, the night, the cold, and the endless walking
Brought on a kind of ecstasy.
I went as if pursued, trying to warm myself.

There was the East River; there was the Hudson.
Their waters shone like oil in sanctuary lamps.

Something supreme was occurring
For which there will never be any words.
The sky was full of racing clouds and tall buildings,
Whirling and whirling silently.

In that whole city you could hear a pin drop.
Believe me,
I thought I heard a pin drop and I went looking for it.

Evaluation of an Unwritten Poem
Wislawa Szymborska

In the poem's opening words
the authoress asserts that while the Earth is small,
the sky is excessively large and
in it there are, I quote, "too many stars for our own good."

In her depiction of the sky, one detects a certain helplessness,
the authoress is lost in a terrifying expanse,
she is startled by the planets' lifelessness,
and within her mind (which can only be called imprecise)
a question soon arises:
whether we are, in the end, alone
under the sun, all suns that ever shone.

In spite of all the laws of probability!
And today's universally accepted assumptions!
In the face of the irrefutable evidence that may fall
into human hands any day now! That's poetry for you.

Meanwhile, our Lady Bard returns to Earth,
a planet, so she claims, which "makes its rounds without eyewitnesses,"
the only "science fiction that our cosmos can afford."
The despair of a Pascal (1623–1662, *note mine*)
is, the authoress implies, unrivalled
on any, say, Andromeda or Cassiopeia.

Our solitary existence exacerbates our sense of obligation,
And raises the inevitable question, How are we to live et cetera,
since "we can't avoid the void."
"'My God,' man calls out to Himself,
'have mercy on me, I beseech thee, show me the way ...'"

The authoress is distressed by the thought of life squandered so freely,
as if our supplies were boundless.
She is likewise worried by wars, which are, in her perverse opinion,
always lost on both sides,
and by the "authoritorture" (*sic!*) of some people by others.
Her moralistic intentions glimmer throughout the poem.
They might shine brighter beneath a less naïve pen.

Not under this one, alas. Her fundamentally unpersuasive thesis
(that we may well be, in the end, alone
under the sun, all suns that ever shone)
combined with her lackadaisical style (a mixture
of lofty rhetoric and ordinary speech)
forces the question: Whom might this piece convince?
The answer can only be: No one. *Q.E.D.*

Urgent Telegram to Jean-Michel Basquiat
Kevin Young

HAVENT HEARD FROM YOU IN AGES STOP LOVE YOUR
LATEST SHOW STOP THIS NO PHONE STUFF IS FOR BIRDS
LIKE YOU STOP ONCE SHOUTED UP FROM STREET ONLY

RAIN AND YOUR ASSISTANT ANSWERED STOP DO YOU
STILL SLEEP LATE STOP DOES YOUR PAINT STILL COVER
DOORS STOP FOUND A SAMO TAG COPYRIGHT HIGH

ABOVE A STAIR STOP NOT SURE HOW YOU REACHED STOP
YOU ALWAYS WERE A CLIMBER STOP COME DOWN SOME
DAY AND SEE US AGAIN END

Endless Structures

To suggest the great variety of structures, and to see what practicing poets have to say about how structure informs and animates their own work, fourteen contemporary poets were asked to choose one of their own poems and discuss its structure. Their poems and responses comprise this section of *Structure & Surprise*.

As these brief responses show, there is a tremendous range of structural possibility. Some of the included poems have clear links to the structures already discussed. For example, Patrick Phillips' "Elegy Ending in a Dream" is a new elegy; Wang Ping's "The Price of a Finger" is a new emblem poem; and Jeffrey McDaniel's "The First Straw," which radically shifts its focus from love to politics, presents a mid-course turn. Additionally, a number of the poems are "difficult" poems that begin to unfold as their subtle structural maneuvers, their substructures, are revealed.

Several poems present altogether new structural possibilities. Susan Wheeler uses the structure of her poem to craft a significant response to a previous poem. Denise Duhamel borrows the structure of a stand-up comedy routine for her poem "Win's Chinese Buffet." Rachel Zucker goes so far as to suggest a whole new kind of poetic structure, and the fact that other poems in "Endless Structures" employ the delay-reveal pattern of what she calls the "Epiphanic" structure suggests that she may have identified a vital structure for poets working now.

However, for all of this variety, some common threads and even some trends begin to emerge in this conversation. For some of the contributors, structure is central, a guide for the whole of their creative crafting; for others, structural concerns mainly are reserved for the later stages of composition, as a method of giving final shape to the poem. Additionally, attentive to the various details of a poem's progress, many of these poets recognize that their poems not only make significant, large-scale turns but also make vital, smaller turns from line to line, stanza to stanza.

As always, structure should not be understood as the end of a conversation or investigation, but rather as a way to continue and deepen inquiry.

Poem with Citations from the *OED*
Francisco Aragón

First: *voz* because I recall the taste
of beans wrapped in a corn
tortilla—someone brings it
to me, retrieves what's left
on the plate, the murmured vowels

taking root, taking hold—mi
lengua maternal. Then later learn
another spelling, label the "box"
where sound's produced, draw too
the tongue, the teeth, the lips. *The voyce*

that is dysposid to songe and melody
hath thyse proprytees: smalle,
subtyll, thicke, clere, sharpe ...
in thirteen ninety-eight. But what
of the deaf-mute, his winning shout

—BINGO!—knocking me over?
Huxley noted: *voice may exist*
without speech and speech may exist
without voice. The first time I spoke
with my father was on the phone, so his

was all I had to go on: that,
and what he'd say—things he'd hear
"inside." In *Doctor's Dilemma*
Shaw wrote: *When my patients*
tell me they hear voices

I lock them up. The pitch, the tone, the range:
a way of trying to know him. Now hers
and his are the pages of a book:
Un baile de máscaras by Sergio
Ramírez, his characters echoing

words, rhythms I heard
until she died, hearing them as well
for months after whenever I spoke

with him. *Who hath not shared that calm*
so still and deep, The voiceless thought

which would not speak but weep.

COMMENTARY

Robert Pinsky has a poem called "Poem with Refrains" in which he in-
terweaves, at regular intervals, lines from the work of, among others, the
English Renaissance poet, Fulke Greville (1554–1628). According to Pin-
sky, including some of the most gorgeous lines of poetry in the English
language ("ear candy" he calls it) was a strategy that allowed him to take on
a subject that remained a touchy one—namely, his complicated relation-
ship with his mother. His strategy became mine, but inadvertently so:
"Poem with Citations from the *OED*" began as a prompt. Poet John Matthias
said, "Write a poem that incorporates definitions of a word found in the
OED [*Oxford English Dictionary*]." But his prompt became something
more. It led me to address, however slightly, my unconventional relation-
ship with my father, and his mental illness. Thus, the compositional strat-
egy and goals that I developed for making this poem were something like
this: to interweave at regular intervals seemingly unrelated, outside mate-
rial as at once a sort of buffer, one that provides necessary distance between
me and my subject, *and* as a way of *allowing* me to write about what I
deemed a risky or unapproachable topic—something I might have thought
too sentimental, too personal, too painful.

Crucial, of course, is *what* one chooses as outside material, and *how* one
places such outside material in the body of the poem, how one *structures* it.
I continue to be drawn to, and obsessed by, the word "voice." It served,
then, as my lantern as I journeyed through my stanzas, and I start with its
Spanish spelling ("voz") as an homage to my earliest memory, and the lan-
guage I mostly heard as an infant and child. Though the *OED* provided me
with a wealth of material to use for my poem, I selected and arranged these
references to voice so that they would increasingly engage the issue of my
father's mental health. So the first citation is emotionally neutral—it is
simply an example of how the word was used in 1398, and thus it is impor-
tant for how distant it is from the heart of the matter. The second citation
offers the idea that voice can exist without speech and so opens onto the
issues of my father, who heard voices inside his head. This citation leads
the poem to its real, though delayed, subject, which the third citation

reinforces and confirms. The final citation concludes the poem because it removes the poem's avoidance strategy and puts in its place the emotional admissions, the revelation of the underlying sadness, that so far had been put off.

There's much my poem doesn't talk about, such as the whole narrative of how my father's mental illness became known to me. But I needed to start writing about this subject somehow. Starting with a strategy, a writing procedure, and some partially-formulated goals, I wrote a poem in and through which the real subject slowly emerges; gradually revealed through the poem's structure, this subject is now central to other poems.

The Game
Mary Jo Bang

Begins with hints of menace, birth violence first, then
Struggle ensues until: At last,
The hero or heroine pulls a sword and then
There is the blood that signs the end

Of life as we knew it—afraid and more
Afraid. Darling sleep and Doris Day
Cheerfulness now follows
Us to the other end

Which is happy and handholding.
But eventually we wake to No (know)
It's only sleep so must be done again.
The story circles

Its tail, just missing its mouth, over and over,
A moving production of *At last, At last, At last*—
Each "At Last" followed by waking
To a day and dodging the enemy which looks like a face

In a mirror—two ears, two eyes, and an act.
Until we get to feeling
Who cares anymore
About virtuosity and we lay down the sword

And say to the ghost we are giving it up,
We are stopping. And we do

And finally we are happy after—and finally
Fatally so. Please close the game board.

Please hide the little pieces.

COMMENTARY

The poem was prompted by an old Mickey Mouse game piece that is now divorced from its original context. Mickey, printed on cardboard with bendable side tabs that make it possible for the piece to stand on its own, brandishes a sword; he is positioned beneath a speech balloon that states "AT LAST YOU VILLAIN!"

"The Game" presents the life span—birth to death punctuated by inevitable moments of difficulty and periodic diurnal dreamscape escapes—in the form of a board game where token swashbuckler musketeer or pirate players make their way around a roughly circular course. Formally, the long sentences and frequent use of enjambment at line ends and across stanzas echo the game's incessancy. Structured as an extended metaphor the poem attempts to concretize the notion that "Life is but a game." The game turns serious at the end, eliciting the poem's final two very direct pleas ("Please . . . Please . . .") for some form of intercession in this over-determined cycle.

Throughout "The Game," the declaration "At last" acts as the *sine qua non* of dailiness with its surmounted obstacles, until that point, at the very end, when it isn't anymore. The last "At last" represents life's ultimate conclusion. Now the Freudian rivalry between Eros and Thanatos is played out once and for all; now the game-*comme*-life arrives at its logical extreme. Here we encounter death, the fixed ending, both happily ("We are stopping...finally...finally") because it brings a welcome relief from the game's exhausting again and again, and sadly, because it contains the unacceptable fact that the game will be forever *over*. This is where, within the world of the poem, the metaphor must paradoxically be abandoned, in a sense because it has done its work too well. When the speaker meets death, she flinches, recoils, and entreats an imaginary player to fold up the game board, and make safe the tokens.

Win's Chinese Buffet
Denise Duhamel

Nick and I were hungry—he'd been driving
all morning. The strip mall didn't look promising,
but the windows of Win's Chinese Buffet were clean,

not greasy, which is our main eatery-choosing criteria
when we're on a long road trip. Inside, the food bar
glistened with all the usual glutinous sauces

and we each filled our plates. When Nick went
for a second heap of rice, a waiter came to refill
our water and asked me: *What kind of a guy*

is that guy? I blinked. *Happy?* I answered,
meaning my husband loved Win's General Tso's
chicken. *Happy Korean?* he asked. And I got it.

No, I said, *Happy Filipino. Oh*, he said, *very good.*
I wanted to ask the waiter what kind of a guy he was,
but he was off with his pitcher, ice clinking,

to other tables. I wondered what kind of customers
he was serving, what kind of men, what kind of women,
what kind of kids. I guessed two little girls

were with their dad, who I guessed was divorced
since the girls were dressed up, not saying much, cutting
their egg rolls into small polite bites with forks and knives.

Nick came back with his rice, two construction workers
with beach ball bellies following behind. I wondered
what kind of Win family would open

their restaurant here, how the Wins came to the states—
Columbia, SC in particular. Nick stretched, anticipating
the long afternoon of driving ahead. His shoulder

hurt, but I thought he said his soldier hurt, and it
was one of those times in our marriage that I wish
we could hit rewind, since I was sure what I heard

was right. I wondered what kind of general Nick
would be, probably not a very good one,
since he didn't like conflict and his soldier/shoulder hurt.

General Tso, on the other hand, has been compared
to American Civil War leader Stonewall Jackson
as an inspiration to the soldiers under his command.

And what kind of a couple was that icy couple
across from us? Two well-dressed seniors,
the man dabbing his lips as though his napkin were cloth

not paper, the woman tapping her cigarette pack
on the table, signaling she was ready to go
and have a smoke in the parking lot.

They were restrained, on the edge of a dispute,
I could tell. And I wondered whose families had once
fought whose, how we were now all brought together

in Win's by this plentiful chowmein. Nick's fortune
said that his happiness was intertwined with his outlook
on life. Mine said it was a good time to look

at what has been familiar in a new way. I studied Nick,
vowing to have a better answer next time someone asked
what kind of guy my guy was.

COMMENTARY

Ever since Mark Twain's humorous monologues, literature and stand-up comedy have been intertwined. Stand-up (unlike theatrical comedy, which relies on character and plot) is dependent upon the voice or persona of the deliverer. In this way, stand-up is particularly fitted to poetry—one voice intimately dispensing information. I have been interested in using elements of comedy in my work for some time: heightening punch lines with line breaks; incorporating word play, misunderstandings, and surprise. In writing "Win's Chinese Buffet," I attempted to use the elements of stand-up in a more deliberate manner.

I consciously used the structure of a stand-up comedy routine to develop the poem. A comic's monologue begins with a narrative. I began with the set-up (the first four stanzas), then the punch (line 13). Once the punch was established, I moved on to the "tags," which are simply more jokes based on the same premise or set-up. My tag "what kind of guy" is repeated and mutated throughout the poem. The offshoot or spin-off narrative of the monologue begins on line 31: "I wondered what kind of general Nick / would be," which riffs on General Tso (who the chicken dish is named after) and brings in historical facts about the South, the setting of the poem. I ended with a "callback," a word or phrase from the earlier punch line ("what kind of"). The "callback" brings the monologue full circle. This, of course, is the equivalent to closure in poetic terms.

Subtitles Off
Eric Gamalinda

The lords of largesse anoint you with their yes
Safe passage for the boy whose small body you lay
bleeding on the kitchen tiles

The world is as wide as a letterbox screen
You sit in the dark with the subtitles off
What is unknowable can't exist but

God slogs in outer space, wish he were not love
but logic, wait long enough and he may yet
expose himself, a bleep, a bang, an intelligent

Design, like Ginol, supreme headhunter
of Papuan cannibals, who revised the universe
five times, devouring the last, imperfect one

Sorrow seeks its own reflection among the living
I'll remember your apocalypse if you'll remember mine
It will be a holiday of the senses

It's all quiet now in the epicenter of your
(yearning) (desolation) (boredom) (religion)
If A then B: If Jesus died for your sins

Then rest your ruins on the glorious mysteries
Strangle the pedophile in his jail cell
You're on death row anyway

COMMENTARY

On its surface, "Subtitles Off" seems largely fragmented. This is inten-
tional. In most of my poems, I use gaps and silences to approximate the
thinking process, which is non-linear, seemingly chaotic, and only pulled
into logic by language. I borrow the idea of fragmentation from experimen-
tal cinema. Scenes seem to come out of nowhere, defying conventional nar-
rative logic; they appear disjointed, unconnected, like random parts of
different narratives. As Antonioni once said of his films, these differences
are what tie them together.

However, I often do use structural devices to shape my poems. At the
level of the stanza, I often use the three-line stanza as an extension of the
haiku form (minus the seventeen-syllable regulation, which I think works
in Japanese but doesn't really work in English). By using the principle of
haiku, I can compress each stanza into three elements: idea-counterpoint-
revelation, or image-juxtaposition-surprise. In "Subtitles Off," I extend
this structure further by sequencing several stanzas and letting them
bounce off each other in a similar fashion. The first two stanzas introduce
violence and unknowing into the poem. The middle stanzas juxtapose such
a close-up view with a cosmic perspective, one that suggests, with the inclu-
sion of details from the Papuan cannibal myth of continuous creation, the
universe truly may be a chaotic place.

As one expects from a haiku, the end of the poem contains a number of
revelations and surprises. First, it suggests that our world is only a reflection
of larger, cosmic orders, and that those orders are not kind but rather sor-
rowful. Additionally, the mention of the death of Jesus, the "Son" of God
"the Father," pushes the violence of the poem into truly taboo territory,
and the end of the poem, with its stark imperative and rationale, suggests a
violent resolution for existence in this irrational world. Of course, there is
still mystery at the poem's end—we are forced to find a connection be-
tween the opening slaughter, God, Ginol, and the pedophile, but perhaps
no connection exists—this strange universe won't simply give up its an-
swers and so easily console. This mystery is an effect created by the use of
both fragmentation and structure: the universe seems to tremble most vio-
lently not when simply given over to chaos but when pulled between chaos
and order.

Human Memory Is Organic
Peter Gizzi

We know time is a wave.

You can see it in gneiss, migmatic
or otherwise, everything crumbles.

Don't despair.

That's the message frozen in old stone.

I am just a visitor to this world
an interloper really headed deep into glass.

I, moving across a vast expanse of water

though it is not water maybe salt
or consciousness itself

enacted as empathy. Enacted as seeing.

To see with a purpose has its bloom
and falls to seed and returns

to be a story like any other.
To be a story open and vulnerable

a measure of time, a day, this day one might say
an angle of light for instance.

Let us examine green. Let us go together

to see it all unstable and becoming
violent and testing gravity

so natural in its hunger.

The organic existence of gravity.
The organic nature of history.

The natural history of tears.

COMMENTARY

    The structure of "Human Memory Is Organic" is metaphoric insofar as
it is metamorphic. The poem's content is also concerned with metamor-
phosis, with the processes by which one thing changes into another. Mig-

matic gneiss, the rock with which the poem begins, is one of the oldest known rocks on Earth; it is a metamorphic rock, a rock that through the natural processes of heat and pressure changes form. As the structure of "Human Memory Is Organic" itself is metamorphic—changing, shifting—this structure is the metaphorical equivalent and enactment of the poem's subject matter.

The poem's structure has at least three major parts, or movements.

The poem's first movement is concerned with observation; it begins with a kind of thesis statement: time is a wave. We think of waves as occurring in fluid—or in astrophysics as particle waves—but in the next line the wave is related to stone. To see a wave pattern, a striation, in stone is to see an historical process at work: it is time made visible. The narrator imagines that the message caught in stone is "Don't despair." That is to say, we're all subject to the same processes of change; i.e. metamorphosis. In this way, we are visitors to a much older process, a process that is organic but not personal or punitive.

In the more self-reflective second movement of the poem, the speaker acknowledges that he is an interloper who is reading a larger process in which he himself is caught, "headed deep into glass." The strange, simultaneously reflective and transparent qualities of the glass, which can make it seem like other things (including "consciousness itself"), lead to reflections centered largely on seeing: "To see with a purpose."

The final movement of the poem begins with an invitation to the reader to see (or "examine"), together with the poem's speaker, the green, organic world. That is, to see the world in its process of becoming, of becoming another thing, of changing. In the poem's final turns the processes of geologic and human history are intertwined, as are the processes of seeing and becoming. The content of the poem literally shifts from stone to tears.

Although an early draft of the poem was written in a notebook after visiting the American Museum of Natural History in New York, the deepest part of the poem is, I think, concerned with my mother—and my being affected by the fact that she is aging and that her memory is rapidly changing—though I only realized this a few weeks after I'd finished the poem.

I mention this because I do not write "about" things but "with" things or "out of" things. And I certainly do not map out a poem before I write it as the above note might suggest. I often learn after the fact of writing a

poem what it may ultimately mean, and often even that notion of meaning
shifts as the poem and I move through time.

The Parenthesis Inserts Itself Into the Transcripts
of the Committee on Un-American Activities
Gabriel Gudding

                    "Senator (I have never lain with rubrics,
               nor am I among the indicted's
          swart date books: I am the anchorite's
          punched lips. Small-lunged boys
           who duck in the old beds from dogs
                have lain low in me;
     rabbits, I think, have bolted here
          who smell a cold hole
               in the fuck-all blurry middle
          of a life sprint. The ant
     comes to me for its mortar: I am the divots of the
          ballpeens, cane marks
          outside libraries. I fell from a tree planted on a hill
     of the earth's early ticker tape; I cracked open,
          a walnut of ticker tape. I am a tick
          in the hide of the book, seed
     of the monograph: Yesterday the dewpoint fell
     and a big fog issued from the comma—meadows
in the semi-colons filled with tractors, the plow's tines
     are made of me, as were the eyelashes of Elijah, fingernail moons
          of Coltrane—my heelmarks
are scattered in the mesquite tree, I was abused
          by cummings.
               The day the pennies pitched their tents
on the banks of the math books,
     I became their tent stakes. Queens
     have walked in me for I am smoother
than a dashboard: Jerusalem
     is just this booth in the heat, but I'm
          the backrooms of Nineveh, cowry's arcature. I respect the oyster
for being the grotto of a single mood—but in me

a canyon's filled with stones
sweetly immobile, in me an old man's laundry
sculls on the slantlight. I am a small girl's middle, suitcase
of the vivid poor—farthest cousin
of a thistle's tribe, having struck and hung on
in this most drifting soil: my whole family was born
in an un-neutral footnote
and was taken out into the wire and weeds
and shot in the gravel; it is on gravestones that I am
the cradle of years,
and) I have to say
it's a pleasure
to appear before you
in this honored room."

COMMENTARY

Few poetic structures could be more obvious than the one employed here: it's a frame. Here, an emphatic and rococo parenthetical interjection is inserted into the phatic speech genre of a formal greeting, which is in turn, as the poem's title suggests, nestled inside a political melodrama.

The parenthetical interruption allows for a second voice—poetic, political, emotional, historical, personal—to be interjected surreptitiously into a setting that is dysfunctional, abusive, totalitarian, and cradled with corruption, power, silencing, and coercion.

What's more, here the parenthetical is personified: this interjection is actually voiced, post facto, by a textual parenthesis in the transcripts, showing that the speaking situation was so coercive and dangerous that the human speaker wasn't even able to speak his or her truth in the moment.

My Last Night on Nova Scotia
Timothy Liu

was spent onboard the Lady Janet I—

a wreck tied up on the end
of a long wharf where no other

tourists (to be seen) wanted

to venture—half of its paint
flaking off or eaten out by rust—

parked there long enough for weeds

to have seeded themselves on deck
where moisture had rotted wood—

its one gang plank an invitation

for adolescent townies to leave
their bottles, graffiti, condoms,

but this was a fishing village

in the middle of the South Shore
where not a single police cruiser

bothered to make the rounds, this

was my last night on Nova Scotia
after downing half a dozen oysters

washed down with a local ale

followed by long tokes on a Grande
Montecristo that seemed the envy

of a town whose streets I strolled

just as it turned dark, drawn
to a war memorial's stone columns

fashioned after what still stands

in the Roman Forum, a gigantic
octagonal gazebo with no one

lounging in it the place I thought

best to reflect before opting out
for the empty swings just uphill—

seats still wet with afternoon rain,

what did I care about a wet ass,
the jeans I wore what he borrowed

in order to look more presentable

in a Parisian bistro exactly thirty
days ago, jeans I couldn't bring

myself to wash, we who were

the same size, the exact fit,
and if I pissed off the dock

behind a shack, it was only to

keep on smoking all seven inches
down to its stump of white ash,

and at first, it seemed I couldn't

board that ghost ship for fear
of getting caught, its masts gently

creaking, packs of sea rats darting

through my mind, the boats tied up
adjacent with sundry portholes lit—

surely someone would see me testing

those aluminum steps for slickness,
would call out, or worse, report me

to whatever authorities would arrive

out of nowhere into my vacation
so I moseyed back on up the hill

past the burnt-out Anglican church

that's been miraculously restored
plank by plank, pew by pew—

it would take four years alone to set

the stained glass back into its arches—
this then the proof that anything

is possible, no arsonist in our time

able to level a national monument
which gave me courage to return

to that other wreck and risk

getting caught red-handed, pants
and boxers down to my ankles

somewhere on the aft deck, and if

you saw the silhouette of a man
fervently about his business

at the end of a long trip, embracing

his sense of finally being alone,
if you saw after much concentration

a shudder run through his body, heard

the secret name he cried out
into the bay where the fishing boats

harbored distant voices anchored there

for the night, perhaps you'd imagine
all the other nights that would lead

to this very moment, the deck glazed

with rain on a massive trawler
rocking and moaning just a little more

on that sea it would never sail again—

COMMENTARY

     Last summer, I returned from a romantic interlude in Paris com-
pletely forlorn. So I decided to take a drive all the way up from Cape May,
New Jersey, to Cape Breton, Nova Scotia. The two thousand-mile trek
alone worked its wonders, but there was also no way of entirely escaping
how much I continued to miss my Beloved. So "My Last Night on Nova
Scotia" mimics that motion of circling back to something that I couldn't

initially face: in this case, engaging in an autoerotic act aboard a rusted-out trawler as compensation for what was missing. That's the shape of desire filled with ambivalence: approach, retreat, approach, until one is finally able to embrace the thing itself.

Narrative poems are able to reflect such shapes. My poem begins with setting: a description of a ship at anchor. Then I—or, a version of myself—hesitate to board the vessel, continuing instead on my evening cigar-lit stroll. This retreat leads me to a new setting: the swings in the park. Such pendular motion once again triggers the memory of my now missing Beloved. Emboldened with such memory, the idea of transgression, of trespass, of "board[ing] that ghost ship," arises again, but not without further caution: "surely someone would see me." It takes a third encounter, that with a restored church, to lend me the courage to return and finally perform the fantasized act where the sacred and profane are conjoined as one.

On his lunch hour, Frank O'Hara would leave his office at the Museum of Modern Art in New York, and in the process of grabbing lunch would jot down "this and that" before returning to his place of employ. These peripatetic ruminations are full of spontaneous delight, and it is only after many re-readings of poems like "A Step Away From Them" and "The Day Lady Died" that one begins to suspect that the ease in which the poems seem composed may in fact not be one-draft wonders at all but poems carefully wrought until the made thing reads as if it were conceived in less than a moment's thought. Though my poem might seem to stray, I have worked hard to craft the feel of something discovered spontaneously.

The First Straw
for Christine Caballero
Jeffrey McDaniel

I used to think love was two people sucking
on the same straw to see whose thirst was stronger,

but then I whiffed the crushed walnuts of your nape,
traced jackals in the snow-covered tombstones of your teeth,

I used to think love was a non-stop saxophone solo
in the lungs, till I hung with you like a pair of sneakers

from a phone line, and you promised to always smell
the *rose* in my kerosene. I used to think love was terminal

pelvic ballet, till you let me jog beside while you pedaled
all over hell on the menstrual bicycle, your tongue

ripping through my prairie like a tornado of paper cuts.
I used to think love was an old man smashing a mirror

over his knee, till you helped me carry the barbell
of my spirit back up the stairs after my car pirouetted

in the desert. You are my history book. I used to not believe
in fairy tales till I played the dunce in sheep's clothing

and felt how perfectly your foot fit in the glass slipper
of my ass. But then duty wrapped its phone cord

around my ankle and yanked me across the continent.
And now there are three thousand miles between the *u*

and *s* in esophagus. And being without you is like standing
at a cement-filled well with a roll of Yugoslavian nickels

and making a wish. Some days I miss you so much
I'd jump off the roof of your office building

just to catch a glimpse of you on the way down. I wish
we could trade left eyeballs, so we could always see

what the other sees. But you're here, I'm there,
and we have only words, a nightly phone call—one chance

to mix feelings into syllables and pour into the receiver,
hope they don't disassemble in that calculus of wire.

And lately—with this whole war thing—the language machine
supporting it—I feel betrayed by the alphabet, like they're

injecting strychnine into my vowels, infecting my consonants,
naming attack helicopters after shattered Indian tribes:

Apache, *Blackhawk*; and West Bank colonizers are settlers,
so Sharon is Davy Crockett, and Arafat: Geronimo,

and it's the Wild West all over again. And I imagine Picasso
looking in a mirror, decorating his face in war paint,

washing his brushes in venom. And I think of Jenin
in all that rubble, and I feel like a Cyclops with two eyes,

like an anorexic with three mouths, like a scuba diver
in quicksand, like a shark with plastic vampire teeth,

like I'm the executioner's fingernail trying to reason
with the hand. And I don't know how to speak love

when the heart is a busted cup filling with spit and paste,
and the only sexual fantasy I have is busting

into the Pentagon with a bazooka-sized pen and blowing
open the minds of the generals. And I comfort myself

with the thought that we'll name our first child Jenin,
and her middle name will be Terezin, and we'll teach her

how to glow in the dark, and how to swallow firecrackers,
and to never neglect the first straw, because no one

ever talks about the first straw, it's always the last straw
that gets all the attention, but by then it's way too late.

COMMENTARY

Before I can address structure, I must touch on impulse, because the
structure evolved out of that. I decided I needed to write a love poem for my
long-term girlfriend. In the early stages of courtship I besieged her with
love (infatuation?) poems, but once the relationship became serious, the
poems stopped. This embarrassed me. We had been together for six years,
and I hadn't written her a love poem in almost five. I aspired to write a
piece that depicted love in practice (admitting flaws and conflict) and not
love in some idealized theory (where the "you" gets levitated to near holy
status). This is why the phrase "I used to think love was" is followed by "but
then" or "till" six times in the poem's first ten couplets. The speaker's ro-
mantic illusions are being revised, so there's a small-scale structural mini-
reversal in each of those sentences. I should say the piece was not con-
structed in a linear fashion. I had over sixty epigrammatic strips that I'd as-
sembled over months. I had the epigrams on slivers of paper; if they could
not stand on their own as charged pieces of language, I discarded them in
the same way that someone building a boat only uses planks of wood that
meet a certain standard of durability. I assembled, re-assembled, looking

for an associative thread. Occasionally I'd supply connective language to seal the fragments together, to give the piece a narrative silhouette.

Nine couplets into the piece there is a narrative turn: the couple gets physically separated, and the relationship becomes long-distance. This was a way to inject longing and helplessness into the equation. Also it reduced the couple's interaction to merely words, which laid the groundwork for what in my mind was the poem's major turn: the speaker's swerve away from his beloved and towards the language he is using to woo her. I was conscious of writing a love poem that turned into a political one.

The piece was constructed about six months after the 2001 World Trade Center attacks, which I witnessed. In the aftermath of the attack, as the U.S. government became increasingly bloodthirsty, I became acutely aware of how language was being effectively manipulated, by the government and in the media, to advance a militaristic agenda. The speaker feels conflicted about using the same alphabet that the military machine uses, about using a language—a language he thought was his—that itself doesn't resist, that is, in fact, cheating on him. In the first half of the poem, the speaker experiences helplessness due to separation from his beloved. In the poem's second half, the helplessness is political: the speaker is unable to do anything meaningful, despite his love affair with language. The speaker's indignation in the second half doesn't turn so much as amplify into the climactic image of the generals' heads blowing open. There is a dramatic release of tension after that, creating space in the last four couplets for the poem's second major turn: the speaker swerves away from hopelessness and rage, and turns his attentive gaze back to the beloved, imagining the child he and she might have, how they will raise her to be a kind of superhero who will be cognizant of language's power and consequently able to see through lies as they are forming, which may make it possible for her to do what the speaker can't: perform meaningful acts.

Eclogue
Susan Mitchell

> *Soprano*
> Oh universe in which the measured blues and violets

A little too high for you?
Should I come down an octave?

Lately, I've been thinking about the problem
of what is singable.

Piano
There is a sound we call music.
Does it mean the world
is insufficient, its saps, its flow still flowing
insufficient?
                    And the instruments
like weapons laid on the grass.

Soprano
What does it mean to sing
when the intervals spread out like an archipelago?
Between are long pauses when nothing is heard.

Piano
Clouds are part of it, vast fields of air, bubbles
shivering the surface, icing
the amphitheaters of mauve and turbulence

Soprano
pieces of broken and churned over

Piano
                    And smoke-
filled bars (are you with me?), the turnpikes and malls
of your itinerary or mine, cantankerous
dialogues that break into trills and interruptions.

Composer
Should I be ready to record what I don't
understand, even what I don't hear, but only suspect?

Piano
There is a sound we call music, does it mean
other sounds are insufficient?
                                        Etceteras of water,
ampersands of rain and wind?

Composer
And if one language gives out, should I rush
to where another like a spring starts up?

Should I include the silences, begin with
them because someone might hear
                              below or above
my hearing, a going-on, a persistence?

                    Soprano
And if there is a hole in listening
no sound has filled? Will I
know it when I
                    Piano
Or something knocking
against something metal or plastic, noise

of many, a multitude; what
it broke off from, the jaggedness
still sounding

COMMENTARY

   I grew up in a very large family, and since we all lived within blocks of
each other in New York City, weekend gatherings at my parents' apartment
were enormous—cousins, aunts, uncles, all four grandparents crowded to-
gether with, of course, many conversations going on at once. As a child, I
moved with delight from conversation to conversation, sometimes trying
to take them all in with one big auricular gulp. After my third book of po-
ems, *Erotikon*, was published, I started to play with the idea of multiple con-
versations as a structure for a poem, maybe even a group of poems. There
was ready to use a very old pastoral mode, the eclogue, which introduces
shepherds engaged in conversation. The mode originated with the idylls of
the Greek poet Theocritus, then was used in more sophisticated ways by the
Roman poet Virgil and, after him, a long line of English and American
poets, including Edmund Spenser, W.H. Auden, and Robert Frost.
   Though I made use of an old mode for my "Eclogue," I did not simply
follow tradition. Where the eclogue was originally pastoral, mine is urban
with its references to turnpikes, malls, and smoke-filled bars. Instead of
shepherds as my speakers, I use a Composer, a Soprano, and a Piano.
Where the shepherds talked about love, my speakers talk about music
theory, performance, and composition, topics which are analogous to my
concerns as a poet. Most important, I changed the structure of the old pas-
toral eclogue. In the older eclogues, the speakers, usually two, focus on a

single topic. I was interested in a more complex structure that would keep three topics going at once, the way a juggler manages to keep three or more balls up in the air.

When I wrote "Eclogue," the challenge for me was to have many swerves or turns, and yet have a coherent poem. How much difference, how many topics, how much complex thinking could the structure hold without breaking? Since my speakers rarely respond to each other's concerns, but instead continue on their own thought-tracks, there is a turn or discontinuity nearly every time the conversation is taken up by a new speaker, which means that the reader has to be ready to move from the Soprano's concern (Is everything singable?), to the Piano's concern (Why do we need art?), to the Composer's concern (If material comes to the artist in a new form, will the artist recognize it as potentially art?). These are, of course, all-important questions for me as a poet. But there are even more discontinuities or turns in the poem because sometimes breaks occur within the dialogue of a single speaker. The Soprano begins the poem by singing a line from a fictitious opera, then immediately shifts to a question about her performance. Her question, "A little too high for you?" can be understood both literally and figuratively. Understood figuratively, her question suggests that she is afraid what she is singing may be too highbrow, or even highfalutin'. An indication that she accepts her own criticism precipitates still another turn, this time to her matter-of-fact statement, "Lately, I've been thinking about the problem / of what is singable." Given the way I have structured "Eclogue," it is a poem paradoxically held together by its turns and breaks, the interruptions a strategy the reader comes to count on, even when they come as a surprise.

Elegy Ending in a Dream
Patrick Phillips

I thought it was like being broken.
It's like being filled with cold sand.

I thought it was fleeting, like passion.
All night in your place the plate shines.

I thought love was the meaning of heaven.
Even heaven turns to shit on my tongue.

I thought *we die* meant like the sun.
All day the sun sinks in the limbs.

I thought a squirrel's nest had blown down.
And found nestled inside it your hands.

COMMENTARY

I began "Elegy Ending in a Dream" after helping my father-in-law fight an agonizing and ultimately failed battle with cancer. That experience was so far beyond words that at first I found it impossible to write anything adequate to my feelings. My only ambition was to write a poem that did not betray my friend's memory, or the experience of watching him die. When I had almost decided it was an impossible task, structures minor and major did, in fact, evolve and help to make the poem possible.

One of those structures is the call-and-response of prayer. I grew up hearing my father preach in Methodist churches, and every Sunday as I waited for my wafer and my sip of wine, he would boom out his part of the "Prayer of Thanksgiving" as the people around me chanted theirs:

> *The Lord be with you.*
> And also with you.
>
> *Lift up your hearts.*
> We lift them up unto the Lord.

Only very late in the writing process did the lines of "Elegy Ending in a Dream" fall into the cadence and alternating voices of a "call and response"—the first structure I had ever known to speak about a mystery. As I revised the poem I found that its difficult subject could be approached not only by what was said by the two voices but also by the silence between them.

The other structure at the heart of the poem is elegiac. Like so many traditional elegies, my poem moves from expressions of loss (in the first three stanzas), to a realization of the speaker's own mortality (in the fourth); it ends with a gesture towards consolation in the final line. At the time, I was not consciously filling the poem with the required elements of an elegy. But it also seems clear now that this structure—moving from lament to self-reflection to consolation—offered a way out of the profound silence with which I began and made it possible for me to speak about the unspeakable experience of grief.

The Price of a Finger
Wang Ping

The Price of a Finger

Injuries are common in Yongkang, China's hardware manufacturing center.

INJURY	COMPENSATION
Loss of a thumb, or any finger past a joint	6 months salary
Two fingers	10 months salary
Four fingers, or a thumb and three fingers	14 months salary and 70 percent pay*
Forearm, or both thumbs	18 months salary and 75 percent pay*
An arm, or hand and the thumb on opposite hand	20 months salary and 80 percent pay*
Both arms	24 months salary and 90 percent pay*

*Through retirement age

Source: Zhejiang Department of Labor and Social Security

China makes 80 percent of the toys sold in America.

With your right hand, you slip strips of metal under a hammer backed by 4,000 pounds of pressure; with your left, you sweep molded parts into a pile. You do this once a second for a 10-hour shift, minus a half-hour lunch. You must concentrate. You must not lose a beat, or it's all over.
— *Wang Chenghua, migrant worker with crushed fingers*

Construct the World's Biggest Market Build an International Shopping Heaven
— *Neon banners on Yiwu World Trade Center*

You tell them to pay attention and they don't listen. They have no culture or education. They are told many times to be safe and they just don't get it.
— *Shi Yanxin, owner of Hua Xin Electronics*

Yiwu, the most sizzling city in Zhejiang Province, makes trinkets that fill stores the world over. 500,000 migrant workers live in and around this city of 640,000 residents.

At 14, my son left to work in the city. 15 years passed, he still borrows money to look for jobs. To make money, you have to leave the village. Nobody has made much, but we can't go back. Nothing left at home. Everything is broken, broken.
　—*Cai Songquan, farmer from Caijia Village*

Yongkang, the hardware capital of China, with 7,000 private-owned factories making hinges, hubcaps, pots, power drills, thermoses, plugs, headphones, filling the shelves of Wal-Marts with products that get better and cheaper each year. "Eternal health" in Chinese, Yongkang is also the dismemberment capital, with 2,500 accidents each year, and thousands more unreported.

The riskiest jobs, as in war, go to green recruits, fresh from the farm. Young migrants are hired at the train station to run metal-stampers, molders, and high-pressure hammers driven by flywheels. Few workers last a month.

We have always met the government's standard for safety. Otherwise, they would not let us operate.
　—*Kang Ziying, lawyer for Lucky Gem and Jewelry*

Of course life has improved. We couldn't have imagined any of this 10 years ago. This small town with mud houses now has an airport, a world trade center, skyscrapers, hundreds of factories, hotels, including two Middle Eastern restaurants with belly dancers. We hardly had any

schooling, but our daughter studies marketing at college.
—*Jin Xiaoqin, Yiwu factory owner*

From their rice paddies, the villagers watch trucks whiz by on the new cross-national superhighway, carrying goods made by their teenage sons and daughters far away, goods they will never see.

And they've been pushing down the rates. We used to get 3.5 fen per toy but now they are just paying 2.5 fen, less than one-tenth of an American penny. When the orders are high, we work 14 hours a day, 7 days a week, and might clear $120 in a month. More typical is $90 a month and in a slow month, $50. It's not enough to get by.
—*Cai Gaoxiang, migrant worker at Yiwu Toys*

You have no right to speak. You have no right to organize.
—*Hu Xu, owner of Xu Xing Metals*

Each eyelash is assembled from 464 inch-long strands of human hair, placed in a crisscross pattern on a thin strip of transparent glue. It takes an hour to complete a pair. We work 14-hour shifts, but can't make enough for a bonus.
—*Wei Qi, 16, migrant worker from Anshan*

Kin Ki and other big producers have come under greater pressure to adhere to global labor codes. They open their doors to foreign inspectors to assuage concerns that products used to entertain children in rich countries are not made under oppressive conditions in poor ones.

Life was poorer under Mao—you were lucky if you had a pair of pants, but it was more equal.
—*Cai Songquan, farmer from Cai Jia Village*

The goal conflicts with price pressures in commodity industries like toys, where manufacturers command no premium for good labor practices. China alone has 8,000 toy makers competing fiercely for contracts by shaving pennies off production costs.

I keep this job because my parents and my daughter depend on the money I earn. No one likes to work in these conditions, but I have no choice.
—*anonymous migrant worker*

Kin Ki stays competitive, workers say, by paying them 24 cents an hour in Shenzhen, where the minimum wage is 33 cents. When the Etch A Sketch line shut down in Ohio just after the Christmas rush in 2000, wages for the unionized work force there had reached $9 an hour.

Ours is a typical story. From small to big, from middleman to producer of goods, from a mud house in the country to a four-story house in town, from carry goods on our shoulders to a motorcycle eight years ago and, last year, a van.
—*Jin Xiaoqin, owner of Yiwu Toy*

I came to China about a decade ago because Korean companies could no longer compete in the market for false eyelashes, which sell for as little as 50 cents a set in Asia and the USA.
—*Lee Yo Han, South Korea entrepreneur*

I summon my boy to my bed. He starts crying before I open my mouth. He knows he must now quit his dream for college and find a job. He's 14, time to help the family. I start crying too. But what else can we do? I'm on the threshold of death and our money is running out. This is our only choice. This is our fate.
—*Hu, migrant worker with silicosis*

Caijia Village, once the incubating ground for the Communist revolution in Jiangxi Province, provides young people for the booming industrial towns on the coast, joining the 100 million migrant workforce nationwide from China's interior.	
	Mary and Jesus are hot. Sell like crazy. We ship them in giant containers. The real problem is the eyes. To do it right, you have to paint them by hand. That's what Americans care about, the tears in Mary's eyes, the sorrow. —*Jin Xiaoqin, owner of Yiwu Plastic Factory*

No nearby exit from the rutted road.

COMMENTARY

"The Price of a Finger" is a collage prose poem that attempts to portray what is happening in China since it opened its market to the global economy and what is happening to 100 million migrant workers—all bankrupt peasants who left their families and lands behind and poured into cities to work in the most horrific conditions for extremely meager pay. The poem's fragmentation is important in that it symbolizes that China's boom in the global economic system is built upon the severed bodies of Chinese migrant workers, upon their broken villages, their loss of land. The isolating column-borders represent the chicken wire around the factories where the migrant workers toil, and the villages where the peasants are stuck in poverty. Such fragmentation also echoes so much of what is produced with the tears and blood of millions of children who left school and home to work twelve hours a day, seven days a week to make costume jewelry, fake eyelashes, inexpensive toys, and other assorted cheap goods to line the shelves of Wal-Mart in order to support their families and the global economy.

Though seemingly a sprawling list created with diverse materials such as the voices of migrant workers, document clippings, quotes from factory owners, foreign investors, and government officials (voices I gathered through research and interviews conducted over the past three years), the personal stories, official numbers, and facts are carefully juxtaposed with and against one another to create an atmosphere charged with controversy and emotion, to jolt the readers out of their comfort zone, to get the reader to start seeing and thinking from different perspectives. Though it may not seem so at first, every word is set to explode at its own time, its own place.

For example, I open the piece with a compensation chart for work-related injuries issued by the Labor and Social Security Department of Zhejiang, China's most successful province that gathers the country's largest population of rich businessmen and poor migrant workers. The visual images are startling and the numbers are shocking, even without knowing that the official figures are almost always ignored by factories or that injured workers often receive little or no compensation at all.

While there's not a hard-and-fast organization to them, the fragments that follow this opening also are carefully arranged. Many of the opening fragments establish context, making clear the real dangers of being a migrant worker, and they combine these terrible facts with the ironic mention of what often is made from such sacrifice: trinkets. Then come the lawyers' and owners' voices, which claim that work is safe, that life has improved: "We have always met the government's standard for safety," "Of course life has improved." Such remarks are followed, however, by counter-evidence: descriptions of the grueling workdays and poor compensation. And at the poem's end, all hope is dashed: the penultimate fragment shows how Communism, once the hope of workers, has been subsumed by global competition, and the final fragment shows that religion is often at best a hollow consolation and at worst one more part of this terrible system.

A Filial Republic
Susan Wheeler

And out on the plaza, there were more people
Than had been expected: the aviators, with their
Thick dark muffs; the women in red, clapping
For Coca-Cola; the small trumpet player,
Leaning on the fender of the car which was not his;
The mechanics, spreading flat the manuals
For timing and for gaps; the blue majorettes;
The mother, who wished so hard she broke in two;
Those divided against the rule; Mick Jagger;
The security-green police; the gentle inquisitor;
The woman who had not yet found the voice for tragedy;

The exercise cadet, with Adidas and cassettes;
The deaf man, elegant, who bends to tie
His shoe; the grocery clerks, hanging back,
Aloof; the girls who clutched their T-shirts
From behind; the model with the cordless telephone;
The guests of honor, in their limousine;
The *New Yorker* hack; the derelicts, smitten with their
Own advice; the shampooer; the plasterer; the
Dishwasher; the drunk; the man so sodden with sex
He reeled; the crook; the benevolent sister;
The priest, wistfully; Alan Funt;
The father, crying with desire; the great
Conquistadors; the dreamers, who looked past the crowd
As it rolled in the sun; the children:
Exclaiming together, as one hut and then another,
South, on the horizon, burst into fire.

Rise up, from where you are seated, smoking,
At a wooden desk. There has been a terrible dream
In the apartment above you, and the tenant is pacing.

COMMENTARY

   The structure of the poem is apparent; the turn in its rhetoric is unmis-
takable. The first stanza, one complex compound sentence, uses—as most
list poems do—parallelism; one equivalent clause follows on the last in its
massing of people on the plaza, using asyndeton to emphasize the form's
repetition throughout the long list. The turn comes in the full two sen-
tences of the brief second stanza, where the form of address breaks from de-
scription to a direct command (sentence one) and then to an explanation
for that command (sentence two).

   Why these turns? The poem is a response to a searingly beautiful poem
by Alvin Feinman, a poem that—in Stevensian fashion—affixes spirituality
to aestheticism. I wanted to challenge that coupling; I wanted a call to ac-
tion as a chastening to the aesthete's contemplation. In Feinman's "No-
vember Sunday Morning," the speaker "sits, and smokes, and lingers out
desire." In my poem, the "you," a solitary voice, would become crowded
out by the press of figures on the plaza, and would—momentarily—feel
relief in the turn toward a personal address. That the address commands
involvement in the nightmare-ridden neighbor's dark plight is the poem's

second turn, one that begins in the release of the oppressive parallelism and ends with the plunge right back into the "fires on the horizon."

Ferns, Mosses, Flags
Elizabeth Willis

We all live under the rule of Pepsi, by the sanctified waters of an in-ground pond. Moss if it gathers is a sign of shifting weathers, the springing scent of consensual facts. A needle's knowing drops into focus while you sleep in its haystack. A boy on the road, a guileless girl disguised as a brook. Even trees deploy their shadows, embossing your skin with the sound of freedom breaking. No one mistakes choice for necessity. Look at the pilgrims in your filmy basket, illustrious eyebrows colored with chalk. The lake is panicking. A latent mystery detected in sepia is quaking to its end. I too have a family astonished, unsaintly. Asleep, I saw them. A porcelain dome insisting on trust, jeweled with telepathy. I don't know how to pour this country from a thinner vessel. Or account for the era of Martian diplomacy, its cheap labor glossily wigging. Little bridges connect every century, seasonally covered with the rime of empire. Can you successfully ignore the eyes in the painting? Can you recount the last three images in reverse order? I read the picture and did what it told me, ducking through the brush with my tablet and pen, following some star.

COMMENTARY

As the title suggests, the overall structure of this poem is paratactic: one thing after another. Each sentence suggests narrative elements that are linked to other narrative elements in the poem by associative, figural, or sonic resemblances rather than by a causal progression. I was interested in the wandering quality of Charles Baudelaire's prose poems, the way they make use of the apparent randomness of the poet's meandering through the city. Baudelaire's Parisian wanderer crossed class boundaries, initiated philosophical dialogues with strangers, and speculated on commercial culture, public tastes, and private desires.

In "Ferns, Mosses, Flags," the territory traversed is not a specific cityscape but a discursive landscape composed at least partly of scenes from American history, some of them experienced directly, others read through their representations in the media. In wandering through the truncated narratives of this image bank, the speaker speculates on various forms of relation—between individual and commerce, individual and state, individual and family; between experience and its representation; and between inherited tropes and the subjective reality one struggles to represent through them. In that sense, a rhetorical turn occurs between virtually every line, as the poem moves from generalization to illustrative example, or from political to personal framework, and so on.

But the poem also follows the trajectory of a quest: it shows a process of getting lost, enduring trials while looking for and interpreting signs, attaining a vision, and finally arriving at a sense of direction and purpose. The poem is initially situated not in Dante's dark wood but in the long shadows cast by a well-lit, image- and ad-driven corporate world. Reading signs that indicate that change is possible, the poem then involves a flight from domination and a search for more directive "signs," even if they are as hard to find as a needle in a haystack. Throughout this process the poem's hero wanders, sleeping as a vagabond and meeting others along the way: a boy, a girl, fellow "pilgrims."

The poem's shift to the first person brings on a dream-vision. This vision features an encounter with a familial, telepathic knowing that helps the hero read the seemingly inscrutable signs in her path. If in conventional quests such supernatural guidance may bring about the founding of nations, in this poem the goal is more simply survival—and the survival of art. The poem moves from overt political concern to looking closely at issues of representation. We are still in the realm of politics, but politics at a different level. The poem's final gesture is a turn from the reception of art to its production: the image-maker cannot escape all forms of government ("I read the picture and did what it told me"), but at least she can replace "the rule of Pepsi" with the resilient and complex knowledge that art makes available. Having left the "rule" of corporate positioning and market-thinking, this poem finally suggests that we have to write our way out of our quest with only the most ancient technology at our disposal: a tablet and pen and the guidance of "some star."

The Death of Everything Even New York City
Rachel Zucker

Even if there are Starlings, well, I can't write "starlings."
And Blackbird? sorry. Mockingbird? nope. Robin,
Bluebird, Warbler, Mourning Dove—you're
kidding, right? Even the Coot, Vulture, Cowbird,
House Finch—the whole bird world is used up.

Even babies and lovers and language—might as well forget
flowers. The most contaminated flower in the world is too
beautiful, the worst marriage too romantic, the most malicious
baby too acutely precious and untrustworthy.

Today the government told us not to drink the water, not
to breathe the air so when I do drink and breathe I've no one
to blame and to write instead of the early morning playground,
the glorious breeze, feathered vertebrae isn't credible and
that's a shame, because Starlings, charming name notwithstanding,
are a nuisance—noisy, nasty to other birds—a nice metaphor
for our sons, the way they *%&)@(&#!

but we're both terminally sick of "the way a"
and whatever comes afterwards.

Today I say shut down the Holland, Lincoln, and Midtown tunnels! I say
lock down the bridges and roads and waterways against the way anything
is like anything else. Say no! to fish named after colors, birds named
after mammals, flowers named after men. Even the names of diseases
are too clever, keen, apropos, disconcertingly lyrical. Eradicate adjectives
and all words beginning with "a": anemia, areola, arroyo—they are all too
elegiac—and continue thus through the many alphabets which are passé.

The *New York Times* reports that since 1886 more than 200 species of birds
have been spotted in Central Park. The Great Blue Heron and Mute Swan
are year-round inhabitants. The Chimney Swift flies over daily in summer.
so what?

it's too late to describe the world.

Poor Bobolink. Bobwhite. Buzzard. Chickadee. Falcon.
Kingfisher. Solitaire. Sparrow. Thrush. We are all fed up of you.
Bloated. Stuffed. Sated and dissatisfied.

Once I said something to you so sincere it was pure, whole, heartfelt.
It was spontaneous and there was no crisis of language, no semiotic
hassle. Anomia was the name of a stubborn child and malignancy
didn't have a nice ring to it because it wasn't invented
and used on-line and in print 500 million times.

But that was just a dream. I won't write about dreams.

But I swear: one day, perhaps not in our life time, we'll finally see
the death of everything and then, o' then, I'll be able to say once
a priori, before tropes and isotopes, the pastiche and list poem,
the rant and dirge, appropriation of French words into English,
to you, my husband, that in this toxic urban aviary especially
because of the contamination, because finally, when the death of
everything and the only bird left is the Cormorant and then that's
gone and Central Park is no longer a simile for the country because
there is no country is no farmland no park to offset the streets nor
streets the blocks and blocks of buildings, skyscrapers, low rises,
air rights, underground water mains because there is no water no air
nor micron of habitable atmosphere and then when the death of everything
and language is pure and there is not a single living man or woman to
say anything not even 'primordial soup' or 'big bang' I'll say
I love you and it means something and you'll know it always did.

COMMENTARY

"The Death of Everything Even New York City" attempts to subvert the
classic structure of the epiphanic poem. Think of James Wright's "The
Blessing" or "Lying in a Hammock at William Duffy's Farm in Pine Island,
Minnesota," or Rainer Maria Rilke's "Archaic Torso of Apollo." The
epiphanic structure is simple: description followed by a short burst of
rhetoric. "The Blessing" presents two Indian ponies "munching the young
tufts of spring in the darkness." The poet, who has stepped over barbed
wire to get closer to the ponies, is moved to caress the pony's "long ear,"
which is "as delicate as the skin over a girl's wrist." In "Lying in a Ham-
mock," Wright describes what he sees and hears around him: "a butterfly,
cowbells," "a field of sunlight between two pines," "the droppings of last
year's horses / blazing up into golden stones," and a chicken hawk flying by
overhead "from his prone position." Rilke's poem describes how Apollo's
torso, though lacking "eyes like ripening fruit," has a "brilliance from in-

side, / like a lamp, in which the gaze now turned to low, / gleams in all its power" and how the stone seems to "glisten like a wild beast's fur." All three poems contain, within the description, a sense of heightened awareness. There is a reason the poet crosses the barbed wire to see the ponies. The late afternoon warrants Wright's close attention just as the headless statue must be marvelous to so dazzle Rilke. But despite the density of language and acute attentiveness, nothing in the description prepares the reader for the poems' last lines: "Suddenly I realize / That if I stepped out of my body I would break / Into blossom," "I have wasted my life," "You must change your life." Of course, one is not supposed to be prepared.

The pleasure in this kind of poem lies in the surprise (an ambush really) of the turn and the following resolution. The sudden utterance at the end of the poem, sounding very much like a *non sequitur*, collides with description like a driver running a red light. Whiplash, double take, brief confusion ensues, but in this case, almost as soon as confusion registers, the rhetoric of the last line aggressively co-opts the description and defines the entire scene. What seemed at first a rogue bit of language is suddenly manifested as the essence of the poem. Dissonance gives way (rather quickly) to a feeling of rightness, of inevitability. The realization at the end of the poem is the latent "true form" within the sculptor's unmarred stone. The experience of looking closely at the ponies, the scene at William Duffy's farm, or Apollo's torso manifests a sudden perception of the essential nature of the poet's life. The Epiphanic structure (as opposed to presenting the realization first and then recalling the scene) is mimetic of the experience in that it allows the reader to experience a jolt of illuminating discovery.

Anxiety arises, however, when the reader suspects that perhaps she has been duped. The poems, in the end, are *about* "breaking into blossom," wasting your life or changing your life (and about the experience of having a profound realization while looking closely at the world). The ponies, farm, and torso, all lovingly apprehended, hardly matter in the end. Worse still, the reader suspects that the poet's attention to the world was manipulative. Maybe the ponies don't have anything to do with breaking into blossom, the scene at the farm with wasting your life, the torso with changing your life. Would any grand statement tacked on to the end of a careful description sound profound, meaningful, true? If so, we (writer and reader) have allowed two wrongs: we have lulled ourselves into embracing false rhetoric and we have poisoned the real world (or at least description of the real world) with our ill-usage. Our cavalier use of the real world to advertise or propagandize exposes our compulsive need to grandly declare, to manipulate everyone and everything in service of our ideas. Exposed as imperialists or at least egocentric finaglers, we are ashamed. All comparisons (description/epiphany is really just a mode of metaphor) become suspect and untrustworthy; all proclamations become tyrannical, imperious.

And, yet—oh, dear—without description, without comparison, without declaration, how can a poet say she loves her husband? If I describe the world and say I love my husband do I defile the world and expose my declaration as fraudulent and worse, symptomatic of acute megalomania? Can it be that I *cannot* say I love my husband? (Is there anything else more worth saying?) Can comparisons no longer contain sincerity? Have we truly come to such a state of deprivation? Perhaps, the poet theorizes, if I could destroy all the expected component ingredients in the description/idea=love recipe all the obvious Love-triggers like beauty and birds, the natural world, as well as all the love antitheses like government, terrorism, the *New York Times*, literary criticism, linguistics, pollution, ideas themselves, comparative language, even the urge to make comparisons, then perhaps I might speak?

Of course, in the end, Death, in "The Death of Everything Even New York City," is just a utopian fantasy, and the poem enacts the very structure it seeks to nullify. The beginning describes or witnesses a state (albeit imagined) of systematic annihilation. Then, in this shadowy nothing, this razed onceland, Epiphany bursts forth.

The Epiphany pretends to exist in a world free of description. "The Death of Everything" has some mini-turns along the way that don't lead to epiphany. These apparent dead ends allow the poet to assert a world where nothing necessarily means anything else and the conjunction of ideas or the passage of time or the movement between states of consciousness don't lead to *la petite morte*. The extended bird foreplay, the poem's mini-turns, discursiveness, repositionings, and the long swelling climax might lead one to say that this version is more female than the more traditionally male epiphany, but both are clearly ejaculatory. Perhaps, despite all my doubts and distrust, there is no righter, more sincere structure for a love poem than the Epiphanic. When she comes, Love, that great finagler, catches you unaware and believes only in her own agency.

Inspiration, Guides, Exercises

Inspiration, Guides, Exercises

The study of poetic structure is, for the working poet, a pragmatic undertaking. While each poetic structure, in response to the questions "What do poems do?" and "How do poems work?," offers up its part of the larger and always incomplete answer, poetic structures more specifically offer templates for writing poems, breaking poems down into their constitutive parts so that they can be used, to a fuller extent, as models.

Any poet trying to figure out where to go with a draft of a poem can benefit from examining his or her poem for its structural turns. For example, working on a draft of a meditation, a poet could dramatize the idea by contextualizing it and showing how it affects the poem's speaker's perceptions using the descriptive-meditative structure. Or, using the emblem structure, the poet might choose to describe an object from which the meditation might arise. Another approach would be to argue the antithesis of the idea to create an ironic poem or a dialectical argument. Many options are suggested simply by considering various structural moves.

In terms of its usefulness for the composition of poems, structure's particular strength is in revision; it generally is not a very helpful prewriting method. The exercises suggested in this section of *Structure & Surprise* can be used profitably alongside other kinds of writing exercises. For example, while many poetry-writing handbooks have a chapter on writing poetic lists, and though these handbooks often suggest wonderful ways to generate raw material, *Structure & Surprise*'s chapter on the retrospective-prospective structure can take the exercise a step further, offering some ideas about what might be done with such a list, how such a list could be brought to completion. And, of course, *Structure & Surprise* can supplement any work on the sonnet, providing detailed options for that form's vital, albeit single, structural feature: the turn.

An awareness of structure enlivens a poet's work. The patterns for poetic structures are everywhere—any process, whether natural or human-made, physical or psychological, that involves a transition from one state to another can serve as the basis of poetic structure or substructure. Once a poet is alerted to such possibilities, the sources are endless. For example, science texts reveal the stages material goes through in order to form a star, and how a snake sheds its skin. Psychology texts describe mental processes, including those that shift from mania to depression, or from initial uncertainty to resolve to efforts at controlling post-decision dissonance in the decision-making process. Anthropology texts explicate rituals, the steps to be taken in various cultures to ensure the favor of the gods, to divine the future, or to talk with the dead. Law books explain how to organize legal briefs. Logic textbooks teach inductive and deductive arguments, hypothetical syllogisms, and fallacies, too. All of these turns can be used to inspire, guide, and craft poems.

Below are some examples of specific exercises that take poetic structure into consideration. While these exercises are generally organized to follow the order of *Structure & Surprise*'s chapters, no strict parallel is possible—there are simply too many similarities between and interactions among the structures. These exercises, which are based on and further reveal the overlap and interaction of the structures, further encourage the mixture of subjects and structures, revealing the different structural turns that similar material can take and emphasizing how helpful and yet how flexible a tool structure can be.

- Mix and match structures and subject matter. Write an elegy for the moth in Robert Frost's "Design" (p. 29). Use Sharon Olds' "35/10" (p. 106) as a prompt to write your own concessional poem in praise of turning 35. Write a dialectical argument about both the drawbacks and the merits of your own previous poems.

- Write an ironic poem in which you repeatedly—at least eight times—fill in the phrase, "I want ..." Then, turn the poem by adding "But ...," and suggest why your desires won't be fulfilled. This poem likely will work best if your subject matter also changes at the turn, switching from cosmic, universal matters to personal, mundane matters, or vice versa.

- Add an ironic ending to one of your own poems. Now revise the rest of the poem towards that "discovered" end.

- To create a new kind of emblem poem, imagine a museum devoted to a specific abstraction: The Museum of Envy, The Museum of Life, The

Museum of Chance, The Museum of the Future. Carefully describe at least ten of the museum's exhibits—paintings, photographs, sculptures, dioramas. Then, at the poem's end, describe what happens *after* this tour. For example, what happens, what does one perceive, upon leaving The Museum of the Future? Does everything glow with possibility or is everything made to seem already obsolete when seen in light of the future? Or else, describe the gift shop at The Museum of Envy. Note: If you use the phrase "The Museum of . . ." as the title of your poem, you won't have to explain a lot in your poem—you can trust your images and the poem's turn to do most of the poem's meaning-making.

- If your poetic material feels familiar to you, it likely will feel familiar to your reader, so research an unfamiliar object for an emblem poem. Find objects to describe and meditate on that you have never heard of before: small but important parts of the anatomy or construction materials. For your meditation you might consider: What does it mean that your notion of Self or your sense of Place depends on such small things, things you never even knew about until you looked them up? If you do write an emblem poem on something familiar—the moon, eyes, a chambered nautilus—you should describe that object in new ways so that the poem might develop a new meditation.

- Meditations often seem daunting. Perhaps it's the name; *meditation* seems weighted with cosmic, religious significance. However, while meditations, like most of those included in the emblem structure chapter, may have such lofty ambitions, it is more accurate to think of the meditation as virtually any act of mind: musing, considering, imagining, dreaming, speculating, doubting, wondering. These activities are not unfamiliar; we do them all the time. Take some time to jot down some of your own musings, from serious ideas to secret speculations to interior debates. Indulge your thinking, be detailed, and let your writing go. For inspiration, you might use a game such as Table Topics, which supplies a large number of questions to get dinner party conversations started. While such an activity is designed to get people talking in groups, it also can get you writing by yourself. For some very different inspiration, try to answer one of the surreal questions poet Pablo Neruda poses in *The Book of Questions*.

• Invent a creature to describe as a preface to one of your meditations. Attach your description and meditation to make a new emblem poem.

• Describe one object in at least two radically different ways. You might describe the object as a cubist might paint it; or as something that appeared to you in a nightmare; or lovingly, as would the object's lover; or with the dispassion of a scientist. Use these different descriptions to write two very different emblem poems with very different meditations.

• Write an emblem poem on someone meditating or on something that is clearly meaningless and insignificant: a typo, a dust mote, a do-hickey, or a thing-a-ma-bob.

• Think of something you love that almost no one else does: your ratty flip-flops; your ancient, rusted-out Chevy Impala; your pet salamander; hot, muggy days; having a roommate; the month of March. Write a concessional poem in praise of your love.

• Write a reverse-concessional poem. Instead of trying to argue for something it seems everyone dislikes, argue against something it seems everyone likes. For example, write a poem against television or the latest summer blockbuster. At the poem's end, install your vision of what's better than these things: listening to a ballgame on the radio, a bicycle ride in the country at night, video games. Or you could end with a tirade against this common love. If the concessional poem shapes a kind of unlikely ode, the reverse-concessional poem makes a kind of idiosyncratic curse.

• Write a concessional poem about a subject you are afraid to write about. Concede all your fears; list every single thing you're afraid might happen as a result of saying what you want to say, and make sure to follow those fears to their far conclusions. Then, say what you have to say. Or else write a poem like Francisco Aragón's "Poem with Citations from the *OED*" (p. 188), Timothy Liu's "My Last Night in Nova Scotia" (p. 200), or Rachel Zucker's "The Death of Everything Even New York City" (p. 220) in which you write about all the ways you avoided talking about your subject, listing everything you've done and even creating some new ways to avoid the subject before you finally succumb and offer up the truth. Remember: These structures work in large part due to the contrast between gradual admission/avoidance and revelation. Let your writing highlight this contrast—employ wild, jumpy, detailed writing in the first part and smooth, calm, fearless, resolved writing at the end.

- Look over your previous poetry. Is there anything you haven't written about that you think is significant? Or is there a way you haven't written, a style or poetic approach—wild and surreal, or plainspoken and straightforward—that you think perhaps you should try? List the ways you've avoided this important subject. What other subjects do you write about instead? Or list the ways your style has held you back from expressing or revealing something important. Use your list as the basis for the first part of a poem employing the retrospective-prospective structure. For the second part, make clear what it is you will write about, or how you will write, in the future.

- Try an exercise similar to the one above with a single poem, a poem with which you are dissatisfied. Using a method similar to that employed in Wislawa Szymborska's "Evaluation of an Unwritten Poem" (p. 182), investigate the poem line-by-line and stanza-by-stanza for its weaknesses, its mistaken assumptions, its unearned assertions or subtle avoidance strategies. If the writing you create from this pre-writing begins itself to be of interest, perhaps you might make a poem with a substructure like Szymborska's. Otherwise, try shaping your ideas into a retrospective-prospective structure using Muriel Rukeyser's "The Poem as Mask" (p. 67) as a guide.

- Consider further subjects for an elegy. Write an ironic elegy for a fictional character whom one can, by watching reruns, renting the DVD, or rereading the book, easily bring back to life. Or, write an elegy for an abstraction that you believe is disappearing, or deceased: civility, opposition, attentiveness.

- Write a descriptive-meditative poem using the sestina form. Because of its repeating words, the sestina form can help weave the structure's descriptions and meditation. Because of its demands for turns, the descriptive-meditative structure offers helpful guidance to the sestina form which, left to its own devices, often ends up rambling.

- John Keats' famous poem "Ode on a Grecian Urn" combines emblem and dialectical structures. The speaker of this poem examines an ancient Greek vase which has two very different pictures on it—one of lovers in chase and another of a ritual sacrifice. He then presents, as a kind of synthesizing meditation, the famous words inscribed upon the urn and the speaker's own take on that inscription: "'Beauty is truth, truth beauty,—that is all / Ye know on earth, and all ye need to know.'" Most scholars agree, however, that Keats invented the urn. Invent your own object—perhaps a two-sided medallion or amulet, or a ring with designs on both inside and outside—that offers antithetical images, describe those images, then meditate on the synthesis of those images. If you want, feel free to include a synthesizing inscription on your object, too, and employ it in your meditation.

- Write a poem with a hybrid structure: a descriptive-meditative poem that employs an elegiac structure for its meditation; a dialectical poem that ends with an ironic punch line instead of a synthesis; an emblem poem with a long list of concessions attached.

- Following the example set by Charles Simic's "The Initiate" (p. 180), use a journey as the substructure of a poem. The journey can be short or epic, easy or difficult. It could be, for example, a trip to the corner store or a trek from the deep interior of a rainforest to an icy floe in the Arctic, or a spelunking expedition. Or else, use a fictional journey from television, movies, or literature for your substructure.

- Following the example set by Francis Ponge's "The Lizard" (p. 177), write out a very complex "argument," or structure, for your poem, one that twists and turns in various ways from one's inner self—one's own thoughts and emotions—to the outside world and large-scale abstractions such as "language." You might write a poem about a creature—perhaps a goldfish or a hummingbird—that actually follows the structure you've laid out. Or write a poem that significantly, perhaps ironically, fails to follow the declared "argument."

- In a reversal of the expectation that a poem will develop in increasingly sophisticated ways, write a poem using the "inverted pyramid" structure of newspaper articles. That is, write a poem that begins by giving out all of the important "facts" of the poem, and then adds supporting material, including quotes from bystanders, in order of declining importance—a technique that allows newspaper editors to easily cut an article down to a size that will fit the paper. Watch out, though: As the final lines can have the effect of undercutting the poem, this kind of writing may encourage a kind of ironic poem. Revise toward or away from this effect as you desire or as your material tends.

- Employing Gabriel Gudding's "The Parenthesis Inserts Itself into the Transcripts of the Committee on Un-American Activities" (p. 198) as a model, use some other platitude or ritual statement, such as "I'm . . . fine" or "I . . . do," as the frame for idiosyncratic, revelatory, and more deeply truthful language.

- Write a poem structured like a legal proclamation, a structure that turns from giving reasons to proffering a resolution. Open your poem with numerous statements that begin with the word "Whereas," and then, following the phrase "It is hereby resolved . . . ," conclude with your resolution. This structure may work well in combination with subjects mentioned in the retrospective-prospective structure chapter.

- Write a poem with a sudden break at the end. You might give a "recap" of the poem, or you might use this turn as an opportunity to shift the poem radically, even ironically. For example, you might end your poem with "a word from our sponsors." If your poem is serious, use the advertisement to add humor, but if your poem is generally lighthearted, employ this opportunity to reveal the forces and assumptions that make their way—often invisibly—into your poem: Family Pressure & Co.; Political Ideology, Inc.; The Firm of the Effort to Still Say Something Meaningful and New.

- Invent a new kind of turn by taking your writing further than it might usually go. For example, write a poem in which you instruct an artist about how to create your portrait. What materials should be used? What style should be employed? What objects should appear around you? But then, at the poem's end, give instructions about how and where—in a shrine? directly across from another work of art? in a closet?—your portrait should be installed, suggesting what effect, if any, this work might have. Or, write a poem in which you construct a fantastic object or machine, a magical mechanism called "The Desire Vaporizer" or "The Memory Box." Employ lots of odd, specific details. At the end of the poem, turn the machine on and say what happens. Of course, it could be interesting if nothing, or something very unexpected, happens. If so, you may have a draft of a poem employing the ironic structure.

- Remember, you can write almost any of the above poems as a dramatic monologue, a poem in which you speak in the voice of another. In fact, assuming another's persona may be a very helpful creative act, providing you with a specific perspective for describing objects and/or developing meditations and arguments.

Further Reading

The following works form a core required reading list on structure.

- Stephen Dobyns' "Writing the Reader's Life" (in *Best Words, Best Order: Essays on Poetry*. New York: St. Martin's, 1996).

- T.S. Eliot's "Andrew Marvell" (in *Selected Essays, 1917–1932*. New York: Harcourt, Brace and Company, 1932).

- A.D. Hope's "The Discursive Mode: Reflections on the Ecology of Poetry" (in *The Cave and the Spring: Essays on Poetry*. Chicago: University of Chicago, 1970).

- Randall Jarrell's "Levels and Opposites: Structure in Poetry" (in *Georgia Review*. 50.4 (1996): 697–713).

- Mary Kinzie's "The Rhapsodic Fallacy" (in *The Cure of Poetry in an Age of Prose: Moral Essays on the Poet's Calling*. Chicago: University of Chicago, 1993).

- Ellen Bryant Voigt's "The Flexible Lyric" (in *The Flexible Lyric*. Athens: University of Georgia, 1999).

Taken together, these essays lay the groundwork for a broad and lively debate about poetic structure and its possibilities. One difficulty, however, arises from the fact that key terms—including "structure," "form," and "mode," a name generally used for more-encompassing poetic traditions such as "ode" or "lyric"—are not the same in each essay (and, indeed, *Structure & Surprise*, which has grown so directly from these essays, establishes its own terms in an attempt to be as clear as possible). As there is no agreed-upon nomenclature, one is best served not by skimming these works for terms but rather by reading these works with an eye to understanding the ideas they share.

Works Cited

INTRODUCTION

Dobyns, Stephen. "Writing the Reader's Life," *Best Words, Best Order: Essays on Poetry*. New York: St. Martin's, 1996.

Eliot, T.S. "Andrew Marvell," *Selected Essays, 1917–1932*. New York: Harcourt, Brace and Company, 1932.

Hope, A.D. "The Discursive Mode: Reflections on the Ecology of Poetry," *The Cave and the Spring: Essays on Poetry*. Chicago: University of Chicago, 1970.

Jarrell, Randall. "Levels and Opposites: Structure in Poetry," *Georgia Review*, 50.4, 1996.

Kinzie, Mary. "The Rhapsodic Fallacy," *The Cure of Poetry in an Age of Prose: Moral Essays on the Poet's Calling*. Chicago: University of Chicago, 1993.

Voigt, Ellen Bryant. "The Flexible Lyric," *The Flexible Lyric*. Athens: University of Georgia, 1999.

CHAPTER ONE: THE IRONIC STRUCTURE

Fairchild, Hoxie Neale. *The Romantic Quest*. New York: Columbia University Press, 1931.

Kennedy, X.J. *An Introduction to Poetry*, 2nd Edition. New York: Little Brown & Co., 1971.

Mellor, Anne. *English Romantic Irony*. Cambridge: Harvard University Press, 1980.

CHAPTER TWO: THE EMBLEM STRUCTURE

Browne, Sir Thomas. *Religio Medici. Selected Writings*. Ed. Geoffrey Keynes. Chicago: University of Chicago Press, 1968.

CHAPTER THREE: THE CONCESSIONAL STRUCTURE

Cioffi, Frank L. *The Imaginative Argument.* Princeton: Princeton University Press, 2005.

Hejinian, Lyn. *The Language of Inquiry.* Berkeley: University of California Press, 2000.

Raiffa, Howard. *The Art and Science of Negotiation.* Cambridge, Massachusetts: The Belknap Press of Harvard University Press, 1982.

Vendler, Helen. *The Art of Shakespeare's Sonnets.* Cambridge, Massachusetts: Belknap Press of Harvard University Press, 1999.

CHAPTER FOUR: THE RETROSPECTIVE-PROSPECTIVE STRUCTURE

Collins, Billy. "My Grandfather's Tackle Box: The Limits of Memory-Driven Poetry." *Poetry*, August 2001.

Leader, Mary. Personal interview, November 20, 2005.

CHAPTER FIVE: THE ELEGY'S STRUCTURES

Proust, Marcel. *The Past Recaptured.* Trans. Blossom. The Modern Library Edition. 1932.

CHAPTER SIX: THE DIALECTICAL ARGUMENT STRUCTURE

Hegel, Georg Wilhelm Friedrich. *The Phenomenology of Spirit.* Trans. A.V. Miller. Oxford: Oxford University Press, 1977.

Ostroff, Anthony, ed. *The Contemporary Poet as Artist and Critic.* Boston: Little Brown, 1964.

Plato. *Euthyphro.* Trans. G.M.A. Grube. *Complete Works.* Ed. John Cooper. Indianapolis: Hackett, 1997.

Sophocles. *Antigone.* Trans. David Grene. *Greek Tragedies.* Vol 1. Ed. Richmond Lattimore and David Grene. Chicago: University of Chicago Press, 1991.

CHAPTER SEVEN: THE DESCRIPTIVE-MEDITATIVE STRUCTURE

Abrams, M.H. "Structure and Style in the Greater Romantic Lyric." *Romanticism and Consciousness.* Ed. Harold Bloom. New York: Norton, 1970.

Harper, G.M. "Coleridge's Conversation Poems." *English Romantic Poets.* Ed. M.H. Abrams. Oxford: Oxford University Press, 1975.

CHAPTER EIGHT: THE MID-COURSE TURN

Aquinas, Thomas. *Summa Theologica*. Trans. Fathers of the English Dominican Province. New York: Benziger Brothers, 1947.

Holman, Hugh C. *A Handbook to Literature*. 4th Edition. Indianapolis: Bobbs-Merrill, 1972.

Wallace, Robert. *Writing Poems*. 3rd Edition. New York: Harper Collins, 1991.

CHAPTER NINE: SUBSTRUCTURES

Burt, Stephen. "Close Calls with Nonsense: How To Read, and Perhaps Enjoy, Very New Poetry." *The Believer*, April 2004.

Shahn, Ben. *The Shape of Content*. Cambridge, Massachusetts: Harvard University Press, 1957.

Wright, Charles (with J.D. McClatchy). "The Art of Poetry XLI." *Quarter Notes: Improvisations and Interviews*. Ann Arbor: The University of Michigan Press, 1995.

Notes on Contributors

FRANCISCO ARAGÓN is the author of *Puerta del Sol* (Bilingual Review Press, 2005). His poems and translations have appeared in various anthologies and journals, and he also is the editor of *The Wind Shifts: New Latino Poetry* (University of Arizona Press, 2007). For more information, visit http://franciscoaragon.net/.

CHRISTOPHER BAKKEN studied creative writing at Columbia University and the University of Houston. He is the author of two books of poetry, *Goat Funeral* (Sheep Meadow Press, 2006) and *After Greece* (Truman State University Press, 2001; T.S. Eliot Prize for Poetry). He is also the co-translator of *The Lions' Gate: Selected Poems of Titos Patrikios* (Truman State University Press, 2006). Bakken teaches at Allegheny College.

MARY JO BANG is the author of four books of poetry, including *Louise in Love* (Grove Press, 2001) and *The Eye Like a Strange Balloon* (Grove Press, 2004). She is an associate professor and director of the Creative Writing Program at Washington University.

JOHN BEER's poems and essays have appeared in many periodicals, including *Barrow Street*, the *Canary*, *Chicago Review*, the *Chicago Tribune*, *Colorado Review*, *Crowd*, *Denver Quarterly*, the *Iowa Review*, *Verse*, and *Xantippe*. He is a Ph.D. candidate in philosophy and social thought at the University of Chicago.

DENISE DUHAMEL's most recent poetry titles are *Two and Two* (University of Pittsburgh Press, 2005), *Mille et un Sentiments* (Firewheel Editions, 2005), and *Queen for a Day: Selected and New Poems* (University of Pittsburgh Press, 2001). She is an associate professor, teaching poetry at Florida International University.

ERIC GAMALINDA is the author of *Zero Gravity* (Alice James Books, 1999), a collection of poems which won the Asian American Literary Award in

2000. He recently published a new collection, *Amigo Warfare* (WordTech Communications, 2007).

PETER GIZZI is the author of four books of poetry, including *Some Values of Landscape and Weather* (Wesleyan University Press, 2003).

GABRIEL GUDDING is the author of *A Defense of Poetry* (University of Pittsburgh Press, 2002) and *Rhode Island Notebook* (Dalkey Archive Press, 2008).

JERRY HARP's books of poems are *Creature* (Salt Publishing, 2003), *Gatherings* (Ashland Poetry Press, 2004), and *Urban Flowers, Concrete Plains* (Salt Publishing, 2006). He is co-editor of *A Poetry Criticism Reader* (University of Iowa Press, 2006). His reviews and essays appear regularly in *Pleiades*. He teaches at Lewis & Clark College.

TIMOTHY LIU is the author of six books of poems, most recently *Of Thee I Sing* (University of Georgia Press, 2004) and *For Dust Thou Art* (Southern Illinois University Press, 2005). An associate professor of English at William Paterson University and a member of the core faculty in Bennington College's Graduate Writing Seminars, Liu lives in New York City.

COREY MARKS' *Renunciation* (University of Illinois Press, 2000) was a National Poetry Series selection. He teaches at the University of North Texas.

JEFFREY MCDANIEL is the author of *The Splinter Factory* (Manic D Press, 2002), *The Forgiveness Parade* (Manic D Press, 1998), and *Alibi School* (Manic D Press, 1995). He teaches at Sarah Lawrence College.

SUSAN MITCHELL is the author of three volumes of poetry, most recently *Rapture* (Harper Perennial, 1992), which won the Kingsley Tufts Poetry Award and was a National Book Award finalist, and *Erotikon* (Harper Perennial, 2001). Her many awards for her poetry include fellowships from the National Endowment for the Arts, the Guggenheim Foundation, and the Lannan Foundation. She teaches in the M.F.A. Writing Program at Florida Atlantic University where she is the Mary Blossom Lee Professor in Creative Writing.

PATRICK PHILLIPS' first book, *Chattahoochee* (University of Arkansas Press, 2004), received the 2005 Kate Tufts Discovery Award. He received a Discovery/*The Nation* Prize from the 92nd Street Y, and he recently completed a doctorate in Renaissance Literature at New York University and teaches at Maritime College.

D.A. POWELL is the author of three books of poems, most recently *Cocktails* (Graywolf Press, 2004), a finalist for the National Book Critics' Circle Award in Poetry. He teaches at the University of San Francisco.

PRAGEETA SHARMA is the author of *Bliss to Fill* (Subpress, 2000) and *The Opening Question* (Fence Books, 2004). She currently teaches in the graduate creative writing program at The New School and in the low-residency B.A. program at Goddard College.

MARY SZYBIST is the author of *Granted* (Alice James Books, 2003), which won the 2002 Beatrice Hawley Award and was a finalist for the 2003 National Book Critics Circle Award. She is the recipient of a Rona Jaffe Foundation Writing Award and was the 2004 winner of the Great Lakes Colleges Association's New Writers Award in Poetry. She teaches at Lewis & Clark College.

MICHAEL THEUNE studied creative writing at the University of Iowa and the University of Houston. His poems, essays, and reviews have appeared in various journals, including the *Iowa Review*, the *New Republic*, *Pleiades*, and *Verse*. He teaches English at Illinois Wesleyan University.

WANG PING was born in China and came to the U.S. in 1985. Her publications of poetry and prose include *American Visa* (Coffee House Press, 1994), *Foreign Devil* (Coffee House Press, 1996), *Of Flesh and Spirit* (Coffee House Press, 1998), *New Generation: Poems from China Today*, (Hanging Loose Press, 1999), *Aching for Beauty: Footbinding in China* (Anchor, 2002), and *The Magic Whip* (Coffee House Press, 2003). She won the Eugene Kayden Award for the Best Book in Humanities and is the recipient of a fellowship from the National Endowment for the Arts and the Bush Artist Fellowship for poetry. She is associate professor of English at Macalester College.

SUSAN WHEELER's most recent books are *Record Palace* (Graywolf Press, 2004), a novel, and *Ledger* (University of Iowa Press, 2005), a collection of poetry. She teaches creative writing at Princeton University.

ELIZABETH WILLIS' books include *Meteoric Flowers* (Wesleyan University Press, 2006), *Turneresque* (Burning Deck, 2003), *The Human Abstract* (Penguin, 1995), and *Second Law* (Avenue B, 1992). Currently she teaches at Wesleyan University.

MARK YAKICH is the author of *Unrelated Individuals Forming a Group Waiting to Cross* (Penguin 2004), a National Poetry Series selection, and *The*

Making of Collateral Beauty (Tupelo Press, 2006), the recipient of a Snow-bound Chapbook Award. He is an associate professor of English at Loyola University New Orleans. His website is http://markyakich.com.

RACHEL ZUCKER is the author of *The Badwife Handbook* (forthcoming from Wesleyan University Press) and two other collections of poems. She lives in New York City with her husband and two sons. For more information, please visit www.rachelzucker.net.

OTHER T&W BOOKS YOU MIGHT ENJOY

Handbook of Poetic Forms, edited by Ron Padgett. This bestselling handbook includes 76 entries that succinctly define the forms, summarize their histories, quote good examples (both ancient and modern), and offer professional tricks of the trade.

Poetry Everywhere: Teaching Poetry Writing in School and in the Community by Jack Collum and Sheryl Noethe. *Poetry Everywhere* contains 65 surefire exercises, more than 400 example poems, and innumerable writing tips and reflections on teaching the craft.

What Is Poetry: Conversations with the American Avant-Garde by Daniel Kane. Over a four-year period, Kane interviewed many of the most interesting and daring contemporary poets about their work, including John Ashbery, Robert Creeley, and Fanny Howe.

The T&W Guide to Walt Whitman, edited by Ron Padgett. Fifteen poets—including Allen Ginsburg, Kenneth Koch, and Anne Waldman—joined forces to create this first and only guide to teaching Walt Whitman from kindergarten to the college level.

The T&W Guide to William Carlos Williams, edited by Gary Lenhart. Seventeen innovative essays by Julia Alvarez, Allen Ginsberg, Kenneth Koch, and others explore imaginative ways of using the work of Williams in the writing classroom.

Luna, Luna: Creative Writing Ideas from Spanish, Latin American, and Latino Literature, edited by Julio Marzán. In these 21 lively essays, Julia Alvarez, Martín Espada, Naomi Shihab Nye, and others share their experiences teaching literature from both Spain and the Americas. They discuss the work of Sandra Cisneros, Federico García Lorca, Pablo Neruda, and others.

Sing the Sun Up: Creative Writing Ideas from African American Literature, edited by Lorenzo Thomas. Twenty writers present original methods for inspiring students to write through readings of James Baldwin, Gwendolyn Brooks, Rita Dove, Zora Neale Hurston, and Jean Toomer.

Classics in the Classroom: Using Great Literature to Teach Writing, edited by Christopher Edgar and Ron Padgett. The unusual range of literature discussed in *Classics in the Classroom* includes Homer, Sappho, Rumi, Shakespeare, Basho, Charlotte Brontë, and Twain.

The Circuit Writer: Writing with Schools and Communities by Margot Fortunato Galt. *The Circuit Writer*, Galt's account of thirty years as a visiting writer teaching in the Upper Midwest, offers a range of exercises for use in creative writing classes.

To Order or for More Information about T&W Books
1-888-BOOKS-TW
www.twc.org

Printed in the USA
CPSIA information can be obtained
at www.ICGtesting.com
LVHW012130011223
765291LV00003BA/187